The Urban Poor in Latin America

D1316961

The Urban Poor in Latin America

Marianne Fay, Editor

THE WORLD BANK
Washington, D.C.

ISBN-10: 0-8213-6069-8
ISBN-13: 978-0-821-36069-9
eISBN-10: 0-8213-6070-1

Cover photos: Edwin G. Huffman/World Bank (background); Michael Brennan/Corbis (foreground).

Library of Congress Cataloging-in-Publication Data

The urban poor in Latin America/Marianne Fay (editor)
    p. cm. – (Directions in development)
  Includes bibliographical references and index.
  ISBN 0-8213-6069-8
    1. Urban poor–Latin America.   I. Fay, Marianne. II. Directions in development (Washington, D.C.)

HV4050.5.A5U74 2005
362.5'098'091732–dc22

                                                                                    2005043244

Contents

Foreword xi

Acknowledgments. xiii

Overview 1
   Marianne Fay

1 Urban Poverty in Latin America and the Caribbean:
   Setting the Stage 19
   Marianne Fay and Caterina Ruggeri Laderchi

2 Working One's Way Up: The Urban Poor
   and the Labor Market 47
   Caterina Ruggeri Laderchi

3 Keeping a Roof over One's Head: Improving Access
   to Safe and Decent Shelter 91
   Marianne Fay and Anna Wellenstein

4 Violence, Fear, and Insecurity among
   the Urban Poor in Latin America 125
   Caroline Moser, Ailsa Winton, and Annalise Moser

5 Keeping Healthy in an Urban Environment:
   Public Health Challenges for the Urban Poor. 179
   *Ricardo Bitrán, Ursula Giedion, Rubi Valenzuela,
   and Paavo Monkkonen*

6 Relying on Oneself: Assets of the Poor 195
   Marianne Fay and Caterina Ruggeri Laderchi

7   Calling on Friends and Relatives: Social Capital 219
    Michael Woolcock

8   Public Social Safety Nets and the Urban Poor 239
    Marianne Fay, Lorena Cohan, and Karla McEvoy

Boxes, Tables, and Figures

Boxes
1.1   Five Views of the Connection between Social Relations
      and Urban Poverty in Latin America 22
1.2   Measuring Urban Poverty 29
2.1   Voices of the Poor: How the Urban Poor in Mexico View
      the Connection between Work and Poverty 49
3.1   How the Poor Typically Acquire Housing:
      Progressive Housing 95
3.2   The Central City Slum of Santo Domingo 97
3.3   Risk-Adjusted Housing Strategies in the Slums of
      Santo Domingo 103
3.4   A Brief History of Housing Policies Since the 1950s 105
3.5   Reforming the Rental Market in Colombia 107
3.6   Using Housing Microfinance: The Micasa Program
      in Peru 108
3.7   Costa Rica's Direct Demand Housing Subsidy Program 110
3.8   Minimizing Deaths from Natural Disasters through
      Good Planning: The Case of Cuba 116
3.9   Providing Catastrophic Insurance to the Poor:
      The Experience of Manizales, Colombia 117
4.1   The Difficulty of Measuring Crime and Violence 130
4.2   The Inter-American Development Bank's Approaches
      to Measuring the Costs of Violence 140
4.3   The Health Costs of Violence in Latin American Cities 143
4.4   Community Policing in Hatillo, Costa Rica 148
4.5   Reducing Crime and Violence in Bogotá 157
4.6   Preventing Gang Violence in El Salvador:
      The Homies Unidos Program 158
5.1   Improving Hygiene Practices as part of a Water Supply
      and Sanitation Project in Peru 189
5.2   Providing Preventive Health Services in Low-Resource
      Communities in Brazil 190
6.1   How the Poor Save and Draw on Their Assets:
      Illustrations from *The Children of Sánchez* 198

6.2   Drawing on Assets Following the 2002 Economic
       Crisis in Argentina and Uruguay 201
6.3   Low-Income Homeownership: Examining the
       Unexamined Goal 205
6.4   How Profitable Is Small-Scale Landlordism? 208
6.5   Informal Savings Institutions in Mexico: *Tandas*,
       Clubes, and *Cajas de Ahorros* 211
7.1   Participatory Budgeting in Bolivia: Getting Top-Down
       and Bottom-Up Right 229
7.2   The Astonishing Success of Villa El Salvador
       in Lima, Peru 231
8.1   Does Social Protection Address the Needs of the
       Urban Poor in Latin America and Caribbean? 243
8.2   How Do the New Poor and the Chronic Poor Cope
       with Macroeconomic Crisis? 244
8.3   How Effective Was Argentina's Jefes Program
       During the 2002 Crisis? 245
8.4   Who Are "At-Risk Youth"? 248
8.5   Argentina's Experience with Workfare:
       The Trajabar Program 250
8.6   Types of Targeting Methods 251
8.7   Expanding a Model Cash Transfer Program from
       Rural to Urban Areas: Mexico's Oportunidades 253
8.8   Latin America's Costly—and Regressive—Social
       Insurance Systems 258

Figures
1.1   Growth in the urban population implies further increases
       in the number of urban poor, even if urban poverty
       rates remain constant 26
1.2   The incidence of poverty decreases as city size increases 27
1.3   Poverty rates in Mexico decline as settlement size increases. . . . 27
1.4   Whether urban or rural areas are more unequal depends
       on the country as well as the segment of the income
       distribution 33
1.5   Inequality generally increases with city size. 33
2.1   Labor income accounts for more than 85 percent of the
       income of the urban poor in Latin America and
       the Caribbean 48
2.2   Very poor men and women are more likely than
       others to have only low-level skills 52
2.3   Returns to education are lower for Rio de Janeiro's
       favela residents 54

2.4   In Mexico the percentage of the urban poor employed
      in good jobs fell between 1991 and 2000. 58
3.1   Services with lower coverage are the most
      unequally distributed 99
3.2   Utilities represent a substantial share of household
      income or expenditures, especially for the poorest:
      The case of Argentina, 2002 101
3.3   Poor people are at greatest risk of suffering physical
      damage from a natural disaster 103
4.1   The cost of violence varies significantly across countries
      but is high throughout Latin America. 142
5.1   Noncommunicable diseases represent an increasing
      share of the disease burden in Latin America
      and the Caribbean. 180
5.2   The urban poor fare as badly as or worse than the rural
      poor in many countries. 183
5.3   Health indicators in urban areas vary widely
      across income groups 185
5.4   Access to basic services rises with income
      in Rio de Janeiro, Brazil 188

Tables

1.1   Poverty is urbanizing in Latin America and
      the Caribbean 20
1.2   Latin America and the Caribbean will continue to
      urbanize, but at varying speeds across subregions 25
1.3   Urban poverty is more responsive to growth than
      rural poverty 30
1.4   The consumption patterns of the urban and rural poor
      are similar: An illustration from Guatemala, 2002 34
1.5   The urban poor generally have much greater access
      to basic services than the rural poor 35
1A.1 Distribution of Household per Capita Income:
      Inequality Indices 40
1A.2 Population, Urbanization, and Poverty Estimates,
      by Country, 1998 41
1A.3 Urban Population Distribution across Latin America 42
2.1   Unemployment is higher among the heads of poor
      households in selected Latin American countries 48
2.2   Argentine households used a variety of
      labor-market-related strategies to cope
      with the 2001–2 Crisis 61
2A.1 Sources of Household Income in Urban Areas,
      by per Capita Household Income Quintile 67

2A.2   Sources of Household Income in Rural Areas,
       by per Capita Household Income Quintile 69
2A.3   Percentage of Employed and Unemployed Adults
       in Urban Areas, by Gender and per Capita
       Income Quintile 71
2A.4   Percentage of Employed and Unemployed Adults
       in Rural Areas, by Gender and per
       Capita Income Quintile 73
2A.5   Percentage of Female Adults by Education Level
       and per Capita Income Quintile 75
2A.6   Percentage of Male Adults by Education Level
       and per Capita Income Quintile 77
2A.7   Percentage of Employed Adults and Youth by
       Education Level 79
2A.8   Percentage of Urban Adults Employed in
       the Informal Sector or Self-Employed,
       by per Capita Income Quintile 81
2A.9   Percentage of Rural Adults Employed in
       the Informal Sector or Self-Employed,
       by per Capita Income Quintile 83
3.1   Latin America has very high rates of homeownership 92
3.2   Homeownership has been stagnant or fell in the 1990s
       for the poorest 93
3.3   Only about half of poor homeowners have formal
       title to their homes or their property 96
3.4   High average access to water obfuscates the
       situation of the poor 98
4.1   Urban violence in Latin America and the Caribbean
       takes many forms 128
4.2   Violence imposes significant costs on Latin America........ 141
4.3   A variety of approaches and interventions are used
       to reduce urban violence 145
4.4   The Khayelitsha Violence Prevention through Urban
       Upgrading Project includes many components 152
4.5   Budget allocations in violence reduction projects funded
       by the Inter-American Development Bank vary 155
4.6   Colombia and Guatemala have tried to reduce violence
       by increasing capital 158
4A.1   Categories of Violence 161
4A.2   Types and Sources of Violence Data 162
4A.3   Incidence of Sexual Abuse of Women in Selected
       Latin American Cities 163
4A.4   Preventing Crime: What Works, What Doesn't,
       What's Promising 164

4A.5   Features of Inter-American Development Bank Projects
       to Reduce Violence in Four Latin American Countries 166
5.1   Health indicators in rural and urban areas
       of Peru, 1997 182
5.2   Correlation between illness and poverty-related factors
       in Cali, Colombia, 1999 187
8.1   The pension system in urban Peru is highly
       regressive—and has become more so over time 241
8.2   Noncontributory assistance pensions in Latin America
       cover a significant proportion of pension recipients 259
8A.1   Targeting Instruments for Safety Net Program in
       Urban Areas 261

Foreword

Poverty remains a key challenge for Latin America and the Caribbean, where 175 million people—36 percent of the region's population—live in poverty. That such a high level persists despite decades of initiatives to reduce poverty shows how complex the problem is. As we adjust our policies to advance poverty reduction efforts, we must confront and accommodate some important changes in the economic and social reality of the region and its poorest inhabitants.

One such change is the fact that Latin America has become a largely urbanized region. Three-quarters of its population now reportedly live in towns and cities (although official figures may overstate the extent of urbanization). And while what is described as "urban" runs the gamut from villages to megacities such as São Paulo or Mexico City, most urban dwellers live in medium and large cities.

Urbanization is usually associated with economic growth and development, in Latin America as elsewhere. While the urban share of the region's population increased from half to three-quarters between 1960 and 2003, GDP per capita almost doubled. For many people from the countryside, cities of various sizes have offered a way out of poverty, with more employment possibilities and better access to services.

As the population has become more urban, so has the poverty that endures. Today, more than half of Latin America's poor live in cities. The challenges and opportunities they face are quite different from those of their rural counterparts, for whom many traditional poverty reduction programs have rightly been formulated. Designing better policy instruments to tackle urban poverty requires a clearer appreciation of its distinctive dynamics.

This report serves a timely need in refocusing the Bank's poverty reduction efforts in the region on an urban context. That is where the poor will increasingly be and where a good deal of the battle must be fought.

Danny M. Leipziger
Director for Finance, Private Sector
Development and Infrastructure
Latin America and the Caribbean Region

Guillermo Perry
Chief Economist
Latin America and the
Caribbean Region

Acknowledgments

This report was funded by the Regional Studies Program of the Office of the Chief Economist and the Finance, Private Sector and Infrastructure Department of the Latin America and the Caribbean Region. Marianne Fay managed the report, with the help of Caterina Ruggeri Laderchi, under the leadership of Maria Emilia Freire and Guillermo Perry. Other team members included Judy Baker, Ricardo Bitrán, Bernice Van Bronkhorst, Lorena Cohan, Leonardo Gasparini, Ursula Giedion, Somik Lall, Karla McEvoy, Paavo Monkkonen, Annalise Moser, Caroline Moser, Rubi Valenzuela, Anna Wellenstein, Ailsa Winton, and Michael Woolcock.

The team is grateful to peer reviewers Christine Kessides, Ellen Hamilton, Sonia Hammam, and Michael Walton. It also gratefully acknowledges the comments and suggestions of Andrea Brandolini, Christopher Chamberlain, Isabella Danel, Francisco Ferreira, Ariel Fiszbein, Francis Ghesquiere, Margaret Grosch, Gillette Hall, Sonia Hammam, Theresa Jones, William Maloney, Helena Ribe, Jaime Saavedra, Luis Servén, Jordan Schwartz, and Tova Solo. Finally, we thank Lic. Concepción Steta Gándara for documentation and insights on the expansion of Oportunidades in urban areas.

The production of this report was superbly managed by Karina Kashiwamoto, with the help of Leah Laboy. The team is also thankful to Mary Morrison for her editing.

Overview

Marianne Fay

With three-quarters of its population living in cities, Latin America and the Caribbean is now essentially an urban region. Higher urbanization is usually associated with a number of positive developments, such as higher income, greater access to services, and a lower incidence of poverty. Latin America is no exception: today the urban poverty incidence, at 28 percent, is half that of rural areas, and the incidence of extreme poverty, at 12 percent, is one-third that of rural areas.

Despite this relatively low poverty incidence, the number of poor people is high, and most studies agree that about half of the poor in the region live in urban areas. The World Bank's own estimates suggest that 60 percent of the poor (113 million people) and half the extreme poor (46 million people) live in urban areas.

Tackling urban poverty requires answering a number of questions. What is specifically urban about poor people living in cities? Are there different determinants of poverty in urban areas? Is the type of deprivation suffered by the poor in cities different from that in the countryside? And, most important, are the instruments to help the poor different in rural and urban areas?

Reviewing what is specifically urban about poor people living in cities reveals a number of facts that are salient to understanding the challenges facing the urban poor and the means to address these challenges. It also reveals three myths that tend to cloud judgment about urban poverty. All three spring from the common misperception that urban statistics are representative of the urban poor. In fact, because of the relatively low incidence of poverty in cities and Latin America's high inequality, urban statistics are almost never representative of the urban poor.[1]

Myth 1: The greater availability of social insurance (unemployment and health insurance and pensions) in cities makes social assistance less necessary. Social insurance is usually available only to workers in the formal sector. Less than a third of the employed urban poor work in the formal sector, and the employment rate of the urban poor is only about 72 percent (see table 2A.3). This means that at the most about 20 percent of poor urban households in Latin America have coverage. And in many countries the figure is much lower: only about 6 percent of poor urban households in Mexico and 4 percent in Peru have access to pensions. Even in Chile, the country

1

with the highest social insurance coverage in the region, more than half of urban households are without social insurance.

Myth 2: An urban bias in health and education expenditures implies that social expenditures favor the urban over the rural poor. An urban bias may exist in some countries, but in the two (Chile and Mexico) in which the health and education budgets were recently scrutinized, none was found (see Glaeser and Meyer 2002 for Chile, World Bank 2004 for Mexico). More generally, even if an urban bias exists, the poor targeting of health and education expenditures in Latin America means that it is likely to favor the rich.

Myth 3: Social assistance is more widely available to the poor in cities. This may be true for some or even most countries, but the data are not available to support it. And evidence from Mexico shows that there at least it is not the case (World Bank 2004).

How Are the Urban and Rural Poor Different?

Urban and rural poverty differ in several important ways. First, and most important, the urban poor are much more integrated into the market economy. The positive side of this is that urban poverty is more responsive to growth: indeed, the elasticity of poverty with respect to growth averages –1.3 in Latin America's urban areas but only –0.7 in rural areas. This suggests that sustained poverty reduction could be possible.

But greater integration in the market economy also implies greater vulnerability to fluctuations in the economy. This, in turn, implies that household coping mechanisms are of particular importance. For the urban poor the transmission of a macroeconomic shock is usually through the labor market, and the loss of work is typically one of the most devastating shocks they can face. Unemployment in Latin America is very much an urban phenomenon: urban unemployment rates in the region average 15 percent, five times rural rates. Finally, the greater integration in the market economy implies a higher monetization of food consumption. Food consumption is thus more sensitive to income and price fluctuations. In contrast, food consumption by the rural poor is more sensitive to changes in household size (Musgrove 1991).

Second, while urban areas are not systematically more or less unequal than rural areas, they are much more heterogeneous socioeconomically and with respect to economic activities and processes.[2] This makes it harder to target the poor in urban areas or to predict how different socioeconomic groups will be affected by a shock.

Third, heterogeneity notwithstanding, Latin American cities tend to be highly segregated. As a result, social exclusion coexists with (relative) physical proximity to wealth, services, and opportunities. This gives rise to negative externalities, or neighborhood effects, that reduce access to jobs and depress educational achievements and earnings. These negative externalities have been particularly well documented in the *favelas* of Rio de Janeiro (Cardoso, Elias, and Pero 2003).

Fourth, social networks are less stable in urban areas, with relationships based more on the quality of reciprocal links between individuals and friends than on familial obligations. This has two important implications. It implies that informal mutual arrangements, such as rotating savings and credits associations, face greater enforcement challenges. And weaker family ties mean that many more elderly people are without family support. Evidence from Chile—which is consistent with that found elsewhere—shows that relative to rural areas, only half as many urban respondents expect some sort of care by their children in old age (Gill, Packard, and Yermo 2004).

Fifth, urban living means much greater exposure to organized crime, drugs, and gang violence. This is true for the population as a whole, but it has particularly dismal implications for the poor living in the slums of Latin America's large cities, where narco-traffic is now pervasive. Combined with weaker family ties, greater diversity, and higher population density, it implies greater social risk in child rearing. Three-quarters of Latin America's youth live in cities, where they are disproportionately affected by poverty and violence, both as perpetrators and victims.

Finally, the urban poor are faced with overwhelmed rather than absent services.[3] Coverage rates for infrastructure are consistently much higher for the urban than the rural poor, although gaps remain that disproportionately affect poor neighborhoods. But quality and reliability are often so poor that they offset many of the benefits of services. This is particularly true for water and sanitation, which affect poor neighborhoods much more than richer ones, with dismal public health implications. The increased water coverage and improvement in quality that occurred as a result of the privatization of the water utility in Argentina resulted in a significant decline in child mortality, particularly in poor areas (Galiani, Gertler, and Schargrodsky 2005).

Structure of the Report

The underlying hypothesis of this report is that the causes of poverty, the nature of deprivation, and the policy levers to fight poverty are to a large extent site specific. Living in a city means living in a monetized economy, where cash must be generated to survive. This in turn requires the poor to integrate into labor markets. Obstacles to this integration have perhaps less to do with lack of jobs and opportunities (as is the case in rural areas) and more with lack of skills, the inability to get to work (because of inadequate transportation or child care), and social/societal issues (lack of social relations, the stigma associated with living in a slum, cultural norms precluding women's participation in the labor force).

At the same time, urban areas present a number of opportunities for the poor. Indeed, this is the very reason why the incidence of poverty is so much lower in urban areas. Labor markets are much broader, opportunities are greater, and access to services (infrastructure, but also health and education) are higher (even if the quality may not be very good). For certain social groups or individuals, living in a city may mean freedom from oppressive traditions.

The organizing principle of the report is that strategies to address urban poverty should allow the urban poor to make the most of the opportunities offered by cities while helping them cope with the negative externalities. The report focuses on the key challenges and opportunities facing the urban poor, with the goal of highlighting policy implications for each set of challenges. These challenges include earning a living (chapter 2), keeping a roof over one's head (chapter 3), protecting oneself from crime and violence (chapter 4), and keeping healthy (chapter 5). The report then examines the means available to the urban poor to handle shocks and improve their lots, namely, building up their asset base (chapter 6); relying on friends and family, by drawing on social capital (chapter 7); and depending on the public social safety net (chapter 8).

Challenges Confronting the Urban Poor

Labor income accounts for about four-fifths of the urban poor's income in Latin America.[4] A key question is then whether people are poor because the economy fails to create a sufficient number of (good) jobs or because their characteristics do not allow them to obtain the (good) jobs that exist. Not surprisingly, the answer is: a bit of both.

Earning a Living

Recent labor market developments in the region include a decline in "good" jobs for low-skilled workers, notably in manufacturing and the public sector, as well as a rise in open unemployment. In Peru, for example, manufacturing declined from 13 percent to 9 percent of employment between 1994 and 2000. Heads of poor households are more likely to be unemployed than nonpoor ones, and in most countries poverty would drop if unemployment or underemployment were to fall. In the case of Costa Rica, Trejos and Montiel (1999) estimate that urban poverty would decrease from 14 percent to 8 percent if the poor participated in the labor markets as much as the nonpoor. Overall, poor urban men exhibit lower employment and higher unemployment than their rural counterparts (participation rates are 88 percent among poor urban men and 94 percent for poor rural men). For poor women, participation is systematically higher in urban areas (see tables 2A.3 and 2A.4).

Some characteristics of the poor make it harder for them to access the relatively few good jobs that exist. About 70 percent of poor adults are low-skilled, as opposed to 50 percent for the urban workforce as a whole. This is due to lower enrollment among poor children in formal education but also to the lower quality of the education and training they can access. In contrast to high-income OECD countries, there is no systematic connection between skill levels and employment status: poor low-skilled households exhibit higher unemployment rates in Brazil but lower rates in Chile and Mexico (see table 2A.6). In addition, the poor may be disconnected from the social networks that command access to "good" jobs.

The lack of good jobs is a particularly severe problem for women, whose substantially increased participation in the workforce in the 1990s was mostly in low-quality jobs. This could be due to the decline in better quality work, gender discrimination, or low educational levels, although the need to combine paid work and child care is likely to be the most important determinant, as child care options are extremely limited for poor households.

A strategy to increase access by the urban poor to better quality jobs should include interventions to help women balance their household and market activities. Child (and possibly elder) care play a crucial role in this respect, especially if designed to accommodate flexible working hours. In addition, general interventions targeting tangible barriers to entry (such as affordable and reliable urban transport) and intangible ones (such as actions to reduce discrimination) are likely to have positive effects. Improving skills and the quality of education and training poor people can increase poor people's employability and earnings. But these interventions tend to have longer term impacts. To help people cope with immediate crises, these measures need to be complemented with other measures, such as social insurance (notably unemployment insurance), workfare, and job-matching services, a low-cost intervention with which high-income OECD countries have had success (Martin 1998).

Keeping a Roof over One's Head

High density and congestion, combined with failed land and housing policies, mean that finding housing that provides adequate shelter and physical safety is one of the greatest challenges confronting the urban poor. Most poor people in urban areas resort to informal housing, often located in marginal areas that are poorly served by public services or utilities and vulnerable to natural disasters. In most countries, formal housing is out of reach for the majority of households: in Brazil and Mexico, for example, formal housing is unaffordable to households in the bottom 70 percent of the income distribution.

Housing and Disaster Mitigation

The informal housing market allows the poor to acquire housing progressively: a plot of land is first acquired, and the house is gradually built and services added as resources allow. Access to informal housing partly accounts for the high rate of homeownership in Latin America, which exceeds 60 percent in most low-income settlements. Very few of these homeowners have formal titles, although the proportion varies across settlements and countries.

Poorly functioning land markets, urban sprawl, and poor public transportation push low-income households to settle in disaster-prone areas. The 20 largest cities in Latin America are located in areas of steep slopes, swamps, floodable land, or seismic activities. As a result, many of the 90 or so disasters that have hit the region over the past three decades—with an annual average loss of 7,500 lives—have hit cities. The poor are at heightened risk from disasters because of the more hazardous locations in which they live and the lower quality of their dwellings. Information for metropolitan San Salvador and Tegucigalpa shows that the share of households affected by landslides and floods declines steadily as income rises (World Bank 2002). There is also evidence that the poor quality of infrastructure in poor communities increases vulnerability (World Bank 2000). The poor are also less able to recover from natural disasters, both because of their lack of resources and because of public policies that may favor economic infrastructure in wealthier or more business-oriented parts of a city.

Policies to improve access to shelter for the urban poor are fairly well understood, and a few countries, including Chile and Costa Rica, have had reasonable success implementing them, although reaching the poorest has been difficult.[5] Policies need to adapt housing and land policies to the constraints of the poor, in an "enabling" environment that respects their need to acquire housing gradually rather than as a finished product. More specifically, they need to convert the poor's housing needs into effective demand by alleviating liquidity constraints through microcredit and household saving schemes. Policies can also address solvency issues through limited use of housing subsidies. They should also tackle supply-side issues, such as land and urban regulations and standards, streamlined permit process, taxes, and subsidies.

Mitigating disasters, especially for the poor, is complex, but there have been a number of success stories, even in poor communities. Cuba, which has withstood a number of devastating storms with minimal losses, shows that much can be done with limited financial resources but good organizational skills. Colombia, with support from the World Bank, is now experimenting with disaster insurance in a way that allows the poor to participate. More generally, a number of countries, particularly in the Caribbean, are experimenting with low-cost infrastructure to protect lives and housing.

Infrastructure Services

As to infrastructure services, access is usually much higher for the urban poor than for the rural poor. But coverage remains incomplete, and high urban averages can hide low access figures among the poor. Household-level data reveal that there are significant inequalities in access between rich and poor but that these differences have been declining over time.

These access figures do not take quality and reliability of service into account, however, and may therefore overestimate effective access. In Tegucigalpa, for example, less than half of households in the lowest income quintile but 78 percent of households in the top quintile have water service more than eight hours a day. This quality issue is most obvious in the case of water and solid waste, where it seems to have a differential effect on the rich and on the poor.[6] In contrast, where they are a problem, blackouts seem to affect all income quintiles almost equally.

Affordability is also an issue. Utilities generally account for a substantial share of poor households' income (16 percent in Argentina). Connection costs can be a heavy burden on poor households, particularly if financing schemes are not available. Lack of affordability can be a strong deterrent to deciding to connect to services. In Guatemala, for example, 20–40 percent of urban households do not connect to a service even if it is available, presumably because of cost.

Unreliability of service and incomplete coverage cause serious environmental health risks in urban areas. This explains why the incidence of diarrhea and acute respiratory infections is equally high among the urban and rural poor, despite much greater availability of health and infrastructure services in urban areas.

Making infrastructure work for the poor requires promoting access while ensuring that the poor can afford consumption. Promoting access usually entails some kind of universal service obligation or connection targets for operators. It may also include measures to reduce connection costs (such as cross-subsidies or allowing households to opt for a less expensive technology) or make them more affordable (by offering financing schemes to spread the cost over time). Consumption can be made affordable by reducing the size of bills (through targeted subsidies or a re-balancing of fixed and variable tariffs); by cutting the cost of services (by letting consumers opt for a lower quality of service, for example); and by facilitating payments though more frequent billings or prepayment schemes.

Protecting Oneself from Crime and Violence

With homicide rates five times the world average, Latin America has the highest level of violence of any region. There are, however, significant variations across countries. Colombia, El Salvador, and Guatemala have the highest levels of homicide, while homicide rates in Argentina and Chile are below the world average. Within countries, violence is usually most severe in large urban areas. City-level differences in homicide levels across the region are striking, however, with rates ranging from 6.4 per 100,000 inhabitants in Buenos Aires to 248 in Medellín (Piquet Carneiro 2000). Cities such as Rio de Janeiro and São Paulo, Mexico City, Lima, and Caracas account for more than half of all of the homicides in their countries (Briceño-León 1999). Violence rates also vary with age and gender, with the young more likely to be both perpetrators and victims.

Violence can take many forms. With the increasing dominance and grip of the drug trade over Latin American cities, organized drug-related crime is now the most worrisome phenomenon, particularly in large capital cities. In some countries state security forces use extrajudicial systems of informal justice, commonly known as "social cleansing," to retain order and power. Police brutality, which occurs with high levels of impunity, is alarmingly common, especially in urban areas, with racism a major factor. Regarding intrafamily violence, little urban-specific information exists. The phenomenon is widespread in Latin America, however, and a number of contributing factors are particularly prevalent in urban areas.

According to the common stereotype, poverty is the primary cause of violence. In fact, the evidence clearly shows that inequality and exclusion are more important in Latin America. At the same time, in situations of widespread and severe inequality, the daily living conditions of the urban poor can heighten the potential for conflict, crime, and violence (Vanderschueren 1996). Political factors, linked to the legacy of decades of protracted internal civil conflicts in Central America and Colombia, are also tied to the spread of violence. Social factors, such as the media sensationalization of violence, the availability of firearms, and drug and alcohol consumption, all contribute to both violence and the culture of fear.

The costs of crime and violence can be high. They include direct costs from increased expenditures on violence prevention, prosecution, and remediation; decreased investment and tourism; and multiplier effects from forgone activity and the erosion of human and social capital. Estimates for six Latin American countries show that the cost of violence ranges from 5 percent of GDP in Peru to 25 percent of GDP in Colombia (Londoño and Guerrero 1999).

Increased concern with violence across the region has meant that violence prevention and reduction are now a growth industry, with an extensive number of direct and indirect interventions. These can usefully be divided into two types: sector-specific approaches and cross-sectoral approaches. Sector-specific approaches are dominated by the criminal justice approach, which seeks to control and treat violence, and the public health (epidemiological) approach, which aims to prevent violence. Newer approaches, such as conflict transformation and human rights, reflect increasing concern with political and institutional violence. The recent recognition of the importance of more integrated strategies has opened the door for cross-sectoral approaches, such as citizen security, crime prevention through environmental design (CPTED), and urban renewal. Still in the process of development are community-based approaches to rebuild trust and social capital.

Keeping Healthy

Access to health care and infrastructure services is generally much higher in urban than rural areas, even for the poor. But there is growing evidence of an "urban penalty"[7]: in a number of countries some key health indicators for poor urban children are as weak or almost as weak as those for poor rural children, despite the much higher availability of services. This is presumably due to the very different public health challenges that arise from living in higher density areas.

Even in countries that do not exhibit evidence of an urban penalty, the urban poor perform significantly worse than the nonpoor on all indicators—even with regard to circulatory conditions often associated with wealth (Stephen and others 1994). Although the reasons for this have not been completely accounted for, one of the main causes is the physical environment of the poor, including lack of access to basic infrastructure, inadequate hygienic practices, and pollution. The urban poor access health services much less than the nonpoor (though more than the rural poor), and health care systems in Latin America and the Caribbean may have the wrong focus and lack the ability to address urban pathologies.

Background work done for this report highlights the fact that research on public health in Latin America and the Caribbean is sparse and scattered, especially in regard to the urban poor (Bitran, Giedion, and Valenzuela 2003). In addition, research on specific topics tends to concentrate on one region. For example, there is abundant research into urban mental health in Brazil, air pollution problems in Chile, and nutrition in Guatemala. While this reinforces the notion of the heterogeneity of the health sector, it points to a need for more and better integrated research into public health of the urban poor in Latin America and the Caribbean.

Coping and Getting Ahead: The Assets of the Poor

Assets are at the core of households' strategies to survive, meet future needs, improve their lot, and reduce exposure to shocks or minimize their consequences. Part 3 of the report examines the assets of the urban poor, the characteristics of these assets, and the role they play in their liveli-hoods. It first examines physical and financial assets, then discusses social capital, and finally looks at the role of social safety nets—public programs to help households mitigate risk and the effects of poverty.

Physical and Financial Assets

Little research has been conducted specifically on the savings behavior of the urban poor and the type of assets they accumulate.[8] Yet the differences between rural and urban poor discussed earlier imply that savings patterns and instruments differ across rural and urban poor:

- The greater integration of the urban poor in the market economy makes owning financial assets critical.
- The fact that the sources of vulnerability the urban poor face are more market based and less covariant than those faced by the rural poor implies that they adopt different types of coping strategies.
- Savings instruments face different challenges in urban and rural areas. Informal arrangements (either savings or insurance based), for example, are less susceptible to covariant risk, due to the diversification of activities in urban areas, but they are harder to enforce given the lower stability of networks.

The poor clearly save—how else would they become homeowners or cope with the occasional need for lump sums of money? The difficulty comes in measuring such savings, since the poor are usually excluded from financial services. The microfinance revolution has increased access to loans for small businesses and to a lesser extent to low-income households; no similar progress has been made in increasing access by the poor to savings instruments. As a result, they save by accumulating anything from consumption goods (such as food) to semidurable goods (such as clothing) to durable goods (such as furniture, equipment, or housing), as well as cash or contributions to informal institutions or networks of reciprocal obligations. It is therefore difficult to identify whether and how poor people are saving, given that the assets they hold have both consumption and investment value.

Housing is likely to be the most valuable asset held by the poor, but it is not clear how good an asset it is. In particular, it is unclear how buoyant or liquid housing markets are in poor neighborhoods. The evidence suggests that these markets are not very liquid, particularly given that most housing finance systems in Latin America explicitly exclude financing for "used housing" (and usually don't serve the poor). Nevertheless, homeownership does offer a number of advantages. It provides a constant flow of services, frees households from having to generate a fixed sum for rent every month, and can be monetized quite easily by taking in renters. Evidence from specialized surveys on risk management in Chile and Peru finds that investment in housing and other residential property acts as a substitute for formal retirement systems (Gill, Packard, and Yermo 2004).

So while the urban poor do accumulate assets, they are constrained in their choices—by their lack of resources, by their risk aversion, and by the fact that good savings and insurance instruments adapted to their needs are not usually available. As a result, they probably overinvest in housing and durable goods and underinvest in financial assets. Policy measures to both make housing a more liquid asset and increase access to financial services are therefore essential to help the urban poor cope with poverty and vulnerability.

Increased access to financial services can be promoted through approaches that encourage banks to go down market. The U.S. experience has been quite successful in this respect, and some of its experience is adaptable to the Latin American context (World Bank 2003a, 2003b). In addition, in some countries, the reach of microcredit can be increased through adoption of now well-understood best practice approaches (see, for example, www.cgap.org). Microfinance institutions are better placed than formal banks to offer savings services to the poor, given their proximity and cost structure, and they would benefit from the additional sources of funding.[9] Unfortunately, in most countries they are either prohibited by law from offering savings accounts or limited by high amounts of minimum capital required to take deposits. Countries in which the sector is sufficiently mature should contemplate allowing microfinance institutions to accept deposits. Doing so may require a modification in the regulatory structure.

Calling on Friends and Relatives:
Social Capital and the Urban Poor

Like their counterparts elsewhere in the developing world, the urban poor in Latin America rely heavily on their friends and relatives to help them both "get by" and "get ahead." Faced with institutions, policies, and services that are frequently hostile, inadequate, or indifferent to their concerns, the urban poor have little choice but to deploy a range of coping strategies, chief among them being the use of their social networks to provide everything from credit and physical security to information about housing and employment opportunities (Thomas 1995). The norms and networks upholding these support mechanisms are often referred to as "social capital," to distinguish them from other forms of capital, such as technology, material assets, and education (World Bank 2000). Whereas technology, material assets, and education are, almost by definition, in short supply in poor communities, certain forms of social capital—such as kinship and intracommunity ties (popularly referred to as "bonding" social capital)—may be in abundance. Other types of social capital—such as ties spanning spatial and demographic divides ("bridging" social capital) and power differentials ("linking" social capital)—may be lacking.

Urban social networks differ from those in villages in terms of their size, diversity, and primary functional role. Urban regions (especially those where the poor reside) tend to have much higher population densities than their rural counterparts. One consequence of this high density is that urban dwellers face many more choices than their rural counterparts. As a result, the informational requirements of making an appropriate choice are much higher in urban areas. This implies that the role of a network as a means of disseminating information is magnified. Hence networks in urban areas potentially have a larger role in their capacity as sources of information.

Networks in urban regions tend to be less stable than those in rural communities (due largely to the fluidity of urban populations). This may change the ways in which networks operate. In dense urban slums, where many families often live in the same house, social relationships move away from the traditional forms that characterize village networks. Marriages are much less stable, and both women and men are more likely to engage in serial monogamy and consequently have several circles of relatives. Relationships are forged more on the basis of the quality of reciprocal links between individuals and friends than on familial obligations.

A key survival and mobility strategy in poor communities entails managing the tension between the claims of kinship and locality with economic imperatives to build a more diverse "portfolio" of social and political assets. A corresponding policy implication is that in successful community-level development programs, linkages to outside institutions need to be forged. A community's stock of social networks in the form of internal ties can be the basis for launching development initiatives, but it must be complemented over time by the construction of new networks (that is, connections to "outsiders" in possession of additional information and resources, especially as they pertain to labor markets, factor and product markets, and public services). The construction of these networks is the task of both broad public policies that expand economic opportunities and access to services for poor people (that is, making "top-down" institutions more propoor) and specific programs that support front-line field workers as they seek to engage poor communities, building relationships with them that can become the basis for enhancing their confidence and organizational competence (that is, making "bottom-up" initiatives more empowering).

Improved public service provision can play a central role in facilitating this process (World Bank 2003). Implicitly or explicitly, it is this general understanding of the dynamics of social capital that has informed several recent policy initiatives in response to urban poverty in Latin America. Successful slum-upgrading projects from around the region provide ample evidence of the importance of combining public service delivery reform with initiatives to enhance the collective capacity of the poor by expanding their networks and political participation.

Social Safety Nets and the Urban Poor

Social assistance aims to help the poor cope when private mechanisms and social insurance (unemployment, health and disability insurance, pensions) cannot. As such, social assistance needs to be informed by the availability of social and private insurance and build on what is known about the vulnerability and nature of the deprivation affecting the target population.

The urban poor face a different set of risks and opportunities than the rural poor. Understanding these differences is critical to creating effective social safety nets. The urban poor are more integrated in the market economy, which makes them more sensitive to macroeconomic shocks, positive and negative. These shocks are transmitted mostly through the labor market, which argues for a safety net strategy focused on improved labor market participation. The greater economic and physical complexity of cities complicates the design of classic safety net programs, such as workfare or conditional cash transfers. The environment facing the urban poor is also much more diversified socioeconomically, making targeting more difficult. Density and diversity also imply weaker family ties—and therefore more elderly people without family support. Combined with classic urban perils (drugs, crime and violence, gangs), these weaker family ties also make child-rearing riskier.

The implication is that the urban poor need some urban-specific types of safety net programs as well as some adjustments in the design of existing safety net programs. In terms of design adjustment, targeting becomes more complex and more necessary, conditional cash transfer programs may need to adapt their requirements and benefits to the urban reality, and workfare needs to take into account the greater complexity of public works in urban areas and the fact that a fall in real wages rather than unemployment may be the labor market shock it needs to respond to.

The elderly poor are not unique to urban areas, but there are many more of them without familial support in cities, making them a significant part of the vulnerable urban population. In terms of groups requiring specifically urban instruments, at-risk youth stand out—not because children and adolescents are necessarily better off in rural areas but because at-risk young people in urban areas face and pose dangers to others that are quite different from those in rural areas. Finally, the greater integration of the urban poor in the market economy argues for urban safety net packages that focus on facilitating their participation in the labor market. This requires active labor market policies, such as training and job search assistance, as well as associated measures, such as policies on transportation, child care, security of tenure (which frees up household members from having to stay at home to secure a property), and others that encourage human capital investments.

Conclusion

The value-added of this report is twofold. First, it identifies some of the key differences between the rural and urban poor—debunking a few myths in the process. Second, it provides an overview of the key policy interventions most likely to improve the quality of life of the urban poor. To the extent that rural-urban migration is still occurring in Latin America, these interventions are also likely to be beneficial in some ways to the rural poor.

The report provides grounds for countries to develop urban poverty strategies, but it does not offer a blueprint, for several reasons. First, as discussed throughout the report, conditions differ across countries and across cities within countries. Governments may want to emphasize different aspects of an urban poverty strategy. Second, the recommendations involve many agencies and are therefore unlikely to be integrated into a single policy. The particular mix that is picked is likely to depend on the alliances forged to promote an anti-poverty program. Finally, the degree of certainty with which the recommendations are made varies. In some sectors (housing, infrastructure services, and possibly access to financial services and social safety nets), policy recommendations are straightforward and well understood, at least technically (political implementation may be more complex). In other areas, strategies are only beginning to emerge. In the case of crime and violence prevention, for example, it is increasingly clear what does not work, while there are promising signs of what does. But in what is perhaps the most important arena—the poor's integration into labor markets—recommendations remain broad and long term. They essentially entail promoting growth and policies that promote more equal accumulation of human capital.

The report suggests the need for further research on a number of topics. Jobs should be at the center of any urban poverty strategy. But which interventions are most effective in improving the quality and quantity of jobs available to the urban poor? How should urban transport systems and subsidy schemes be designed? How should child care for low-income families be designed and priced, and what is its likely impact? What role do residential stigma and social exclusion play in limiting access to jobs and incentives to "get ahead"? Most of the literature on the neighborhood effect comes from the United States; it is not clear whether and how the results apply to Latin America. The U.S. response has been to promote mixed-income zoning, in which developers of middle- and high-income housing are required to tailor a proportion of the houses they build to a low-income clientele. It is unclear whether and how such an approach could be adopted in developing countries.

Concerning the poor's asset-building strategies, there is a need to learn more about the structure of housing markets in low-income neighborhoods—how liquid and buoyant they are and how this might change over time as a neighborhood formalizes and densifies (or becomes known for crime and violence). Improving the low-income housing market may benefit poor people who are already homeowners at the expense of those who are not.

Very little work has been done on rental markets, so there is little knowledge as to whether there is room for more policy interventions to improve their working. While the U.S. and European literature finds that homeownership positively affects labor market outcomes (rather than hampering labor mobility), it is uncertain whether this finding applies to Latin American slums.

As to the savings behavior of the urban poor, little is known. More research is needed to understand determinants other than income and what the effect of greater access to financial savings instruments might be. (A good question is whether greater access to financial instruments would reduce demand for home ownership in favor of rental.) Nor is it clear whether the U.S. approach of encouraging banks to move down market could be successful in Latin America.

Concerning social capital, the policy implications of research remain vague and need to be further developed. How can policy interventions promote communities' ability to harness communities' energies toward achieving common positive goals? The concepts of bridging and linking social capital should be at the heart of slum upgrading operations, yet it is not clear how to effectively operationalize them.

As to social safety nets, there is a need to collect systematic evidence on whether social services and social assistance are really more generally available in urban areas. Is this notion a myth across Latin America or only in Chile and Mexico?

While the report emphasizes the need for programs to cope with transient poverty in urban areas and describes a number of successful ones, it does not discuss strategies for pulling the poor out of poverty. Perlman's work on the *favelas* of Rio de Janeiro shows that despite major improvements in human capital and physical living conditions (homes and infrastructure services), feelings of exclusion and hopelessness had intensified in the families she had first visited in the 1970s.

Other important topics for further research include the following:

- *Monitoring and evaluation.* Despite the significant and worthwhile investment targeted at alleviating urban poverty, very limited conclusions have been drawn on the relative efficiency of major interventions. This work is urgently needed to yield guidelines for public investment purposes.
- *Leveraging short-term interventions.* How to leverage transfer programs and especially target interventions into longer term results continues to be a puzzling issue. Despite social and well-targeted interventions and transfers, we still do not understand how an influx of cash can lead to more sustainable development and avoid dependency on state subsidies.
- *Weighing short- and longer term concerns.* Most poverty alleviation programs focus on building up human capital (working on the long term), providing short-term safety nets (conditional transfers), and improving labor market conditions. How to integrate these programs and enable a solid foundation to improve the asset base of the poor requires further work.

Endnotes

1. Exceptions are the very few variables for which quasi-universal coverage has been achieved (for example, electricity, some vaccines) and which are therefore homogeneous across the urban population.

2. Inequality refers to the unequal distribution of wealth (or other goods.) Heterogeneity implies that the population is diverse. Thus a society in which all are poor except for one person who owns almost all wealth would be considered unequal but homogeneous.

3. The expression was coined by Michael Woolcock (see chapter 7).

4. The rest includes transfers (13 percent), pensions (5 percent), and capital income, rents, and profits (2 percent).

5. Mexico and Brazil are currently reforming their low-income housing policies along similar lines.

6. In Tegucigalpa and San Salvador, the poor are substantially more likely to experience problems with solid waste management, such as pests and garbage accumulation (World Bank 2002).

7. The term was coined in nineteenth-century England, when urban mortality rates, particularly from tuberculosis, were much higher than rural ones. Public health measures, improved water and sanitation, and socioeconomic change led to declines in infant mortality rates, so that by 1905 rural and urban infant mortality rates were similar (see www. Urbanobservatrory.org for more details).

8. The bulk of the literature on savings and coping behavior of the poor has been rural based.

9. The poor save, but they do so in small, uneven increments. A savings instrument that fits their needs is one that allows frequent deposits with low transactions costs. This requires physical proximity and precludes accounts with high minimum balances.

References

Briceño-León, R. 1999. "Violence and the Right to Kill: Public Perceptions from Latin America." Paper presented at the conference "Rising Violence and the Criminal Justice Response in Latin America: Towards an Agenda for Collaborative Research in the 21st Century." University of Texas, Austin, May 6–9.

Bitrán, Ricardo, Ursula Giedion, and Rubi Valenzuela. 2003. "La problemática de salud de las poblaciones urbanas pobres en América Latina." Background paper commissioned for this report. World Bank, Washington, DC.

Cardoso, Adalberto, Peter Elias, and Valéria Pero. 2003. "Urban Regeneration and Spatial Discrimination: The Case of Rio's *Favelas.*" Proceedings of the 31th meeting of the Brazilian Association of Graduate Programs in Economics, Belo Horizonte. www.anpec.org.br/encontro2003/artigos/F41.pdf.

Galiani, Sebastian, Paul Gertler, and Ernesto Schargrodsky. 2005. "Water for Life: The Impact of the Privatization of Water Services on Child Mortality." *Journal of Political Economy* 113 (1): 83–120.

Gill, Indermit S., Truman Packard, and Juan Yermo. 2004. *Keeping the Promise of Old Age Income Security in Latin America: A Regional Study of Social Security Reforms.* World Bank, Washington, DC. wbln0018.worldbank.org/LAC/LAC.nsf/PrintView/146EBBA3371508E785256CBB005C29B4.

Glaeser, Edward, and John R. Meyer, eds. 2002. *Chile: Political Economy of Urban Development*. Cambridge, MA: Harvard University Press.

Londoño, J.L., and R. Guerrero. 1999. *Violencia en América Latina: Epidemiología y costos*. Working Paper R-375, Inter-American Development Bank, Washington, DC.

Martin, John P. 1998. *What Worked among Active Labour Market Policies: Evidence from OECD Countries' Experiences*. Labour Market and Social Policy Occasional Paper No. 35. Organisation for Economic Co-Operation and Development, Paris.

Musgrove, P. 1991. *Feeding Latin America's Children: An Analytical Survey of Food Programs*. Latin America and the Caribbean, Technical Department Regional Studies Program No. 11, World Bank, Washington, DC.

Perlman, Janice. 2003. "Marginality: From Myth to Reality in the *Favelas* of Rio de Janeiro, 1969–2002." In *Urban Informality: Transnational Perspectives from the Middle East, Latin America, and South Asia*, ed. Ananya Roy, pp. 105–146. Lanham, MD: Lexington Books.

Piquet Carneiro, Leandro. 2000. "Violent Crime in Latin American Cities: Rio de Janeiro and São Paulo." Department of Political Science, University of São Paulo.

Stephen, C., and others. 1994. "Environment and Health in Developing Countries: An Analysis of Intra-Urban Differentials Using Existing Data." London School of Hygiene and Tropical Medicine, London.

Thomas, J. 1995. *Surviving in the City: The Urban Informal Sector in Latin America*. London: Pluto Press.

Trejos, Juan Diego, and N. Montiel. 1999. "El capital de los pobres en Costa Rica: Acceso, utilización y rendimiento." Working Paper R-360, Inter-American Development Bank, Washington, DC.

Vanderschueren, F. 1996 "From Violence to Justice and Security in Cities." *Environment and Urbanization* 8 (1): 93–112

World Bank. 2000. *World Development Report 2000/01: Attacking Poverty*. New York: Oxford University Press.

———. 2002. "Urban Service Delivery and the Poor: The Case of Three Central American Cities." Report No. 22590, Washington, DC.

———. 2003. *World Development Report 2004: Making Services Work for Poor People*. New York: Oxford University Press.

———. 2004. *Public Expenditure Review for Mexico*. Washington, DC.

1

Urban Poverty in Latin America and the Caribbean: Setting the Stage

Marianne Fay and Caterina Ruggeri Laderchi

With three-quarters of its population living in cities, Latin America and the Caribbean is now essentially an urban region. Greater urbanization is usually associated with a number of benefits, such as higher income, greater access to services, and a lower poverty incidence, and Latin America is no exception: the urban poverty incidence (28 percent) is half the rural rate, and extreme poverty (12 percent) is a third of the rate in rural areas.

Despite this relatively low poverty incidence, the absolute number of poor people is high: 60 percent of the poor (113 million people) and half the extreme poor (46 million people) in the region live in urban areas (table 1.1). Demographic trends suggest that the urbanization of poverty will continue: if poverty rates remain unchanged, by 2015 two-thirds of the poor in Latin America and the Caribbean will be living in cities. This trend is in line with Ravallion's finding (2000) that the poor urbanize faster than the population as a whole in developing countries.

Increasingly, Latin American policy makers—typically mayors, as well as a growing number of central government officials—are asking the World Bank for advice on how to design programs and strategies to alleviate urban poverty. Mexico and other countries have started aggressively developing urban poverty programs.

Providing such policy advice requires answering a number of questions. What is specifically urban about poor people living in cities? Are the determinants of poverty different in urban areas? Is the type of deprivation suffered by the poor in cities different from that which occurs in

Marianne Fay is Lead Economist and Caterina Ruggeri Laderchi Economist at the World Bank.

Table 1.1   Poverty is urbanizing in Latin America and the Caribbean
(millions)

	Total poverty		Extreme poverty	
Year	Urban	Rural	Urban	Rural
1986	71	65	26	32
1995	102	79	38	47
1998	102	76	39	46
2000	113	76	46	46

Sources: Siaens and Wodon 2003; World Bank 2004c.

Note: Data for 1986 are estimated from a 13-country sample; data for all other years are from a 17-country sample.

the countryside? Most important, are different instruments needed to help the poor in rural and urban areas?

The underlying hypothesis of this report is that the causes of poverty, the nature of deprivation, and the policy levers to fight poverty are indeed to a large extent site specific. Living in a city means living in a monetized economy, where cash must be generated to survive. To earn cash, the poor need to integrate into labor markets. Obstacles to this integration have perhaps less to do with lack of jobs and opportunities (as is the case in rural areas) and more to do with lack of skills; the inability to get to work (transport, child care); and social and societal issues (lack of social relations, the stigma associated with living in slums, cultural norms precluding women's participation in the labor force). And loss of employment is one of the most devastating shocks that can confront a poor household in urban areas.

A key challenge for poor people living in cities is gaining access to housing. Many slums are built on unsecured land, often located in areas prone to natural disasters, such as flooding and landslides, or in close proximity to environmental hazards, such as landfills. In most cases, this is due to policy failures—housing construction norms and plot sizes that are out of the poor's reach, distorted housing finance systems, and, most important, inefficient land policies and regulations. These failed policies lead to spatial segmentation, a key factor in social exclusion (Gould and Turner 1997; Cardoso, Elias, and Pero 2003).

Basic services tend to be much more widely accessible in urban areas than in rural areas. Most of the poor have electricity, and many have water and sanitation. But quality and reliability are often inadequate. And because of crowding, the public health externalities associated with even a fraction of a neighborhood not having access to sanitation can be enormous.

Another specifically urban issue that disproportionately affects the poor is crime and violence. Crime is not, of course, unique to poor urban neighborhoods. Property crime is common in rich neighborhoods, and violence is sometimes a very serious problem in rural areas, where it tends to be associated with civil war and paramilitary forces. No presumption is made about whether intrafamily violence is more or less severe in poor urban areas than elsewhere (although the stressors may be different). But crime and violence has become the number one concern of many poor neighborhoods in Latin American and Caribbean cities.

Despite these problems, urban areas present a number of opportunities for the poor. Indeed, this is why the poverty incidence is so much lower in urban areas. Labor markets are much deeper, opportunities greater, and access to services (infrastructure, but also health and education) also potentially much better. Many services can be provided more cheaply in the dense setting of a city. Cities may also mean freedom from oppressive traditions for certain social groups or individuals.

The organizing principle of this report is that strategies to address urban poverty should allow the urban poor to make the most of the positive externalities of cities (deeper labor markets, better amenities and services, greater freedom, and possibly less discrimination against certain social or ethnic groups) while helping them cope with the negative externalities. Those externalities include congestion costs, such as the difficulty of securing affordable shelter; the risks to physical safety associated with pollution and environmental contamination, as well as crime and violence; increased isolation; and perhaps reduced social capital.

This study recognizes some of the important insights social scientists have gained over the past several decades and how these views have evolved (box 1.1). It emphasizes the fact that the poor have developed a very rich set of sophisticated economic and social responses to cope with the challenges of urban living, and that interventions to help the poor need to build on their ingenuity and social mechanisms. It also argues, however, that the poor cannot do much unless opportunities—such as employment—are available and that their ability to seize opportunities and rely on their traditional coping mechanisms can be eroded by social exclusion, crime, and violence.

Two important points are worth emphasizing at the outset. First, "urban" in most countries is a heterogeneous concept, including any settlement larger than a few thousand people. This report does not enter into the debate of what constitutes an urban or a rural settlement—whether it should be defined in terms of density of population, settlement size, or predominant economic activity or what the cut-offs should be.[1] That debate is unlikely to provide useful empirical or policy implications. A much more interesting approach, which this study has tried to adopt as far as

Box 1.1 Five Views of the Connection between Social Relations and Urban Poverty in Latin America

Over the past 50 years, five different accounts have been given to explain the connection between social relations and urban poverty in Latin America. These views are not mutually exclusive; indeed, they reflect an evolving understanding that is a product of broader trends in development theory, historical events, and empirical realities. These accounts are instructive, because they show that the core interpretation of empirical evidence has varied over time, radically affecting the policy implications drawn from the evidence.

The Marginality View
The earliest understanding, drawing on the prevailing assumptions of modernization theory in the 1950s and 1960s, was that squalid urban squatter settlements housed those unable or unwilling to adapt to the challenges of modern city living, thereby becoming "marginal" to it. According to this view, the urban poor in Latin America were lazy, passive, and fatalistic, their beliefs, behaviors, and kinship systems a legacy of backward rural livelihoods. The corresponding policy response was to implement slum clearance programs in which entire communities were razed or (at best) resettled. Little or no importance was attached to the many and varied ways in which poor households (and indeed entire communities) deployed strategies to cope with harsh living conditions, and few saw any merit in acquiring a detailed understanding of the conditions under which recent rural migrants maintained, adapted, or discarded coping strategies learned in rural settings.

The Myth of Marginality View
In the mid-1970s, as modernization theory fell into disfavor, the seminal work of Perlman (1976) on the *favelas* of Rio de Janeiro and Lomnitz (1977) on the shantytowns of Mexico City argued that the urban poor, far from being passive, inert, and "marginal," represented a rich mosaic of sophisticated economic and (especially) social responses to persistently difficult circumstances, ones in which networks played a crucial role. In the mid-1970s the key issues facing the urban poor in Latin America seemed to be those associated with health and property rights (not violent crime, drugs, and unemployment), in particular the constant fear that the government or private developers would, without notice or consultation, bulldoze their houses and possessions. Those aligning themselves with the myth of marginality view advocated for policy responses that were more attuned to understanding—and thus complementing—the survival and mobility strategies the poor were using.

The Culture of Poverty View
In the late 1960s and early 1970s, a view inspired by ethnographic studies of urban poverty in North and South America emerged. According to this view, in adapting to their poverty, the persistently poor increasingly took on identities,

expectations, and behaviors that reinforced their plight (Lewis 1961, 1968). Seeing themselves as victims of circumstances largely beyond their control or as trapped in cycles from which they could not escape, the poor were seen as engaging in practices that undermined their capacity to better their lives. Such behavior could be financial (poor spending and savings habits); health related (excessive smoking, bad diet); educational (dropping out of high school); or sexual (becoming a parent while still a teenager).

This approach has since gone in two directions. A more strident and essentialist version has been co-opted by conservatives and neomodernization theorists (such as economist David Landes and former USAID official Lawrence Harrison), who invoke it to claim that poor people, even poor countries and entire regions, are mired in "cultures" that are simply not conducive to development, with its modernist requirements for science, law, and efficiency. In terms of policy, this version perpetuates long-standing imperialist views that behavior deemed inconsistent with "development" must be changed through moral invocation, education, requirements, and (if necessary) force.

A second strand, more faithful to the spirit of the original formulation, has continued to employ detailed anthropological approaches to better understand how and why the poor so often engage in seemingly "nonrational" or counterproductive behavior. Such behavior often makes sense only when understood in terms of the contexts, identities, and normative expectations of those engaging in it (Nussbaum 2001; Appadurai 2004). From this standpoint, a more appropriate set of policy responses is concerned with working through intermediaries who understand something of these contexts, identities, and expectations to help the poor avail themselves of external resources and opportunities, but also help policy makers design programs that poor people want and can use (World Bank 2003b).

The Resources of Poverty View
The fullest expression of the innovative and diverse ways in which the poor respond to poverty in Latin America is encapsulated in the work of Gonzales de la Rocha (1994), who studied residents of shantytowns in Guadalajara (see also Selby, Murphy, and Lorenzen 1990; Pezzoli 1998). More conscious of the role that the broader national and international political economy plays in creating and perpetuating such harsh circumstances, this view nonetheless focuses on documenting how poor households and local community organizations manage to live with a measure of dignity and purpose in the face of trying circumstances. The policy agenda of those subscribing to this view is similar to that of the second strand of the culture of poverty view, but it also calls for national policy reforms that generate more widespread economic opportunities. Many of the "resources" of the poor are, after all, a virtue of necessity: making them "less necessary" through more inclusive economic policies is thus important.

(box continues on the following page)

Box 1.1 *(continued)*

The Poverty of Resources View

The most recent view argues that globalization (at least in post–NAFTA Mexico) has tilted the national and international context away from the interests of the poor to such an extent that their erstwhile "strategies" and "resources" have been rendered almost ineffective. In a strident reversal of her earlier position, Gonzales de la Rocha (2001) now argues that viable employment became so scarce in the late 1990s and early 2000s that the very social foundations of earlier survival strategies were eroded. An understated assumption of her earlier work—and, by extension, that of other scholars writing in a similar vein—was that the "resources of the poor" were conditional on the presence of employment options capable of supporting a family. In a globalized world in which firms seek low-wage and nonunionized workers wherever they can, Mexicans now find themselves at once less competitive in international labor markets and more exposed to the pernicious flow of drugs and violence—a point echoed by Perlman (2003) in a follow-up report on her earlier study of Rio de Janeiro. Moreover, through pervasive advertising and television programs, the poor are reminded on a daily basis of the economic distance that separates them from the rich. Hopes and opportunities have dimmed, and both physical and livelihood insecurity have escalated, leading Gonzales de la Rocha (2001) to argue that the key policy problem is now not so much understanding the "resources of poverty" but coming to grips with the insidious "poverty of resources" available to poor and unskilled workers.

Source: This box was written by Michael Woolcock, Senior Social Scientist at the World Bank.

---

the data allow, is to distinguish cities by their size. Poor people living in a small town of less than 20,000 inhabitants may have more in common with their rural counterparts than with poor residents of a megacity. To the extent that this report is about what is urban about poor people living in cities, it probably has a bias toward poor people living in larger settlements.

Second, this report by no means intends to distract attention from the plight of the rural poor. In fact, by "exploding" the urban categories, it may help improve our understanding of the continuum between rural and urban poverty and the complementarities in corresponding policy interventions.[2] More generally, the report aims to help improve the understanding of the extent and nature of urban poverty and the coping mechanisms used by the poor. Indeed, a goal could be to bring the knowledge of urban poverty closer to that which exists for rural poverty.

Migration is another element in the continuity between rural and urban settlements. This report touches only briefly on the issue, however, because its complexity requires separate treatment.

This report includes three parts. The first (chapter 1) examines urban poverty trends, discusses how they are affected by growth and urbanization, and looks at who the urban poor are and where they live. The second focuses on the key challenges and opportunities facing the urban poor and identifies policy implications for each of these challenges. These challenges include earning an income (chapter 2), keeping a roof over one's head (chapter 3), protecting oneself from crime and violence (chapter 4) and keeping healthy in a highly polluted environment (chapter 5). The third examines the means available to the urban poor to handle shocks and improve their lots. These include building up their asset base (chapter 6), relying on friends and family (chapter 7), and depending on the public social safety net (chapter 8).

Urban Poverty Trends

Urbanization in Latin America is expected to increase from its current rate of 77 percent to about 80 percent by 2015 (table 1.2).[3] Although the expected increase, and that of projected natural population growth, is modest, it implies a 16 percent increase in the number of urban dwellers, representing some 75 million people. Urban population growth is likely to be most rapid in the least urbanized countries in the region (the Central American countries, Bolivia, Ecuador, and Paraguay), where the urban

Table 1.2 Latin America and the Caribbean will continue to urbanize, but at varying speeds across subregions

Subregion	Urbanization rate (percent)		Absolute increase in urban population (million)	Annual rate of growth of urban population (percent)
	2005	2015		
Central America, Bolivia, Ecuador, and Paraguay	57	62	13	2.8
Caribbean	65	68	4	1.4
Mexico and South America (excluding Bolivia, Ecuador, and Paraguay)	81	84	58	1.5
Latin America and the Caribbean	77	80	75	1.6

Source: United Nations 2003.

Figure 1.1   Growth in the urban population implies further increases in the number of urban poor, even if urban poverty rates remain constant

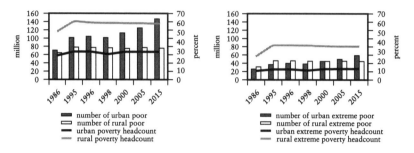

number of urban poor
number of rural poor
urban poverty headcount
rural poverty headcount

number of urban extreme poor
number of rural extreme poor
urban extreme poverty headcount
rural extreme poverty headcount

Sources: Authors' calculations based on data from UN (2003), Siaens and Wodon (2003), and World Bank (2004b).

Note: Data for 2005 and 2015 are projections, based on the poverty rate remaining constant at its 2000 level.

population is projected to increase 2.8 percent a year, twice as fast as the 1.4–1.5 percent rate predicted for the rest of South America, Mexico, and the Caribbean. Nevertheless, because of the size of the existing urban population, the vast majority of the absolute increase will occur in Brazil, Mexico, and to a lesser extent the other large countries of South America. More than a third (23 million) of the absolute increase in urban population will occur in Brazil, despite the modesty of the increase in its urbanization rate (from 84 to 86 percent).

Unless poverty rates decrease, population growth and continued urbanization imply that by 2015 there will be an additional 22 million poor people in Latin American cities, 9 million of whom will be living in extreme poverty (figure 1.1). Continued urbanization does imply lower overall poverty, however, because the poverty incidence is lower in urban than in rural areas.

Latin America's experience with urban poverty is similar to that of high-income OECD countries, where the rapid urbanization of the postwar period resulted in a massive shift in the proportion of poor people living in cities, from 44 percent in 1959 to 78 percent in 2000. Although the incidence of urban poverty rose, the overall poverty rate declined, because urban poverty rates remained much lower than rural ones (Brandolini and Cipollone 2003).[4]

The lower incidence of poverty in urban areas reflects a continuum in which the incidence of poverty generally decreases as settlement size increases and is least severe in metropolitan areas (figure 1.2). This point

Figure 1.2 The incidence of poverty decreases as city size increases

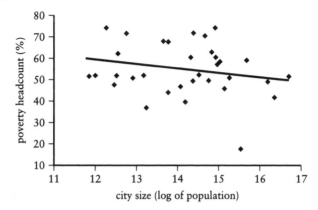

Source: Baker and Lall 2003.
Note: Data cover 39 cities in nine Latin American countries for various years.

is well illustrated by Mexico, where the share of people living in extreme poverty in small cities is three times that in large cities and the share of people living in moderate poverty is 60 percent higher (figure 1.3). But despite the inverse relation between settlement size and poverty incidence, a third of Mexico's poor—some 16 million people—still live in large cities. This is due to the concentration of population in larger urban centers.

Figure 1.3 Poverty rates in Mexico decline as settlement size increases

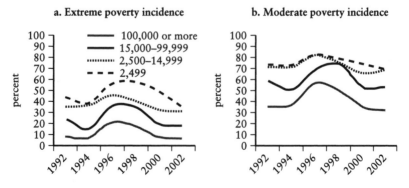

Source: World Bank 2004b.

Figure 1.3 also suggests the need for a differentiated response of poverty to income shocks (such as the 1994 peso crisis) across settlement size. Disaggregated poverty trends between 1992 and 2002 show that the impact of macroeconomic turbulence in the mid-1990s was much more visible in cities, both smaller and larger, than in small rural or semi-urban areas. Across urban areas, the crisis-driven increase in the incidence of poverty was at least as sharp in small as in larger agglomerations, however, and the recovery was slower. Indeed, in 1998 the moderate poverty incidence was as high in small cities as in semi-urban settlements.

While the inverse relation between poverty incidence and settlement size seems to hold for all of Latin America, countries differ as to whether the majority of the urban poor live in large or small towns. In Brazil 62 percent of the urban poor live in small and medium-size cities (World Bank 2001a), while in Mexico about two-thirds of the urban poor live in large cities (World Bank 2002b). International comparisons may be difficult, however, because of the lack of comparable data (box 1.2).

Growth, Inequality, and the Evolution of Urban Poverty

The limited decline in the incidence of poverty during the 1990s reflects the poor growth performance in the region. A by now consistent body of literature (see review in Wodon and others 2001) has measured the impact of growth on poverty reduction and highlighted the important role of inequality in mediating such an impact. In addition, several countries in the region experienced periods of deep crisis, whose impact on urban and rural poverty varied depending on the nature of the shock and the characteristics of the poor in different sectors.

Response of Urban Poverty to Growth

Golan and Wodon (2003) find that the elasticity of poverty with respect to growth is about −1.3 in urban areas and −0.7 in rural areas (table 1.3). These different elasticities translate into similar absolute declines in poverty, however, since the higher incidence of poverty in rural areas offsets the lower elasticity. In contrast to the rural estimates, the urban estimates do not seem sensitive to the poverty line selected (the results are the same for both poverty and extreme poverty).

The negative implication of this higher elasticity of urban poverty to growth is that urban populations are more vulnerable to macroeconomic shocks than rural ones. Morley (1995), who obtains similar results when looking at the effects of the crisis of the 1980s, suggests that this may be because the rural poor are to a large measure disconnected from the economy.

Box 1.2   Measuring Urban Poverty

Analysis done for this report shows that poverty in Latin America is always more severe in rural areas, regardless of where the poverty line is set. However, the extent of the difference depends on which poverty line is chosen—the lower the poverty line (which captures more extreme poverty), the more poverty seems to be concentrated in rural areas—and whether adjustments are made for different costs of living or consumption patterns between rural and urban areas.

Income or consumption measures are the most commonly used measures of poverty. They assess whether households can afford to purchase a basic basket of goods. The basket ideally adjusts for spatial price differentials across regions and urban or rural areas in a given country. This may not always be possible, but it has important consequences. In France, for example, Brandolini and Cipollone (2003) estimate that accounting for Paris' higher housing costs would increase the poverty incidence there to the same level as the rest of France.

The issue of comparability across urban and rural areas (or more generally across regions in a country) is more controversial when the basket is further adjusted to reflect local tastes and consumption patterns. While it is important to capture the different types of goods people can access, it has been argued that comparisons are difficult if baskets used to compute the poverty line are allowed to vary (Ravallion and Bidani 1994; Ferreira, Lanjouw, and Neri 2003).

An additional challenge is posed by the fact that urban areas are very diverse, and data are seldom disaggregated enough to allow for analysis between and within urban areas. This is unfortunate given the significant differences in the issues faced by people in small towns and large metropolitan areas—and perhaps even between different urban slum areas within the same city—and the substantial concentration of poverty within specific urban neighborhoods (typically at the periphery).

Urbanization can also affect estimates of urban poverty trends. In particular, the reclassification of rural areas as urban as they grow may cloud the understanding of what underlies the trend. Similar problems arise when attempting cross-country comparisons of urban and rural poverty rates, due to the differences in definition of what is urban.

Finally, income or consumption measures may not capture some of the features of urban poverty of greatest concern. The urban poor rely heavily on the cash economy, making them more vulnerable to income shocks. They are also vulnerable to the environmental and health hazards presented by crowded living conditions and to the high levels of crime and violence in urban slums. Other aspects of poverty, both rural and urban, relate to access to basic services. Unfortunately, these data are not usually broken down by income level within rural and urban areas, and citywide statistics do not reflect the conditions of the poor. Finally, survey data fail to capture the service problem facing the urban poor, which is generally less one of access than one of reliability, quality, and affordability (nominal access may be high, although "effective" access is low).

Sources: Adapted from Hentschel and Seshagir 2000; Brandolini and Cipollone 2003.

Table 1.3 Urban poverty is more responsive to growth than rural poverty

	Basic model		
Type of poverty	Poverty headcount	Estimated growth elasticity	Implied absolute decline in headcount for 1 percent growth in income per capita
Total poverty			
Poverty	35.0	−1.1	−0.39
Extreme poverty	16.3	−1.5	−0.24
Urban poverty			
Poverty	29.0	−1.3	−0.30
Extreme poverty	11.9	−1.3	−0.16
Rural poverty			
Poverty	53.4	−0.7	−0.36
Extreme poverty	29.8	−1.0	−0.29

Sources: Elasticities from Golan and Wodon (2003); headcount from Siaens and Wodon (2003).

Note: The expected reduction in the headcount is extremely sensitive to the poverty line chosen.

As a result, their income does not fluctuate as much in real terms with growth or recessions, although it is likely to be sensitive to natural shocks (weather related) or changes in the prices of major crops.

The literature on vulnerability offers a more nuanced view. It distinguishes two different kinds of shocks. Idiosyncratic shocks affect one household independently of others and are usually linked to a household's life cycle. Some of the underlying risk factors (such as the risk of contracting a particular illness) may vary between urban and rural areas, as may their consequences. However, it is in the second kind of shock—covariant or aggregate shocks—that systematic differences between rural and urban areas may be found. These shocks affect many households simultaneously, and their likelihood is usually specific to a location or sector. Examples include natural disasters, a decline in the price of a specific crop, or a decline in the demand for a particular industry's product.

The economic characteristics of different groups and the overall economic environment interact in shaping the risk distribution households face.[5] Furthermore, the distribution of the burden of a crisis depends on the nature of the macroeconomic shocks and their impact on the demand for labor in different sectors; the policy measures adopted (for example, whether financial assets are frozen); and the severity and length of the crisis. It is therefore difficult to identify a priori which groups are likely to be more affected by shocks.

Do macroeconomic crises affect the poor more than the rich? Not necessarily. A study of the impact of four recessions in urban Brazil found that only one affected the poorest quintile proportionally more than the others. In two out of three periods of growth in urban Brazil, the poorest deciles benefited more than the richer ones (Neri and Thomas 2000). In urban Mexico after the 1995 crisis, losses classified as "average" were evenly spread across wealth groups (Maloney, Bosch, and Cunningham 2003). A recent survey on household responses to crisis in Uruguay finds that the richest households had the highest incidence of reduction in income, while the poorest suffered least in terms of income decline (Ridao-Cano 2003). These data do not allow a comparison of the size of the shocks across wealth groups, as they reflect households' self-assessment of whether they had experienced a shock.

The limited evidence available suggests that the impact of a crisis tends to be more uniform in rural than in urban areas. This was the case during the 1995 Mexico crisis (Maloney, Bosch, and Cunningham 2003). The evidence is compatible with the notion of a more homogeneous population in rural areas, especially as far as sources of livelihoods are concerned. A note of caution is needed when drawing these comparisons, however, not least because of the linkages between rural and urban areas, through migration and the flow of remittances.

Food insecurity is one channel through which the urban poor are made more vulnerable to macroeconomic crisis than the rural poor. Food expenditures can absorb as much as 60–80 percent of total income among the urban poor (Ruel, Haddad, and Garrett 1999), and their food consumption is much more sensitive to changes in income or food prices than that of the rural poor (Musgrove 1991). Indeed, evidence from Cali shows that the degree of food insecurity is high. About one-third of the population in the poorest income quintile had family members who were hungry at least once during 1998/99 and did not have sufficient resources to purchase food. Sixty percent of parents in the poorest quintile said they had to reduce nutrition for their children because of insufficient resources over a one-year period (World Bank 2002b).[6]

In sum, urban households are more sensitive than rural households to macroeconomic fluctuations. However, vulnerability per se is likely to vary across subgroups, depending on the nature of the shock. Moreover, the studies discussed above focus on income vulnerability rather than well-being. The impact on well-being depends on the type of responses adopted by households, the intrahousehold distribution of the effects of such strategies, and how sustainable these strategies are. The sustainability of a household's coping strategy is in turn influenced by both the intensity of the shock and the resources available to the household. These issues are discussed in more detail in chapter 2, on labor, and in chapter 6, on asset accumulation strategies.

What about Inequality?

Since inequality dampens the effect of growth on poverty reduction, one possible explanation for the greater responsiveness of urban poverty to growth could be that inequality is lower in urban areas.[7] However, the general presumption is that inequality is higher in cities than in rural areas, where people are more homogeneously poor. This appears to be supported by the data: the average Gini coefficients for Latin America and the Caribbean for 1996 were estimated at 0.55 in urban areas and 0.51 for rural areas (Siaens and Wodon 2003).

In reality, however, the pattern of inequality in urban and rural areas varies across countries: the Gini coefficients are higher in urban than in rural areas in 6 out of 16 countries for which data were available, lower in 7, and the same in 3. Even looking at other measures of inequality, no clear pattern emerges.[8] Similar results are found in 20 countries in Eastern Europe and Central Asia, although there a higher proportion of countries have greater inequality in urban areas (World Bank 2004a).

A variety of indices can be used to analyze urban-rural differences in income distribution (see table 1A.1). Two indices of the generalized entropy family can be computed to enhance their sensitivity to inequality at different parts of the distribution. Adopting zero as a parameter results in an index (also known as Theil L) that is very sensitive to inequality at the bottom of the distribution (that is, highlights differences among the poorest). In contrast, choosing 2 as a parameter yields an index that is very sensitive to inequality at the top (that is, highlights differences among the richest).

Combining these measures shows that the results vary across countries: while urban areas are clearly more unequal than rural ones in El Salvador, Jamaica, and Nicaragua, the opposite is true in Colombia, Ecuador, Mexico, and Panama. In other countries, the answer depends on the part of the distribution one is focusing on (figure 1.4).[9]

What about differentials in inequality across cities of different sizes? Inequality, as measured by the Gini coefficient, tends to increase with city size, although not monotonically (figure 1.5). And there is much variation in this finding. In Brazil, for example, the Gini coefficient is 0.54 in Rio de Janeiro (10.6 million residents), 0.61 in Fortaleza (3 million residents), and 0.59 in Brasilia (1.9 million residents).

Figure 1.4   Whether urban or rural areas are more unequal depends on the country as well as the segment of the income distribution

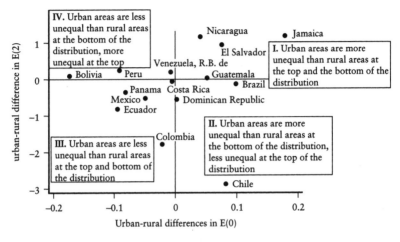

Source: Authors' calculations based on data from table 1A.1.

How and Where Do the Urban Poor Live?

Understanding whether the urban poor have different characteristics from other groups can provide important guidance for policy. It can highlight their needs and yield other valuable information, such as indicators for targeting programs by proxy.

Figure 1.5   Inequality generally increases with city size

Source: Baker and Lall 2003.

Comparisons with Other Socioeconomic Groups

The urban poor share many characteristics with their rural counterparts. An analysis of poverty in Latin America (Wodon and others 2001) finds that most key characteristics are the same in rural and urban areas. Factors increasing the probability of being poor include living in a larger household, with a younger or female head; having less education; and living in a household in which both the household head and the spouse are unemployed (searching for employment rather than "not working").

These similarities between the poor in urban and rural areas are not surprising; others are more striking. Consumption patterns appear remarkably similar between rural and urban poor. In Guatemala food accounts for more than half of all consumption, in both rural and urban poor, followed by "other" (about 14 percent), housing (10–12 percent), and personal goods (about 12 percent) (table 1.4). This is true despite the fact that rural and urban consumption patterns are very different for the population as a whole. Average spending by all urban households is almost three times higher than that of rural households; the differential for the poorest households is much smaller.

Table 1.4   The consumption patterns of the urban and rural poor are similar: An illustration from Guatemala, 2002

| | Proportion of total household consumption (percent) | | | |
Category	All urban	Urban poor (quintile 1)	All rural	Rural poor (quintile 1)
Food	34.0	52.8	51.5	58.1
Housing	16.0	12.8	10.4	10.1
Personal goods	9.3	12.4	9.7	12.3
Education	6.6	3.1	2.9	1.5
Health	4.5	2.0	2.2	1.4
Durable goods	4.7	0.7	2.6	0.6
Transport	7.0	1.9	4.9	2.0
Other	15.6	14.1	15.2	14.0
Services	2.5	.3	0.6	0.2
Total	100.0	100.0	100.0	100.0
Guatemalan Quetzales	10,122	1,681	3,668	1,571

Source: Adapted from World Bank 2003.
Note: Values account for regional price differentials.

Some differences in labor markets are evident, however. Returns to education are somewhat higher in urban areas. Underemployment is a much more significant marker for poverty in urban areas. Self-employment is associated with poverty in rural areas but not in cities. And in both urban and rural areas, migration either in the previous five years or over the life cycle is not associated with a higher poverty rate. This implies that migrants do as well as people from the receiving areas; since migration tends to occur from poorer to richer regions, this suggests that migrants usually do improve their lot by migrating.

In addition, features of urban life, such as greater access to services, result in differences in spending patterns (table 1.4). Education and health spending, for example, are proportionally higher for the urban poor than the rural poor. In education the differences arise primarily from spending on materials and books. For health, a higher proportion of urban residents seek care (and thus incur costs), and they are more likely to use private facilities, which are on average seven times more expensive than public facilities (World Bank 2003). Data for Mexico show similar results, although the urban poor there spend significantly more on housing (11 percent) than the rural poor (6 percent) (World Bank 2004b).

The greater ease of providing services to clustered rather than scattered populations helps explain some of the differences between the urban and rural poor. On average the urban poor fare much better than the rural population (poor and nonpoor alike) in terms of access to water, sanitation, and electricity (National Research Council 2003) (table 1.5). Access is also much more limited in smaller cities than in larger ones.

Despite better access to services in urban areas, the basic service needs of the urban poor are seldom fully met, for several reasons (see chapter 3). First, coverage remains far from universal. Even in relatively wealthy

Table 1.5   The urban poor generally have much greater access to basic services than the rural poor
(percent)

Population	Piped water on premises	Flush toilet	Electricity	Lack of all three services
All rural	31.4	12.6	40.5	46.4
Urban poor	58.7	33.6	79.4	14.4
Urban nonpoor	72.7	63.7	96.4	2.8

Source: National Research Council of the National Academies 2003.

Note: Figures are obtained from probit analysis. Poverty is identified as the lowest quartile of a composite asset and durable index, as there are no monetary measures in the Demographic and Health Surveys, on which the analysis is based. Data are for various years.

Argentina, 47 percent of the urban poor lacked adequate sanitation in 1998 (World Bank 2000). In Cali, Colombia, 20 percent of the poorest did not have the use of a private toilet in 2000 (World Bank 2002b). And half of *favela* dwellers in Rio de Janeiro had no sewerage connection in 2000 (World Bank 2001a). Second, quality tends to be poor, and services are often unaffordable. Third, incomplete coverage and poor quality in high population density areas has severe public health implications. Indeed, it partly explains why infant and child mortality are higher among the urban than the rural poor in a number of countries, despite higher urban access to both infrastructure and health services (see chapter 5).

Access to basic education and health services is higher in urban areas, though not necessarily for the poorest. In Mexico school attendance is almost identical among the rural and urban poor, with a slight difference emerging only among young adults 18 and older (SEDESOL 2003). More generally, the quality of these services in poor areas tends to be very low, as schools in poor neighborhoods tend to be overcrowded and the levels of repetition and drop-out high. In poor urban areas, particularly those on the periphery, accessing secondary education can be problematic. Students often have to travel some distance to attend secondary school, and public transport is not always reliable. School dropouts have few options for entering the labor market. Inactivity has been linked to violence, crime, and teenage pregnancy (see chapters 4 and 7).

Coverage and quality issues are also a problem in health. In poor areas of Montevideo, a city with good social indicators overall, residents living in marginal areas note problems of low quality or nonexistent polyclinic services, limited access to pre- and postnatal care, and lack of coordination in the delivery of services between central and local governments (World Bank 2001b).

Finally, urban living often involves high congestion costs. Land scarcity in urban areas pushes prices up, so that most housing becomes unaffordable to the poor. As a result, many live in unsafe and insecure conditions in order to remain close to the center; others seek cheaper land on the periphery on which to build, often at the cost of long and expensive commutes (chapter 3). More generally, the relatively high cost of housing tends to result in crowded households. In Argentina more than half of urban households in the poorest quintile live with an average of two or more people per room, and 17 percent have three or more per room (Angel and others 2001).

Location Patterns of the Urban Poor

An essential feature of urban poverty in Latin America is that cities tend to be highly segregated. Such segregation takes different forms, ranging from pockets of poor neighborhoods in parts of the inner city to sprawling urban slums covering large areas of the periphery. Within these poor areas, however, there can be significant variation in income. In Brazil, for example, a significant proportion of *favela* residents are not poor, with the figure exceeding 50 percent in some cities (World Bank 2001a).

Most of the processes that led to segregation between rich and poor in Latin America took place over the course of many decades and were linked to the development of motorized transport and suburbanization. There have been, however, examples of rapid change in the patterns of urban settlement, such as the location transition that occurred in Montevideo, Uruguay, between 1989 and 1996 (Baker 2001). Households affected by job losses during the major recession of the mid-1990s moved from the center, where accessibility to jobs and services was good, to the more isolated, undeveloped periphery. This resulted in an increasing pattern of polarization across different areas of the cities.[10] In many cities, such as Buenos Aires and Mexico City, more affluent groups are pursuing a strategy of "proximity and high walls" in gated communities (Caldeira 1996).

The costs of segregation along income and geographic lines have been estimated to be substantial by models that analyze the premium households are willing to pay to live in neighborhoods with given characteristics.[11] In Bogotá a 10 percent increase in average travel time to employment centers reduces the desirability of a location by 2.5 percent (Baker and Lall 2003). Increasing travel time for a poor household from 45 minutes to 90 minutes reduces willingness to pay for housing by $55–$75 a month.

Arguably, however, the concentration of the poor in particular areas has effects stretching well beyond commuting times and rental values. Residential location and neighborhood composition may have a number of far-reaching influences on households' socioeconomic future. A comprehensive review of the evidence finds that a strong neighborhood environment can discourage or sanction disruptive behavior by individual residents and therefore criminal behavior by young people (Gould and Turner 1997).

Building on this type of evidence, Durlauf (2001) suggests that the main effects the social composition of a neighborhood can have on individual behavior are peer group effects (in which individual choices are influenced by the choices of others), role model effects (in which the preferences of older members of a neighborhood influence younger members' preferences), social learning (in which information on some of the choices available is derived from the experiences of others), and social complementarities (in which group members' outcomes are directly affected by outcomes of other members). All these types of interactions are externalities and suggest that policies encouraging socioeconomic mixing may have important "social multipliers."

Neighborhood effects may also be compounded by stigma, which affects poor people's access to jobs and increases other forms of discrimination. In Montevideo residents of peri-urban slums cite stigma as a major problem in securing a job. In Rio de Janeiro 85 percent of slum residents sampled perceived discrimination against people living in *favelas* (Perlman 2003). A recent study of Rio's *favelas* found that residents there earn 10–47 percent less than people from other neighborhoods who work in similar occupations and have the same education, age, and gender characteristics (Cardoso, Elias, and Pero 2003).

Awareness of these negative externalities in the United States has led to policies that explicitly encourage local housing agencies to promote mobility and deconcentration of poor families (Turner, Popkin, and Cunningham 2000).[12] Neighborhood effects, particularly the implications for housing policies that cluster low-income people together, should also be considered in Latin America.

Conclusions

This chapter examined urban poverty trends in Latin America, analyzed how they are affected by demographic and economic changes, and looked at who the poor are and where they live. The main findings can be summarized as follows:

Poverty is urbanizing, but urbanization reduces overall poverty. The urbanization of the population is resulting in an urbanization of poverty, but it is also helping reduce poverty. Poverty incidence is systematically lower in urban areas than in rural areas (at least in developing countries). This is because urban areas tend to be more productive, with economies of agglomeration allowing for higher wages, deeper labor markets, and better opportunities for the poor. The key challenge, then, is to help the poor take advantage of the opportunities urban areas offer.

Poor urban households share many characteristics with the rural poor, with some notable differences. Like their rural counterparts, the urban poor tend to have larger families, lower education levels, and less access to services than richer households. But returns to education are higher and underemployment is a more serious problem for the urban poor than the rural poor, and self-employment is not significantly associated with higher poverty. In terms of services, the urban poor tend to have higher nominal access than their rural counterparts; the key challenge they face is one of quality and effective access. Overall, however, there are tremendous variations in access by the urban poor to services. The availability of services (of good or bad quality) is determined largely by the age of a settlement, with new peri-urban settlements typically underserved.

Urban poverty is more responsive to overall growth than rural poverty. This suggests that sustained poverty reduction could be possible, but much depends on the degree of integration of the poor into the broader urban economy, their ability to access jobs and build up assets to raise themselves out of poverty and rely on during crises, and their access to government programs and institutions. The effects of macroeconomic crisis are likely to be highly differentiated, with socioeconomic characteristics— particularly those pertaining to labor market integration—greatly affecting household vulnerability.

Income inequality is not systematically higher in urban areas than in rural ones, but cities are characterized by great heterogeneity. This can be explained almost mechanically by the lower incidence of poverty in urban areas. The implication is that it may be harder to target the poor or predict how different socioeconomic groups will be affected by a shock. Heterogeneity also springs from the wide array of what is considered urban (from small towns to megacities, from central cities to distant peri-urban areas just being settled).

Heterogeneity notwithstanding, Latin American cities tend to be highly segregated. Exclusion is a key challenge facing the urban poor, despite their much greater proximity to wealth, services, and opportunities. This gives rise to negative externalities, which result in less access to jobs, lower earnings, lower educational achievements, higher crime and violence, and stigma associated with particular neighborhoods. Such a concentration stems from a variety of mechanisms, including the sorting role played by the land and housing markets and the ability of the most affluent to negotiate access to key infrastructure and services. (For a discussion of the positive and negative effects of social interactions in poor areas, and between the poor and their surrounding environment, see chapter 4, on crime and violence, and chapter 7, on social capital.)

Annex

Table 1A.1 Distribution of Household per Capita Income: Inequality Indices

Country/Year	Urban					Rural				
	GINI	CV	E(0)	E(1)	E(2)	GINI	CV	E(0)	E(1)	E(2)
Argentina 2001	52.2	1.276	0.517	0.497	0.814					
Bolivia 2002	54.0	1.573	0.525	0.593	1.237	57.3	1.514	0.699	0.620	1.147
Brazil 2001	57.7	1.787	0.616	0.676	1.596	53.1	1.852	0.519	0.602	1.714
Chile 2000	56.5	1.920	0.577	0.678	1.844	52.4	3.064	0.494	0.719	4.695
Colombia 1999	55.1	1.952	0.560	0.646	1.905	55.0	2.714	0.580	0.717	3.683
Costa Rica 2000	44.2	0.987	0.350	0.344	0.487	44.0	1.040	0.356	0.352	0.541
Dominican Rep. 1997	48.0	1.369	0.407	0.454	0.936	47.5	1.723	0.405	0.480	1.485
Ecuador 1998	52.2	1.655	0.496	0.561	1.370	54.1	2.092	0.591	0.640	2.189
El Salvador 2000	50.6	1.775	0.510	0.529	1.576	46.9	1.107	0.435	0.396	0.613
Guatemala 2000	55.8	1.622	0.569	0.620	1.316	51.8	1.594	0.518	0.550	1.270
Jamaica 1999	54.9	2.091	0.575	0.665	2.185	46.8	1.392	0.399	0.427	0.969
Mexico 2000	50.9	1.552	0.456	0.531	1.205	52.1	1.854	0.505	0.581	1.718
Nicaragua 2001	56.7	2.881	0.584	0.815	4.150	52.2	2.439	0.542	0.581	2.975
Panama 2000	52.2	1.358	0.501	0.516	0.922	54.4	1.597	0.583	0.583	1.275
Paraguay 1999	50.3	1.577	0.450	0.512	1.243	59.9	4.852	0.714	0.941	11.769
Peru 2000	44.0	1.218	0.354	0.389	0.742	47.3	0.988	0.446	0.382	0.488
Uruguay 2000	44.6	1.040	0.347	0.357	0.541					
Venezuela 1998	46.3	1.226	0.381	0.405	0.752	45.4	1.051	0.389	0.370	0.553

Source: Compiled by Leo Gasparini, Universidad Nacional de la Plata, Argentina, based on latest available country household survey.
Note: CV = coefficient of variation. E(1) = Theil.

Table 1A.2 Population, Urbanization, and Poverty Estimates, by Country, 1998
(percent, except where otherwise indicated)

Country	Population (millions)	Share population urban	Poverty incidence Total	Poverty incidence Urban	Poverty incidence Rural	Share poor in urban areas
Argentina	36	88	n.a.	17	n.a.	n.a.
Bolivia	8	62	63	52	82	50
Brazil	166	80	34	27	58	65
Chile	15	85	26	24	43	76
Colombia	41	74	65	55	80	66
Costa Rica	4	58	25	20	29	49
Dominican Rep.[a]	8	63	28	21	37	49
Ecuador	12	62	n.a.	60	n.a.	n.a.
Guatemala	11	39	50	26	66	20
Honduras	6	51	58	41	71	37
Jamaica	3	55	19	14	22	44
Mexico	95	74	26	15	55	43
Nicaragua	5	55	55	45	67	46
Panama[a]	3	55	49	35	74	37
Paraguay	5	55	55	36	77	36
El Salvador	6	58	32	16	53	30
Uruguay	3	91	n.a.	.17	n.a.	n.a.
Venezuela	23	86	44	37	54	81

Sources: Poverty estimates are from Siaens and Wodon (2003). Population and urbanization rates are from the World Bank (2004b), World Development Indicators database.

Note: n.a. = not available.

a. Data are for 1997.

Table 1A.3 Urban Population Distribution across Latin America

City size category	Number of cities	Population (millions) 2000	Average growth rate 1990–2000 (percent)	Mean city size within category	Median city size within category
Small (20,000–100,000)	8 7	5.4	20.8	64,900	64,600
Medium (100,000–500,000)	3 26	65.0	18.7	199,500	169,800
Large (500,00–1 million)	4 0	28.5	20.8	713,100	660,200
Very large (1–5 million)	4 3	87.1	25.6	2,030,000	1,740,000
Mega (more than 5 million)	7	78.4	16.0	11,200,000	10,600,000

Source: Baker and Lall 2003, based on data from the UN World Cities Database on 500 cities in 18 countries.

Endnotes

1. De Ferranti and others (2005) discusses this issue in depth. Changing the definition of what is urban affects what share of the poor are deemed to be urban, but the effect is weaker than that of changing the poverty line. This is because, as discussed in this chapter, there is substantial continuity across settlement sizes, so that any reasonable change in the cut-off will have only a relatively small impact.

2. On this issue, see Tacoli (1998) and the World Bank rural and urban poverty "toolkits," available at http://poverty.worldbank.org/library/view/12995.

3. This section draws heavily on Baker and Lall (2003).

4. The contribution of urbanization was small relative to the improvements in poverty incidence in both cities and rural areas, however (Brandolini and Cipollone 2003).

5. Maloney, Bosch, and Cunningham (2003) show how in urban Mexico even in "normal periods," different types of households faced very different income variability. That variability can be attributed to the characteristics of the microenterprise sector, in which a minority of firms does either much better or much worse than salaried workers and firm mortality is very high. In contrast, over the same period less educated households faced lower variability in income than other groups, possibly because of their limited chances of accessing jobs with wage growth prospects and their willingness to increase household labor supply in times of crisis.

6. This figure may have an upward bias, since some respondents may have thought that answering yes to food insecurity questions would have given the household a chance to access subsidy programs.

7. Indeed, Golan and Wodon (2003) find much higher elasticities once inequality is kept constant. Unfortunately, their results are not disaggregated by urban and rural areas.

8. The annex presents a variety of inequality measures for rural and urban areas for 16 countries for which data are available. These measures capture different aspects of the distribution. While the Gini index is the most widely quoted of the indices, it is most sensitive to inequality in the middle of the distribution, which is just one aspect of inequality.

9. While conclusive inequality comparisons can be obtained from the Lorenz curves only for countries that fall in quadrants I or III, being in either of those quadrants does not imply Lorenz dominance. It is possible that using other indexes would suggest different assessments of relative inequality in urban and rural areas.

10. Such polarization is seen by decomposing income inequality (Theil index) data at the level of census sections or neighborhood clusters into "within" and "between" area components and observing decreases within areas and increases between them.

11. The seminal work of Alonso (1964) and Muth (1969) demonstrates how sorting is defined over the relationship between relative expenditures on commuting and land consumption. An important extension to these models investigates how both preferences for community homogeneity and trips to multiple city centers affects household optimization decisions.

12. The Section 8 Program provides subsidies (equivalent to about 70 percent of rent) to low-income families for renting moderately priced housing.

References

Alonso, William. 1964. *Location, and Land Use: Toward a General Theory of Land Rent.* Cambridge, MA: Harvard University Press.

Angel, Schlomo, N.A. Félix, C. de Hoz, M. Jiménez, S. Lebedinsky, L. Lucioni, N. Pazos, P.A. Pereyra, and M.B. Rudolfo. 2001. *El sector de vivienda y la política de vivienda en Argentina: Una evaluación expeditiva.* Inter-American Development Bank, Washington, DC.

Appadurai, Arjun. 2004. "The Capacity to Aspire: Culture and the Terms of Recognition." In *Culture and Public Action Stanford,* ed. Vijayendra Rao and Michael Walton, 59–84. Stanford, CA: Stanford University Press.

Baker, Judy. 2001. "Social Exclusion in Urban Uruguay." In *Measurement and Meaning,* ed. E. Gacitua-Mario and Q. Wodon. World Bank Technical Paper No. 518, Washington, DC.

Baker, Judy, and Somik Lall. 2003. *Trends and Characteristics of Urban Poverty in LAC.* World Bank, Washington, DC.

Brandolini, Andrea, and Piero Cipollone. 2003. "Urban Poverty in Developed Countries." In *Inequality, Welfare, and Poverty: Theory and Measurement,* ed. J.A. Bishop and Y. Amiel, 309–343. Philadelphia: Elsevier.

Caldeira, T. 1996. "Building Up Walls: The New Pattern of Spatial Segregation in São Paulo." *International Social Science Journal* 48 (147): 55–66.

Cardoso, Adalberto, Peter Elias, and Valéria Pero. 2003. *Urban Regeneration and Spatial Discrimination: The Case of Rio's Favelas.* Proceedings of the 31th meeting of the Brazilian Association of Graduate Programs in Economics, Belo Horizonte. www.anpec.org.br/encontro2003/artigos/F41.pdf

De Ferranti, David, Guillermo Perry, William Foster, Daniel Lederman, and Alberto Valdes. 2005. *Beyond the City: The Rural Contribution to Development.* Washington, DC: World Bank.

Durlauf, Steven. 2001. "The Membership Theory of Poverty: The Role of Group Affiliations in Determining Socio-Economic Outcomes." In *Understanding Poverty,* ed. Sheldon H. Danziger and Robert H. Haveman. Cambridge, MA: Harvard University Press.

Ferreira, Francisco H.G., Peter Lanjouw, and Marcelo Neri. 2003. "A Robust Poverty Profile for Brazil Using Multiple Data Sources." *Revista Brasileira de Economia* 57 (1): 59–92.

Gilbert, Alan, ed. 1996. *The Mega-City in Latin America.* New York: United Nations Press.

Golan, Amos, and Quentin Wodon. 2003. *Nonlinearities in the Elasticity of Poverty Reduction to Growth and Inequality.* Washington, DC: World Bank.

Gonzales de la Rocha, Mercedes. 1994. *The Resources of Poverty: Women and Survival in a Mexican City.* Cambridge, MA: Blackwell.

———. 2001. "From the Resources of Poverty to the Poverty of Resources? The Erosion of a Survival Model." *Latin American Perspectives* 28 (4): 72–100.

Gould, Ellen Ingrid, and Margery Austin Turner. 1997. "Does Neighborhood Matter? Assessing Recent Evidence." *Housing Policy Debate* 8 (4): 833–66.

Hentschel Jesse, and R. Seshagir. 2000. *The City Poverty Assessment: A Primer.* World Bank, Washington, DC.

Lewis, Oscar. 1961. *The Children of Sanchez*. New York: Random House.

———. 1968. *La Vida: A Puerto Rican Family in the Culture of Poverty*. New York: Random House.

Lomnitz, Larissa. 1977. *Networks and Marginality: Life in a Mexican Shantytown*. New York: Academic Press.

Maloney, William F., Mariano Bosch, and Wendy Cunningham. 2003. *Measuring Vulnerability: Who Suffered in the 1995 Mexican Crisis?* Washington, DC: World Bank.

Morley, Samuel. 1995. *Poverty and Inequality in Latin America: The Impact of Adjustment and Recovery in the 1980s*. Baltimore: Johns Hopkins University Press.

Musgrove, Philip. 1991. *Feeding Latin America's Children: An Analytical Survey of Food Programs*. World Bank, Latin America and the Caribbean Technical Department Regional Studies Program No. 11, Washington, DC.

Muth, R. 1969. *Cities and Housing*. Chicago: University of Chicago Press.

National Research Council. 2003. *Cities Transformed: Demographic Change and Its Implications in the Developing World*, ed. Panel on Urban Population Dynamics, M.R. Montgomery, R. Stren, B. Cohen, and H.E. Reed. Committee on Population, Division of Behavioral and Social Sciences and Education. Washington, DC: National Academies Press.

Neri, Marcelo C., and Mark Thomas. 2000. "Macro Shocks and Microeconomic Instability: An Episodic Analysis of Booms and Recessions." *Escola de Pos-Graduacao em Economia da Fundacao Getulio Vargas*. Economic Working Paper No. 391.

Nussbaum, Martha. 2001. *Women and Development: The Capabilities Approach*. New York: Cambridge University Press.

Perlman, Janice. 1976. *The Myth of Marginality: Urban Poverty and Politics in Rio de Janeiro*. Berkeley: University of California Press.

———. 2003. "Marginality: From Myth to Reality in the *Favelas* of Rio de Janeiro, 1969–2002." In *Urban Informality: Transnational Perspectives from the Middle East, Latin America, and South Asia*, ed. Ananya Roy, 105–46. Lanham, MD: Lexington Books.

Pezzoli, Keith. 1998. *Human Settlements and Planning for Ecological Sustainability: The Case of Mexico City*. Cambridge, MA: MIT Press.

Ravallion, Martin. 2000. *On the Urbanization of Poverty*. Washington, DC: World Bank.

Ravallion, Martin, and Benu Bidani. 1994. "How Robust Is a Poverty Profile?" *World Bank Economic Review* 8 (1): 75–102.

Ridao-Cano, Cristobal. 2003. *Household Welfare and Doping Strategies in the Face of Economic Crisis: Evidence from Uruguay 2002*. Washington, DC: World Bank.

Ruel, Marie T., L. Haddad, and J. L. Garrett 1999. "Are Urban Poverty and Undernutrition Growing? Some Newly Assembled Evidence." *World Development* 27 (11): 1891–1905.

SEDESOL (Secretaria de Desarollo Social). 2003. *Programa Institucional Oportunidades*. Government of Mexico, Mexico City. http://www.progresa.gob.mx/pdfs/prog_oportunidades.pdf

Selby, Henry, Arthur Murphy, and Stephen Lorenzen. 1990. *The Mexican Urban Household: Organizing for Self-Defense*. Austin: University of Texas Press.

Siaens, Corinne, and Quentin Wodon. 2003. *Latest Estimates of National Urban and Rural Poverty in Latin America*. Washington, DC: World Bank.

Tacoli, Cecilia, 1998. "Rural-Urban Interactions: A Guide to the Literature." *Beyond the Rural-Urban Divide*. Special issue of *Environment and Urbanization* 10 (1): 3–4.

Turner, Margery, Susan J. Popkin, and Mary K. Cunningham. 2000. *Section 8 Mobility and Neighborhood Health*. Urban Institute, Washington, DC. www.urban.org/url.cfm?ID=309465.

United Nations. 2003. *World Population Prospects: The 2002 Revision*. New York. esa.un.org/unpp/.

Wodon, Q., R. Castro-Fernandez, K. Lee, G. Lopez-Acevedo, C. Siaens, C. Sobrado, and J.P. Tre. 2001. "Poverty in Latin America: Trends 1986–1998 and Determinants." *Cuadernos de Economia* 114: 127–53.

World Bank. 2000. *Argentina: Poor People in a Rich Country*. Report No. 19992-AR, Washington, DC.

———. 2001a. *Attacking Brazil's Poverty*. Report No. 20475-BR, Washington, DC.

———. 2001b. *Maintaining Social Equity in a Changing Economy*. Report No. 21262, Washington, DC.

———. 2002b. *Mexico Urban Development: A Contribution to a National Urban Strategy*. Report No. 22525, Washington, DC.

———. 2003. *Poverty in Guatemala*. Report No. 24221-GU, Washington, DC.

———. 2004a. *Dimensions of Urban Poverty in ECA*. Washington, DC.

———. 2004b. *World Development Indicators*. Washington, DC.

———. 2004c. *Urban Poverty in Mexico*. Washington, DC.

2

Working One's Way Up: The Urban Poor and the Labor Market

Caterina Ruggeri Laderchi

The key asset of the poor is human capital, which they can monetize through the labor market. Gaining employment—particularly employment that pays a decent wage and offers benefits, stability, and prospects for growth—is probably the major challenge facing the urban poor.

Are poor people poor because the economy fails to create a sufficient number of (good) jobs or because their characteristics do not allow them to obtain the (good) jobs that exist (Bartik 1993)? The answer is: a bit of both. Heads of poor households are more likely to be unemployed than heads of nonpoor ones (table 2.1), and in most countries poverty would drop if unemployment or underemployment were to fall. In Costa Rica, for example, Trejos and Montiel (1999) estimate that urban poverty would decline from 14 percent to 8 percent if the poor participated in labor markets as much as the nonpoor. Nevertheless, the characteristics of the poor—low education, weak integration in social networks that provide access to good jobs—have a bearing on their performance in labor markets.

Labor markets, and the poor's ability to get and keep good jobs, are at the heart of poverty dynamics. Long and protracted unemployment can plunge a household into poverty, while marginal and unsafe jobs generally offer no hope of escaping poverty. More generally, labor markets are the key channel of transmission of macroeconomic volatility to the poor. Such linkages between poverty and the labor market can be mitigated by social insurance and safety nets. Unfortunately, as discussed in chapter 7, the urban poor have very limited access to such social protection in Latin America and the Caribbean. This chapter examines the employment

Caterina Ruggeri Laderchi is an Economist at the World Bank. This chapter benefited from extensive inputs from Marianne Fay.

Table 2.1 Unemployment is higher among the heads of poor households in selected Latin American countries
(percent)

Country	Poor	Nonpoor	Total
Argentina	19.1	4.4	10.2
Brasil	11.2	2.1	4.8
Chile	14.8	2.3	4.9
Colombia	8.8	4.6	7.5

Source: Urani 2003.

situation of the poor and the supply and demand factors that may explain their inability to access or keep good jobs. It then looks at recent labor market developments and their impact on the urban poor, examines how the poor draw on labor in times of crises, and draws policy implications.

How the Urban Poor Use Their Key Asset

Labor income accounts for more than 85 percent of the income of the urban poor in Latin America and the Caribbean (figure 2.1). The extent to which the poor use their labor and the returns they receive are therefore

Figure 2.1 Labor income accounts for more than 85 percent of the income of the urban poor in Latin America and the Caribbean

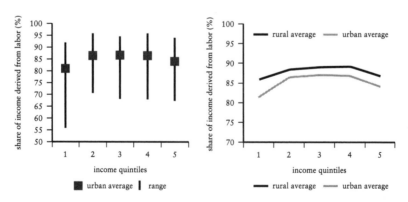

Source: Annex tables 2A.1 and 2A.2.
Note: Range excludes Jamaica, for which the data look suspiciously high. Some of the cross-country differences may be due to different methodology in calculating income and income sources.

key for their livelihoods. It is not surprising, then, that employment is central to the poor's strategies for escaping poverty (box 2.1).

Employment Characteristics of the Urban Poor

The sources of livelihood of the urban poor are more differentiated than those of the rural poor, as evidenced by the fact that their dependence on labor income is slightly lower (figure 2.1). The difference is largest for the poorest quintile (although it is only about 4 percentage points) and is due mostly to the fact that the urban poor receive more pensions and transfers as well as slightly more capital, income, rent, and profits than the rural poor. The slightly lower importance of labor income among urban dwellers seems to be widespread: it holds for 14 of the 17 countries for which data are available (the exceptions are Jamaica, Mexico, and Venezuela).

Box 2.1   Voices of the Poor: How the Urban Poor in Mexico View the Connection between Work and Poverty

A recent survey of poor people's perceptions of poverty and well-being in Mexico underscores the importance of jobs and working conditions. Asked what they perceive is needed to end poverty, poor people cite labor market conditions as the most important factor: 28 percent of urban respondents (21 percent in rural areas) say that more jobs are needed, 27 percent think creating jobs is the most effective government action in reducing poverty, and 25 percent (22 percent in rural areas) identify the need for higher salaries. A quarter of respondents perceive lack of jobs as one of the key problems facing their neighborhood or locality.

Work is seen as the key to improving one's lot: 43 percent of respondents cite working more as the main action they could take to raise their living standard. Other actions mentioned include having jobs compatible with taking care of children (13 percent of respondents) and starting their own business (5 percent of respondents).

Labor markets are also seen as sources of discrimination toward certain groups, and a significant share of the poor views the labor market as a source of insecurity and exclusion. When asked about the specific obstacles poor women face, 30 percent of respondents cite the lack of jobs, and another 27 percent cite discrimination due to child-rearing or pregnancy. Twenty percent of respondents cite losing one's job as a cause of worry over the next 10 years, and 17 percent report worrying about their current lack of work opportunities.

Source: Székely Pardo 2003.

Labor force participation is about 88 percent for poor urban males—somewhat lower than in rural areas (94 percent). The difference reflects the much lower employment rate for poor urban males (72 percent versus 90 percent in rural areas), which is only partially offset by a much higher unemployment rate (15.5 percent versus 3.9 percent in rural areas). In contrast, female participation is higher in urban areas (49 percent) than in rural areas (42 percent). More generally, labor force participation increases with income, largely because employment increases substantially (and unemployment decreases), particularly for women.

Despite the importance of labor for poor people's livelihoods, the region is characterized by great variety in the use of labor by the poor, across both countries and genders (annex tables 2A.3 and 2A.4). Cross-country rates of labor participation vary more among the poorest quintile than for the richer ones, and they vary much more widely among women than among men (participation by poor women ranges from 34 percent in Costa Rica to 77 percent in Jamaica; participation by poor men ranges from 80 percent in Guatemala to 93 percent in Colombia).

The high levels of labor supply by men reflect a range of levels of employment and unemployment. In the bottom quintile in urban areas, the share of adult men employed ranges from 58 percent in Argentina to 85 percent in Mexico, while the share of unemployed is as low as 2 percent in Guatemala and as high as 34 percent in Argentina (annex tables 2A.3 and 2A.4). Such high levels of open unemployment—discussed in more detail below—are a recent development in the region and defy the commonly held notion that open unemployment is a rich country phenomenon. One view is that with inflation having declined in the region, labor markets now tend to adjust through quantity rather than changes in the real wage.

For urban women, the worst employment performance among the bottom quintile is in the Dominican Republic (18 percent), and the best is in Jamaica (73 percent). Female employment and unemployment shares are less closely correlated than they are for men. This seems to reflect the higher likelihood of women resorting to inactivity, although the extent to which they do so varies across countries. Unemployment rates among poor women are 1 percent in Mexico and 18 percent in Colombia, despite very similar employment rates among poor women (42 percent in Mexico and 41 percent in Colombia).

International evidence suggests that skills may be an important determinant of employment performance, with employment rates increasing for higher skill levels (European Commission 2003). But this may not be the case among the urban poor in Latin America and Caribbean. While in Chile employment rates among people in the bottom income quintile rise with skill levels (42 percent for people with low-level skills,

46 percent for people with medium-level skills, and 49 percent for people with high-level), in Brazil the employment rate among this group declines as skills rise (from 54 percent to 49 percent to 47 percent) (annex table 2A.6). Similar trends are found in Argentina and to a certain extent Mexico.[1] Such findings could reflect more limited job growth in high-skill activities (a cause of concern in Mexico) or discouraged high-skilled workers choosing inactivity rather than low-paying jobs. It may also be related to the fact that higher education in some Latin American countries is disconnected from business needs and is therefore perceived to be of low quality.

Job Quality as a Key Element of the Poor's Employment Performance

Finding a job is difficult for poor people. Finding a good job is even harder: most of the jobs to which they have access offer low wages; limited employment security, social protection, or opportunities for advancement; and working conditions that present safety and health risks.

Examples abound of the low quality of jobs accessible to the poor and the implications this has on their earnings and security. Evidence from Peru shows that productivity losses due to ill health are largest among the poor, in part because the poor tend to be employed in low-skill jobs that require more physical effort (Murrugarra and Valdivia 2000). Evidence from urban Mexico shows that the informal sector, which employs a majority of the poor, provides less job tenure, particularly for women.[2] It does, however, seem to be better at allowing women to reconcile family and work responsibility (Calderón-Madrid 2000).

SUPPLY-SIDE LIMITS TO ACCESS TO GOOD-QUALITY JOBS
On average, about three-quarters of the poor have low-level skills, although the figure varies greatly across countries, ranging from 48 percent in Jamaica to 95 percent in Guatemala. Very few poor people have high-level skills (about 2 percent in the poorest quintile, figure 2.2). This figure varies across countries, however: in Argentina, Chile, and Colombia, more than one-fifth of poor urban household heads have at least 11 years of schooling (Urani 2003).

Much of the differences in wages across groups of people can be ascribed to differences in education, suggesting that schooling plays an important role (Arias, Yamada, and Tejerína 2004). Factors that have been linked to the lower educational achievements of the poor, particularly women and nonwhite populations, include the rural-urban divide (which affects access to schools, though there is a great heterogeneity in the quality

Figure 2.2   Very poor men and women are more likely than others to have only low-level skills

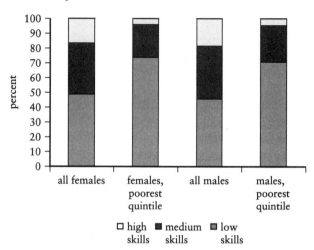

Source: Annex tables 2A.5 and 2A.6.

of schools within both urban and rural areas); racial and socioeconomic discrimination in schools; the intergenerational transmission of low education; and poverty itself, which makes it difficult to afford the direct and indirect costs of education (de Ferranti and others 2004).

Another element suggesting a link between skills and job quality is provided by evidence that most of the linkages between the formal and informal sectors are through the movement of low-skilled workers (Maloney 2002; Calderon-Madrid 2000). This suggests that despite the supposedly higher quality of formal sector jobs, the type of employment low-skilled workers can access is equally poor across sectors. This is supported by the finding that most transitions from formal salaried to informal salaried are voluntary. The high mobility of low-skilled workers across sectors also suggests that they are more fungible and hence less secure, irrespective of the sector of the economy in which they work.

The low quality of the education available to the poor is a major obstacle to accessing better employment. In Chile, where there is little difference in the enrollment of young children across income groups, achievement scores are typically lower at schools serving poorer children (Contreras and Larrañaga 1999). More generally, by international standards the quality of education is low in Latin America and the Caribbean. Weak education systems are likely to have the worst effects on the poor, who are less able to pay for tutoring or private schooling.[3]

Doubts have also been raised about the quality of training in Latin American cities. Saavedra and Chacaltana (2001) document the large variety of training opportunities available in Peru. They find, however, that while training opportunities are available to the urban poor, they are more limited in the poorest regions of the country. Variations in quality between public and private sector training are large, raising concerns about the adequacy of training of people who must rely on public sector training.

DEMAND-SIDE LIMITS TO ACCESS TO GOOD-QUALITY JOBS
The 1990s saw a decline in the number of good jobs available for poor and low-skilled workers in the public sector and in manufacturing. Most countries in the region saw massive retrenchments of the public sector in the past decade, particularly in low-skill jobs. Latin America and the Caribbean may be losing manufacturing jobs to Asian countries with much lower labor and transport costs.

An additional difficulty in accessing good jobs is the spatial distribution of employment. Many of the poor live in distant suburbs poorly connected by public transportation to places of urban employment. Barone and Rebelo (2003) document the influence of limited mobility on the "peripheralization of the poor," high unemployment, and low incomes in marginal areas of São Paulo.

Racial discrimination, gender discrimination, and discrimination related to the stigma of coming from certain neighborhoods may account for the prevalence of poorer people in certain sectors and their inability to move to better jobs. Among workers in Rio de Janeiro with the same number of years of schooling, the returns to labor are lower for residents of *favelas*, even after correcting for race, gender, and distance from Rio's more dynamic employment center (Cardoso, Elias, and Pero 2003) (figure 2.3). This supports the hypothesis of spatial discrimination. It is unclear whether the discrimination occurs through lower pay for the same job (earning discrimination) or by not being able to access the same type of jobs that others with similar nominal qualifications can access (professional segregation).[4]

In Costa Rica, Trejos and Montiel (1999) show that poor people's human capital is rewarded with lower returns. According to them, if the working poor earned average returns, the urban poverty rate would have been 6 percent rather than 14 percent.

Evidence from the United States suggests that discriminatory mechanisms can become internalized by disadvantaged groups, with inner-city African Americans and Latinos tending to self-select themselves out of jobs in white suburban areas and limit their applications to the low-skill

Figure 2.3   Returns to education are lower for Rio de Janeiro's favela residents

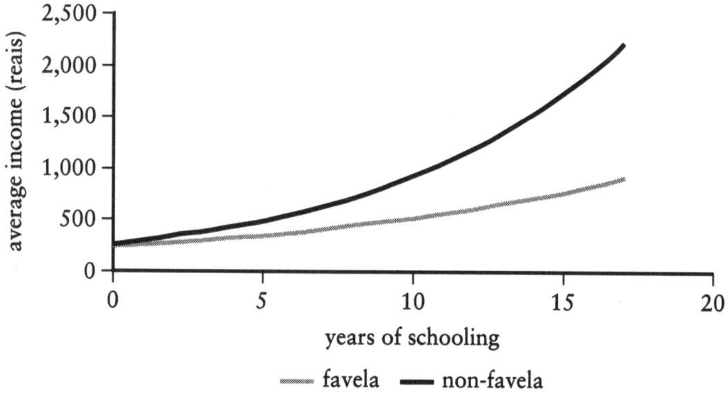

Source: Cardoso, Elias, and Pero 2003.

jobs available in their own neighborhoods. A combination of factors, including poor job information, transportation difficulties, and perceptions of hostility or employer discrimination, explains this phenomenon (Stoll, Holzer, and Ihlanfeldt 1999). The effects of this self-selection on job applications and hiring patterns is reinforced by the reliance on "spreading the word" about vacancies through the social networks of the already employed.

Spatial discrimination in Latin American cities has not been widely explored. Exceptions, such as the work of Nopo, Saavedra, and Torero (2002) on Peru, suggest that some occupational segregation may be taking place. Segregation by ethnic group is higher among wage earners than among the self-employed, though the sector of economic activity, occupation, and firm size explain the greater share of the wage gap across ethnic groups. Arias, Yamada, and Tejerína (2003) find that differences in human capital (including the quality of education and parental education) can account for the lower earnings of nonwhites in urban Brazil in lower paying jobs. At the top of the earnings distribution, however, a 10 percent gap between whites and nonwhites remains unexplained, suggesting the existence of discrimination.

Recent Trends in the Labor Market and Their Impact on the Urban Poor

Labor market developments play a crucial role in shaping the economic environment facing poor households. Such developments include changes in the pattern of utilization of labor, the uses to which such labor is put in terms of sector or type of activities, and the returns that labor can command. An analysis of changes in the income distribution in urban areas of Brazil between 1976 and 1996 highlights the role played by a decrease in average returns to education (Ferreira and Paes de Barros 1999). Despite rising educational attainments, changes in the labor market in Brazil have meant that the poor have been struggling not to lose ground.

The 1990s was a tumultuous decade for Latin America and the Caribbean. The changes that occurred included major labor market developments, some of which are particularly relevant for the urban poor. These include the rise in female participation, which is important inasmuch as having a second income is a key strategy for fighting poverty and diversifying risk; the rise in open unemployment, which was traditionally very low for the poor; the change in the sectoral composition of employment, with a decrease in manufacturing jobs and in jobs supplying services to the middle classes; and an increase in the relative importance of the informal sector.

Increased Female Participation

The most important development in the region's urban labor markets in the 1990s was the increase in female participation (Saavedra 2003).[5] A cohort analysis for urban Colombia based on surveys from 1976 to 1998 estimates that men's participation rate was consistently above 90 percent for all cohorts. In contrast, women's participation increased significantly over time: just 35 percent of women born in 1937 were participating in the work force in 1977, but 65 percent of women born in 1957 were labor force participants (Attanasio and Székely 2002). The increase in female participation has affected all educational levels, but it has been particularly strong among the poor (Duryea and Edwards 2001).

Greater female participation is due to a combination of factors, particularly gains in women's earning opportunities with respect to those of men, a reduction in fertility, and an increase in returns to education. However, in the case of poor women, the key determinant is probably the need to supplement family income when traditional bread winners lose their jobs. In Mexico women who are primarily caregivers enter the informal salaried sectors when faced with increased income risk (Cunningham 2001a). However, when an actual shock occurs and a longer term coping strategy seems to be needed, they enter self-employment or formal jobs.[6] A similar substitution within the household supply of labor is documented in urban Bolivia, where women work longer hours to compensate for a decline in their husbands' wages (Pradhan and Van Soest 1997, cited by Lay and Wiebelt 2001).

There is some evidence that the increase in female participation may have occurred in low-quality jobs. This could be due to discrimination, lower education, or the decline in better quality work, although the need to combine work with childcare is likely to be key.[7] The importance of childcare is underscored by Deutsch's (1998) study of childcare in 15 *favelas* in Rio de Janeiro. She concludes that increased low-cost childcare in Rio's *favelas* raised mothers' labor force participation as well as their use of public care. Deutsch finds that the most expensive care options (and therefore the least affordable to the poorest) are the most effective, because of the greater flexibility they offer mothers in terms of hours they can work.

Perlman (2003) documents the increase in paid at-home employment for women in Rio de Janeiro over the past 30 years. This type of arrangement, which allows poor women to combine unpaid housework and paid work, may have offset the decline in the demand for live-in domestic help, but it comes with greater insecurity in earnings.

Hallman and others (2002) show that increased female participation in Guatemala is mostly in low-quality, high-insecurity, part-time jobs that offer the opportunity of combining work with some childcare activities. About 40 percent of low-income working mothers take care of their children while working. Almost 30 percent leave their children with another household member, and about as many leave them in the homes of relatives or neighbors. The absence of childcare is likely to have a particularly large effect on recent immigrants, who may have weaker social networks. As the economies of Latin America and the Caribbean become more formal, women may find it more difficult to combine working and raising children.

Increased Unemployment

The rise in open unemployment is a relatively recent development in Latin America's urban labor markets, where it has become an increasingly acute problem in Argentina, Colombia, Chile, Uruguay, and Venezuela (Saavedra 2003). The increase, from relatively low levels at the beginning of the 1990s, has been ascribed to macroeconomic stability, which has prevented real wages from adjusting downward (exceptions were the Tequila crisis in Mexico and the 2000 crisis in Argentina, during which real wages fell precipitously and labor markets adjusted mostly through prices). Skill-intensive technological progress and increasing participation following crises, especially by women, may also be driving this trend (de Ferranti and others 2003). Arias (2001) documents how the slow speed of job creation in Argentina and Costa Rica affected older workers and those with higher education, who had difficulties getting reemployed, not only the low-skilled young, who traditionally experience problems entering the labor market.

Changes in the Sectoral Distribution of Jobs

During the 1990s Latin America and the Caribbean saw a reduction in the share of manufacturing jobs, an increase in the share of service jobs (both high- and low-skill), and a decrease in public sector employment (Saavedra 2003). These patterns varied across countries. In Peru, for example, manufacturing declined from 13 percent of total employment in 1994 to 9 percent in 2000. In Argentina unskilled services expanded from 16 percent of total employment in 1992 to 23 percent in 1997, while skilled services' share of total employment declined (from 22 to 16 percent) and manufacturing stagnated (Saavedra 2003).

This shift in employment patterns has been accompanied by increasing demand for skilled workers, especially workers with tertiary education, as foreign direct investment and appreciating exchange rates favored the adoption of new technologies. (Mexico, where low-skilled workers have fared relatively better than higher-skilled workers in recent years, is an exception.) These sectoral changes have been felt strongly in urban areas. For example, the manufacturing share of employment in the six main Brazilian metropolitan areas (Porto Alegre, São Paulo, Rio de Janeiro, Belo Horizonte, Salvador, and Recife) fell more than 16 percent between 1991 and 2002, for a total employment loss of 600,000 jobs (Urani 2003).

Although the brunt of these changes has affected the middle class, and in some cases the upper-middle class, they have had at least second-round effects on the demand for labor of the urban poor by affecting the demand for low-paid, low-skill jobs such as maids, caretakers, and porters. There is also evidence that some form of "grade inflation" (whereby the schooling requirements for jobs has risen) may have taken place for jobs traditionally held by low-skilled workers, such as garbage collectors (Perlman 2003). In Mexico there is evidence of a strong direct effect on the employment of the poor, with the share of the poor employed in manufacturing falling from 26 percent in 1991 to 19 percent in 2003 (figure 2.4).

Increases in Informal Sector Jobs

Informality is not a particularly urban phenomenon: it is more prevalent in rural areas. Arguably, however, in urban areas some of its characteris-

Figure 2.4   In Mexico the percentage of the urban poor employed in good jobs fell between 1991 and 2000

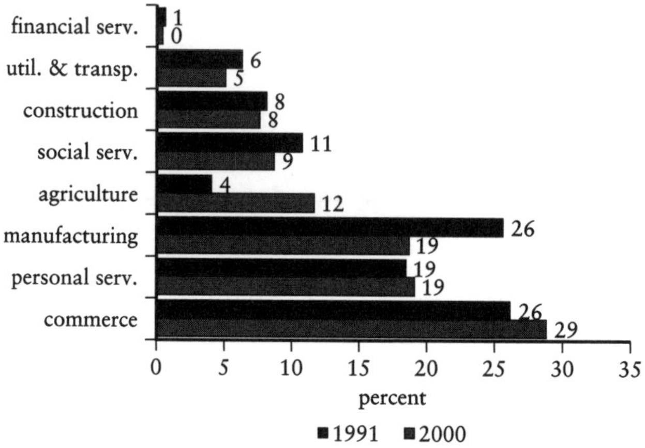

Source: Montes and Santamaría 2004.

tics (such as the lack of worker protection and the ease of dismissal) have a greater bearing on the living conditions of the poor, due to their dependence on the cash economy and the difficulty of diversifying household coping strategies away from selling labor. Access to other strategies, such as relying on informal support networks, may be more limited in urban than in rural areas (see chapter 6).

The informal sector accounts for about 70 percent of the employment of the urban poor, a much higher share than for richer groups (the average for all urban employment is 45 percent, the figure for the top quintile is 32 percent). A monotonic decline in informality by quintile is found throughout the region, with the exception of El Salvador and Jamaica. The lowest shares of adults in the bottom quintile working in the informal sector are found in El Salvador and Venezuela (about 36 percent), while Bolivia, Ecuador, and Paraguay record the highest shares (about 86 percent) (annex table 2A.8).

The expansion of informal employment has been linked to the slowdown of the economy at the end of the 1990s and the rise in nonwage costs (Saavedra 2003). The interpretation of this trend depends on how one views the sector. Some informal activities are low value-added, have low capital requirements, and expand at times of crisis due to the lack of barriers to entry, despite the possible decline in market demand. Some economists claim that in Latin America and the Caribbean the share of informal jobs within urban employment rises especially quickly in the economies most affected by recession (Gilbert 1997).

On the other hand, Maloney (2002) has shown evidence of the pro-cyclical nature of the informal sector in Brazil and Mexico. This supports a more dynamic view of the informal sector. It suggests that the rise of informality should not be seen as a cause of the deteriorating working conditions of the urban poor, which are driven by the low skill level of many urban residents and problems with formal training and apprenticeship systems. Instead, it is the differential between the cost to the employer and the perceived benefits to the workers of social security systems, combined with low national productivity, that makes low-technology and low-capital production a good alternative to formal sector jobs.

At the core of this view is the fact that the informal sector is composed largely of self-employed workers.[8] The evidence (reviewed in Maloney 2002) suggests that these microentrepreneurs have moved voluntarily to the sector rather than being forced into it by the dual structure of the labor market. Such a move is often fostered by having accumulated skills, capital, and contacts by working in the formal sector, by wanting to be "one's own boss," or by facing obstacles to career progression in the formal sector due to low levels of formal education.

The lack of security and social protection that characterizes the informal sector is a source of concern. But the high levels of firm mortality and the need for entrepreneurs to cover their own insurance expenses are common to all small enterprises—formal or informal, in developing or developed countries. Maloney (2002) suggests that as they grow and become more established, small firms start complying with different aspects of regulation and become more formal by degrees.

Concerns remain, however, about the low quality of jobs of salaried workers in the informal sector, who enjoy neither the sense of autonomy of being their own bosses nor the security of a formal sector job, and for workers performing unpaid work in family businesses. The issue is more appropriately framed as one of low quality of work in general for those who have low skills, as there seems to be little difference between the formal and informal jobs they can access. Maloney (1999) reports that in Mexico the urban labor market is fluid and integrated: there is a continuum between formal and informal activities, informal jobs are found in formal enterprises, and workers often hold different types of jobs at the same time.[9] Evidence from both Argentina and Mexico suggests that salaried informal jobs can act as entry points into the labor market for younger workers, who move into formal sector jobs after a relatively brief tenure.

Use of Labor in Times of Crises

Labor markets stand at a crucial junction between the macro and micro environments households live in, a link that is often brought up when discussing the effects of growth on the poor (see chapter 1). Both the specific sources of opportunities and vulnerability that the macro environment offers and the way households respond to them are mediated largely by the labor market.

Based on the literature that shows the positive effects of growth on the poor, one would expect that in the aggregate a crisis would negatively affect them. The literature on the United States offers evidence that growth in the metropolitan economy is particularly pro-poor (Bartik 1993). This result can be explained in a variety of ways. If the labor market is segmented and good jobs are rationed, workers may be required to queue to access them, and the queues may be particularly long for disadvantaged workers. By shortening the queues, economic growth may therefore be particularly beneficial for the poorest workers. Other explanations for the effects of growth on poor people's jobs focus on the supply elasticities of different groups and on the skill intensity of the jobs created or lost.

In Latin America the issue has been analyzed in terms of the impact of shocks on labor markets. Fallon and Lucas (2002) find that total employment continued to rise through the 1995 crisis in Mexico (when GDP declined more than 6 percent) and that it declined by less than 3 percent in Argentina (when GDP contracted 4 percent). Increases in employment can, however, also be consistent with increased unemployment, as households cope with the fall in income due to the crisis by increasing their participation and more people look for jobs.[10]

At the micro level, labor market status affects the specific sources of vulnerability households face, with the sectoral distribution of the shocks and the educational levels of the workforce important elements of the transmission mechanism. In Mexico households whose head was without work before the 1995 crisis experienced much larger proportional reductions in income than other households (Maloney and others 2003). In contrast, other groups, such as workers in the informal sector, did not experience any additional variability relative to their precrisis situation. Other studies confirm that the employment status of household members and changes in their status are likely to be the major transmission channel of macroeconomic crises to households. A study of the 2001–2 Argentine crisis finds that becoming unemployed was the largest shock to household income and that the probability of unemployment varied across sectors and educational levels. Public sector workers were less likely to lose their

Table 2.2 Argentine households used a variety of labor-market-related strategies to cope with the 2001–2 Crisis

Strategy	Percent of all households that used strategy	Percent of households reporting a reduction in income that used strategy
Increase participation of family members in labor market	13.4	16.1
Work more hours	14.8	19.2
Increase home manufacture	59.9	62.6
Dismiss domestic workers or reduce domestic services	35.3	40.4
Migrate	4.1	3.9

Source: Fiszbein, Adúriz, and Giovagnoli 2002.

jobs, while in the private sector, construction workers were the most vulnerable. Better educated people were less likely to become unemployed than people with less education, and households with public sector workers or more educated heads were less likely to suffer income losses (Pessino and Andres 2003).

Given the high macroeconomic volatility the region has experienced, the issue of how households adjust their labor market behavior following crises, and the longer term repercussions of these strategies, have attracted a great deal of attention.[11] During the Argentine crisis, households adopted a variety of strategies (table 2.2). As these decisions are often part of householdwide strategies, their intrahousehold consequences also need to be analyzed.

A few qualitative studies analyze in detail the labor market implications of household coping strategies. Fuchs (2001) finds that 36 percent of workers in Puebla increased their working hours during the 1994–95 Mexico crisis. Blue-collar and white-collar employees resorted to finding alternative jobs. A much lower share of the self-employed held more than one job. Together with intensifying their use of labor, households also increased participation by other family members. Women, whose qualifications are lower on average, found it difficult to enter the manufacturing sector and resorted to informal petty trading activities. Finally, when the crisis meant losing jobs, people changed sector of activity. Those with higher skills as well as some capital provided by severance payments moved more easily than others into self-employment. Less qualified workers often remained unemployed despite vacancies in some textile factories, as wages fell too low to make working worthwhile.

Analyses of coping strategies highlight the importance of the combination of assets households command (Fuchs 2001). A household's portfolio matters for a variety of reasons. First, assets are complementary. Second, shocks affect households through variations in the returns to household assets, particularly human capital, so that portfolio composition affects household-specific sources of vulnerability. In Brazil, for example, education is associated with a lower probability of making a transition into poverty and a higher probability of making a transition out of poverty following a crisis (de Ferranti and others 2000). In other crises, however, the better educated have been more affected (for a discussion of urban Mexico in 1995, see Mckenzie 2003).

The intrahousehold consequences of the labor market strategies adopted by the household have raised significant concern. Cunningham (2001b) documents how increased female participation in work outside the house is accompanied by a decrease of only half of the hours spent doing housework, resulting in both a decrease of the overall time spent on housework activities, which may affect the welfare of household members, and a decrease in women's leisure. Moreover, women's burden may rise through increased reliance on home production, so that working hours may become longer without a visible change in women's work status.

The recourse to children's labor following crises has also attracted a great deal of attention. Theory suggests that the effects of shocks on children's labor supply are potentially ambiguous, as they depend on the relative importance of substitution effects (child labor may become less attractive, due to the lower opportunity cost of sending children to school) and income effects (if there is a subsistence constraint, parents may resort to child labor to boost household income). Which effect will prevail is likely to depend on the circumstances, especially the depth of the crisis. The empirical evidence on this issue is mixed.

The overall evidence suggests that even if child labor does not necessarily increase during crises, children may suffer important disruptions to their learning process. In metropolitan Brazil child labor seems to be at least mildly procyclical, increasing with economic growth rather than at times of crisis (de Ferranti and others 2000; Duryea and Arends-Kuenning 2003). This seems to be the case in Mexico as well (Maloney 2002). It is likely, however, that different groups may be affected differently. The evidence suggests that if the option of working in family-run activities is available, the opportunity cost of studying may be higher, though not enough to withdraw children from school. In Brazil this effect has resulted in increased repetition, which can have longer-term effects for children.[12]

Child labor market status and educational outcomes are not associated in a simple way. Cross-country analysis shows that school enrollment is negatively correlated with income and employment volatility in low-income countries (Flug, Spilimbergo, and Wachtenheim 1998, quoted in Duryea and Arends-Kuenning 2003). But such negative correlation does not necessarily hold. De Ferranti and others (2000) find that in metropolitan Brazil, school enrollment, in contrast to child labor, does not vary over the cycle. And Schady (2002), looking at school attendance in Peru over the 1988–92 period, finds that the crisis did not affect attendance by school-age children, while it increased mean educational attainment. He suggests that declining opportunities in the labor market meant that parents could put more effort into investing in their children's education. This argument points to the complexity of educational outcomes, reinforced by the consideration that these outcomes also depend on a variety of complementary inputs. What happens to these other expenditures can be a cause of concern.

In Uruguay during the recent crisis, 71 percent of households with children (86 percent in the bottom wealth quintile, 49 percent in the top one) declared that they had curtailed educational expenditures during 2002, while only 6 percent admitted to having their children drop out of school or delay entry into the system (Ridao-Cano 2003). It is too early to evaluate the consequences of such cuts in expenditure.

Finally, labor market–related changes can affect the welfare of various household members, through various channels. About 12 percent of Argentines experienced some change in health insurance coverage as a result of the recent crisis, with 60 percent (concentrated in the lowest income groups) losing all coverage (Fiszbein, Adúriz, and Giovagnoli, 2002). Other, more indirect effects are due to changes in expenditure in health and education, which may affect the stock of human capital of household members. Examples include arranging fewer medical checkups for children (a strategy adopted by 37 percent of Argentine households with children under 12 reported) and reducing educational inputs (72 percent of households reduced their purchases of school materials, 2.0 percent substituted private school for public ones, and 3.1 percent turned to cheaper private schools).

Conclusion: How to Make Labor Markets
Work Better for the Urban Poor

Throughout Latin America and the Caribbean, the urban poor are crucially dependent on labor, although the extent to which they use labor, as measured by employment, unemployment, and participation, varies greatly by country and gender. During the 1990s several important changes in the labor market occurred. Female participation rose; open unemployment increased; the sectoral composition of jobs changed, with a decrease of manufacturing and public sector employment; and the informal sector grew. The urban poor are at increased risk of unemployment, and the quality of the jobs they can access is low. Skill levels, and the low quality of education and training available to them, are important barriers to obtaining better jobs. This is particularly worrisome in light of the decline in the sectors with relatively well-paid low-skill jobs. Access to good jobs is also likely to be hindered by lack of appropriate transportation to and from areas where urban poverty is concentrated; by gender, ethnic, and racial discrimination; and by the stigma of coming from an impoverished neighborhood. Access to good jobs is particularly poor for women, both because of their lower skill levels and because the increase in their labor-market participation has come about without significant changes in gender roles or the availability of childcare. The result may be an increased concentration of women in low-paying and casual jobs that offer the possibility of reconciling their market and nonmarket responsibilities.

Labor markets are the main channel through which the urban poor are affected by macroeconomic developments, positive or negative. But the impact of economic crisis on the urban poor and the coping strategies they adopt are context and crisis specific. At the aggregate level, the poor may or may not be the most affected by a crisis, and the way they adapt to the shock—generally centered on intensifying the use of labor—may result in increased employment or unemployment, as more labor is supplied. At the micro level, household vulnerability to a given shock depends on the labor-market status of household members, the sectors in which they work, their educational levels, and the overall composition of their asset portfolios. A key insight that emerges from the analysis of the impact of and response to crises at the household level is that the burden of adjusting household labor supply may fall disproportionately on particular household members. The evidence on the effect of crises on child labor is very mixed. Finally, coping strategies may have a negative impact on the present or future labor market performance of the poor if they result in decreased spending on schooling or other complementary inputs.

What are the policy implications of these results? In particular, what active labor market policies could help increase demand for low-skilled workers or improve their earning ability?[13] With the exception of childcare and urban transport policies, the recommended policies are not urban specific. Instead, they include training and education policies that affect the supply of labor. Evaluations suggest that the impact of training programs is positive, although small. It takes a very large effort to provide sufficient effective training to make a difference.[14] As to broader education policies, they need to focus on increasing quality and improving the skills level of students who will eventually hold low-skill jobs (Freeman and Gottschalk 1998).[15]

Active labor market policies that tackle the demand for labor include policies to reduce the cost of employing the disadvantaged, public employment schemes, and employment regulations.[16] Evidence from the United States suggests that wage subsidies have succeeded in raising demand for youth, albeit only modestly (Katz 1998). In contrast, subsidies to employers to locate in particular impoverished areas have been shown not to be cost effective (Gramlich and Heflin 1998). The conclusion, then, is that subsidy policies should target disadvantaged individuals rather than disadvantaged areas. Public employment programs for targeted groups appear to increase employment of the targeted group, but they have little impact on future wages or skills (Gottschalk 1998). It is not clear how realistic such programs are in Latin America and the Caribbean, given public sector retrenchment and bloated public labor forces. Regarding employment regulations, many Latin American countries could benefit from more flexible hiring rules. (Redesigning social security, including unemployment insurance, to make it available to informal and self-employed workers is discussed in chapter 8.)

Local governments can encourage job creation through local economic development policies. Local economic development has become increasingly popular over the past decade, fueled partly by the decentralization explosion and partly by the well-publicized success of a few cities. It is based on the premises that favorable local business conditions are necessary for achieving prosperity and that local governments have an essential role to play in creating favorable environments for business success and job creation. Local economic development thus requires a partnership between local governments, business, and community interests that seek to reduce the obstacles to growth and attract the investment needed to develop their economic and employment base.

Local economic development efforts that work tend to be the ones that mobilize a city's stakeholders to identify local strengths, bottlenecks, and market opportunities and commit to joint actions. This often includes actions to attract new firms or industries. To be effective these activities should aim to enhance comparative advantage and avoid costly efforts to simply compete with other locations through tax and public investment incentives, which can lead to an expensive race to the bottom. Although there are a number of well-documented successes, they appear to be based on idiosyncratic circumstances and are therefore hard to replicate.[17]

The findings of this chapter suggest a three-pronged strategy for increasing the returns to labor of the urban poor and facilitating their access to jobs, particularly better quality jobs:

- *Increase the supply of labor.* Interventions in this area should include providing women with better ways of balancing their household and market activities. Child (and possibly elder) care play a crucial role in this respect, especially if designed to accommodate flexible work hours. In addition, interventions targeting tangible barriers to entry (such as affordable and reliable urban transport) or intangible ones (such as actions to reduce discrimination) are likely to have positive effects on the labor supply of the poor.
- *Increase returns to labor.* Improving skills and the quality of education and training available to poor people is key to increasing their employability, the returns they can receive for their work, and their flexibility, particularly during crises. Well-targeted and designed training programs can have a positive impact, although their effect is likely to be small.
- *Help poor people find work during crises.* Together with social insurance (notably unemployment insurance), measures are needed to help affected groups find work during crises. Measures include income-generating activities, such as workfare (discussed in chapter 8 in the context of social safety nets) and job-matching services, with which the OECD has had success (see Martin 1998).

Annex

Unless otherwise noted the statistical information for this annex was provided by Leo Gasparini and his team at the Universidad Nacional de la Plata (Buenos Aires). He was commissioned to produce disaggregated urban and rural data from the latest available surveys for Latin America and the Carribbean for a variety of indicators.

Table 2A.1 Sources of Household Income in Urban Areas, by per Capita Household Income Quintile
(percent)

Country	Labor income					Capital, income rents and profits					Pensions					Transfers				
	1	2	3	4	5	1	2	3	4	5	1	2	3	4	5	1	2	3	4	5
Argentina 2001	79.1	80.7	77.4	75.3	78.4	0.9	1.5	1.1	1.6	4.4	9.8	12.6	17.2	18.9	13.2	10.2	5.2	4.2	4.2	4.1
Bolivia 2002	91.2	92.0	89.5	88.7	79.8	1.3	0.6	1.1	2.2	8.0	0.0	0.6	2.5	2.1	4.2	7.5	6.8	6.9	7.0	7.9
Brazil 2001	79.2	81.5	79.5	81.0	77.8	2.7	1.5	1.2	1.5	3.4	15.2	15.7	18.6	16.8	18.3	2.9	1.3	0.7	0.7	0.5
Chile 2000	73.4	79.2	81.5	77.5	81.4	—	—	—	—	—	4.4	7.3	8.0	11.1	6.6	7.5	4.3	1.8	0.7	0.1
Colombia 1999	78.6	83.7	85.2	83.5	79.4	4.9	2.7	3.1	3.6	6.0	0.9	5.1	4.7	7.4	8.5	13.0	6.6	5.8	4.4	5.2
Costa Rica 2000	78.3	83.7	90.1	89.9	88.3	—	—	—	—	—	6.7	9.5	5.2	6.0	7.2	15.0	6.8	4.7	4.1	4.4
Dominican Republic 1997	72.5	83.2	86.1	85.5	85.3	3.5	1.9	1.8	2.0	2.4	3.2	2.7	1.7	1.5	5.0	20.8	12.1	10.5	11.0	7.3
Ecuador 1998	86.9	92.2	94.3	93.5	91.8	2.5	1.8	1.5	1.6	4.7	—	—	—	—	—	—	—	—	—	—
El Salvador 2000	74.0	79.6	83.8	85.9	84.8	1.3	0.9	1.4	0.9	2.8	2.7	5.8	5.9	4.7	6.1	19.1	11.2	6.7	6.1	4.3
Guatemala 2000	88.9	94.6	87.5	89.3	75.6	0.4	0.2	0.5	0.4	5.8	1.3	1.1	3.2	3.4	3.6	9.4	4.1	8.8	6.9	15.1

(table continues on the following page)

Table 2A.1 (continued)
(percent)

Country	Labor income					Capital, income rents and profits					Pensions					Transfers				
	1	2	3	4	5	1	2	3	4	5	1	2	3	4	5	1	2	3	4	5
Honduras 1999	86.9	92.6	94.1	95.5	93.6	2.6	1.2	1.0	1.0	3.4	1.0	0.9	0.7	0.5	0.8	9.5	5.2	4.2	3.0	2.2
Jamaica 1999	100.0	98.3	98.9	100.0	99.2	—	—	—	—	—	—	—	—	—	—	—	—	—	—	—
Mexico 2000	91.8	93.6	93.3	92.8	89.2	0.8	0.4	0.8	0.7	2.4	3.9	3.7	3.9	4.0	6.6	3.5	2.3	2.0	2.5	1.9
Nicaragua 2001	84.3	92.2	92.6	91.9	90.6	0.0	0.8	0.2	0.6	6.0	3.3	1.8	2.9	1.9	1.0	12.5	5.2	4.5	5.6	2.4
Panama 2000	56.2	78.5	78.6	79.4	75.8	0.9	0.7	1.3	0.9	2.1	5.9	7.9	10.4	13.1	16.3	36.6	12.4	8.8	5.8	3.7
Paraguay 1999	75.0	88.4	87.9	88.7	86.4	4.3	0.6	1.5	1.5	3.4	3.1	0.6	2.6	3.4	5.8	17.5	10.4	7.9	6.4	4.5
Peru 2000	83.7	86.5	87.4	86.4	81.6	0.9	1.0	0.8	1.3	3.2	0.8	3.5	4.5	7.5	9.4	14.5	9.0	7.2	4.7	5.8
Uruguay 2000	72.4	70.9	68.3	68.2	67.7	0.3	0.6	1.1	1.6	5.6	14.5	20.9	24.4	25.3	24.3	12.8	7.6	6.1	4.9	2.4
Venezuela 1998	90.3	95.5	94.3	94.9	93.8	1.0	0.5	0.5	0.4	1.0	—	—	—	—	—	8.6	3.8	4.7	4.2	4.9

Note: — = not available.

68

Table 2A.2 Sources of Household Income in Rural Areas, by per Capita Household Income Quintile

(percent)

Country	Labor income					Capital, income rents and profits					Pensions					Transfers				
	1	2	3	4	5	1	2	3	4	5	1	2	3	4	5	1	2	3	4	5
Bolivia 2002	92.7	91.3	91.6	91.4	85.8	0.3	0.8	0.8	0.6	3.5	0.0	0.6	1.4	2.0	3.4	7.1	7.2	6.3	6.0	7.3
Brazil 2001	85.3	79.3	74.0	80.0	81.5	4.4	1.9	1.1	1.9	5.2	9.1	18.2	24.7	17.7	12.9	1.1	0.6	0.2	0.4	0.3
Chile 2000	69.7	74.7	75.7	77.2	76.9	—	—	—	—	—	4.2	6.9	9.6	10.6	5.3	12.3	8.0	4.4	1.9	0.4
Colombia 1999	90.1	91.3	91.5	89.8	89.3	1.5	1.3	1.4	1.9	3.3	0.3	1.2	2.3	3.8	3.8	7.5	5.7	4.3	4.2	3.5
Costa Rica 2000	84.9	91.4	92.9	93.7	89.9	—	—	—	—	—	3.6	3.8	2.9	3.5	3.4	11.4	4.8	4.2	2.8	6.7
Dominican Republic 1997	85.5	87.3	90.4	88.8	83.8	0.9	0.2	0.6	0.6	0.8	1.4	1.6	0.8	0.7	0.6	12.1	11.0	8.2	9.9	14.9
Ecuador 1998	94.0	95.5	96.8	96.5	91.3	0.7	0.9	0.7	0.9	4.5	—	—	—	—	—	—	—	—	—	—
El Salvador 2000	78.9	88.3	90.3	91.0	90.6	0.6	0.1	0.2	0.3	0.5	0.9	0.8	1.7	2.3	1.5	17.3	8.1	5.5	3.6	4.2
Guatemala 2000	93.4	89.5	89.6	87.0	76.9	0.0	0.1	0.1	0.4	1.6	0.5	1.5	1.0	1.3	2.0	6.1	8.9	9.3	11.4	19.5
Honduras 1999	91.0	94.4	96.4	97.2	97.8	1.6	1.1	0.8	0.3	0.5	0.1	0.1	0.4	0.3	0.4	7.3	4.3	2.4	2.2	1.3

(table continues on the following page)

69

Table 2A.2 (continued)
(percent)

Country	Labor income					Capital, income rents and profits					Pensions					Transfers				
	1	2	3	4	5	1	2	3	4	5	1	2	3	4	5	1	2	3	4	5
Jamaica 1999	96.6	96.7	97.5	98.1	95.8	—	—	—	—	—	—	—	—	—	—	—	—	—	—	—
Mexico 2000	81.4	84.3	82.3	85.0	79.6	0.5	0.3	0.5	0.8	1.5	0.8	1.8	2.3	1.8	2.0	17.2	13.6	14.9	12.3	16.8
Nicaragua 2001	93.4	94.5	94.9	94.9	89.4	0.3	0.2	0.5	0.7	3.6	0.3	0.3	0.8	0.6	4.5	6.0	4.9	3.7	3.8	2.5
Panama 2000	63.1	76.7	80.5	80.5	76.9	0.2	0.7	0.8	1.1	2.8	3.3	6.2	8.9	11.0	12.2	32.6	14.9	8.3	5.8	5.0
Paraguay 1999	82.9	85.4	86.0	85.9	90.5	0.4	0.2	0.1	0.7	2.4	0.4	0.7	3.5	4.6	3.4	16.3	13.6	10.5	8.8	3.7
Peru 2000	92.1	93.6	93.5	89.9	83.6	0.4	0.8	0.9	0.8	2.9	0.4	1.3	2.6	3.7	7.2	7.0	4.3	3.1	5.6	6.4
Venezuela 1998	87.2	91.8	92.4	92.7	93.0	1.0	0.9	0.6	0.7	1.7	—	—	—	—	—	10.2	6.3	6.1	5.8	4.6

Note: — = not available.

70

Table 2A.3 Percentage of Employed and Unemployed Adults in Urban Areas, by Gender and per Capita Income Quintile

Country	% female adults employed						% female adults unemployed						% male adults employed						% male adults unemployed					
	1	2	3	4	5	Total	1	2	3	4	5	Total	1	2	3	4	5	Total	1	2	3	4	5	Total
Argentina 2001	34.0	31.6	42.1	54.4	69.5	48.7	12.4	9.5	9.7	6.0	3.5	7.7	58.2	73.6	77.7	81.2	91.3	78.4	33.6	18.0	13.1	10.7	2.9	13.9
Bolivia 2002	50.3	54.9	62.1	71.1	70.5	65.7	4.7	5.5	4.4	2.6	4.5	4.1	82.3	88.1	91.2	90.3	91.1	90.2	10.0	4.1	2.8	4.0	2.3	3.4
Brazil 2001	38.2	45.3	51.9	58.3	65.0	54.4	10.8	7.5	5.6	4.5	2.6	5.4	73.3	81.7	84.4	86.7	88.7	84.6	13.2	6.4	4.3	2.9	1.7	4.5
Chile 2000	23.9	32.6	45.1	51.3	66.5	46.9	10.4	7.4	4.3	3.0	2.3	4.9	67.6	82.0	84.4	86.5	90.8	83.9	21.9	8.9	6.4	4.1	1.7	7.1
Colombia 1999	40.7	39.5	44.8	54.6	64.7	52.8	17.6	15.9	12.8	8.2	5.8	10.2	68.2	76.5	82.7	84.8	86.1	82.3	25.3	16.1	11.0	7.8	5.6	10.3
Costa Rica 2000	26.9	28.0	37.8	49.1	62.6	47.2	7.3	2.8	2.0	1.5	1.1	2.1	70.5	88.3	90.2	90.4	92.7	89.8	13.7	2.1	1.6	2.0	1.3	2.4
Dominican Republic 1997	17.9	30.5	38.5	49.3	61.9	45.1	18.8	18.8	11.9	7.8	6.1	10.8	65.3	84.1	87.5	87.5	93.4	87.3	22.5	9.2	6.2	5.9	2.5	6.6
Ecuador 1998	52.1	49.2	54.4	59.7	73.0	61.4	3.0	3.2	4.4	2.0	1.2	2.4	63.1	89.4	94.5	94.4	97.1	92.7	21.6	2.3	1.9	1.9	0.7	2.8
El Salvador 2000	56.4	57.2	59.6	66.8	70.4	64.2	2.7	2.6	1.8	1.0	0.9	1.5	80.7	77.3	85.5	86.6	88.8	85.5	9.5	9.5	5.8	5.3	2.9	5.4
Guatemala 2000	39.8	37.7	47.1	51.1	60.1	52.5	6.1	0.7	0.6	1.4	1.6	1.5	78.4	92.9	91.9	87.2	90.3	89.5	1.7	1.0	2.0	2.2	1.5	1.7

(table continues on the following page)

Table 2A.3 (continued)

Country	% female adults employed						% female adults unemployed						% male adults employed						% male adults unemployed					
	1	2	3	4	5	Total	1	2	3	4	5	Total	1	2	3	4	5	Total	1	2	3	4	5	Total
Honduras 1999	47.3	46.9	53.0	65.7	72.4	61.4	2.0	2.2	2.3	1.8	1.0	1.7	74.7	86.4	91.6	93.1	95.4	91.5	10.7	7.5	3.3	3.5	1.2	3.6
Jamaica 1999	73.1	75.6	67.3	75.2	87.4	77.8	3.9	8.0	4.4	2.2	1.5	3.4	81.6	82.0	89.7	95.6	97.9	92.6	6.6	7.7	0.0	1.6	0.0	1.9
Mexico 2000	42.3	36.8	40.0	52.4	56.9	47.8	0.6	0.1	0.3	0.3	0.6	0.4	85.5	90.6	91.3	92.8	93.2	91.8	2.3	1.4	1.7	0.8	1.1	1.3
Nicaragua 2001	34.9	46.8	53.3	56.2	65.7	55.8	10.7	3.1	5.4	5.2	3.8	4.9	63.8	82.9	81.9	85.9	87.4	84.0	20.9	12.6	6.7	5.8	4.3	7.2
Panama 2000	26.8	28.3	39.2	53.7	67.0	50.1	11.3	7.5	5.6	3.7	1.9	4.5	61.0	75.3	81.7	85.5	87.6	82.9	25.0	15.7	10.5	4.9	2.8	7.7
Paraguay 1999	34.8	36.2	49.4	57.2	75.6	58.4	4.8	3.2	4.5	3.7	1.6	3.1	62.1	88.3	85.5	89.0	91.8	88.2	22.1	5.8	3.5	3.9	1.7	3.9
Peru 2000	52.6	52.8	51.5	56.7	60.4	56.1	2.7	3.7	4.7	3.7	2.0	3.3	77.6	78.2	88.8	86.2	87.8	85.9	9.6	9.3	4.7	3.7	2.6	4.5
Uruguay 2000	38.3	45.4	56.0	64.3	70.4	56.6	15.1	12.2	7.7	5.5	2.8	8.0	79.3	79.8	83.9	86.5	89.9	84.4	11.8	9.4	5.3	4.0	1.7	6.0
Venezuela 1998	36.8	38.8	56.0	62.8	66.9	60.5	10.2	7.5	4.1	3.8	2.4	3.8	76.5	89.5	84.4	91.5	94.1	91.0	11.7	3.0	9.2	2.6	1.7	3.5

Table 2A.4 Percentage of Employed and Unemployed Adults in Rural Areas, by Gender and per Capita Income Quintile

Country	% female adults employed						% female adults unemployed						% male adults employed						% male adults unemployed					
	1	2	3	4	5	Total	1	2	3	4	5	Total	1	2	3	4	5	Total	1	2	3	4	5	Total
Bolivia 2002	81.5	71.7	61.6	64.0	69.0	73.6	0.4	1.6	2.3	2.1	0.0	1.1	98.3	98.0	97.9	98.3	97.3	98.1	0.0	0.2	0.9	0.0	0.3	0.2
Brazil 2001	67.6	63.7	68.4	72.5	72.1	67.6	1.8	2.0	1.6	1.4	0.4	1.7	94.8	93.6	92.0	95.9	96.2	94.2	1.0	1.1	0.3	0.6	0.3	0.8
Chile 2000	13.2	20.8	29.5	38.8	49.5	23.9	3.0	2.0	1.2	1.0	0.5	2.0	76.1	84.3	87.8	91.6	93.1	84.0	9.1	4.7	2.8	1.6	1.2	5.0
Colombia 1999	30.4	29.9	36.4	47.5	60.5	37.3	4.2	4.7	4.3	2.7	1.7	3.9	89.0	90.0	90.8	92.8	94.8	90.9	4.4	2.1	1.7	1.2	0.8	2.4
Costa Rica 2000	17.2	24.2	30.8	39.9	52.0	30.3	1.5	0.6	1.5	1.4	0.9	1.2	83.0	90.4	94.3	94.6	95.0	91.1	4.5	2.2	1.5	1.8	0.7	2.3
Dominican Republic 1997	13.3	20.2	28.4	45.7	50.4	27.9	12.8	8.9	8.2	3.3	4.3	8.3	83.0	90.4	94.5	95.4	95.9	91.7	10.2	3.3	1.8	0.5	0.6	3.4
Ecuador 1998	60.4	55.3	65.7	75.0	65.7	62.5	0.6	0.6	0.0	0.1	0.0	0.4	95.6	95.6	96.8	98.5	96.6	96.4	0.7	0.7	0.8	0.6	0.7	0.7
El Salvador 2000	31.1	40.7	44.6	59.3	68.7	43.4	1.2	2.0	1.0	0.3	0.4	1.2	85.6	87.3	90.2	89.9	91.1	88.2	7.8	7.0	4.0	3.4	1.9	5.6
Guatemala 2000	27.6	32.8	36.8	45.0	41.7	35.3	0.4	0.0	0.0	0.8	0.0	0.2	92.3	94.0	94.7	95.1	91.2	93.6	0.7	0.1	0.7	0.4	0.1	0.5
Honduras 1999	28.6	31.1	44.2	50.8	64.2	40.5	1.1	0.8	0.0	0.0	0.4	0.5	93.4	95.7	95.9	96.5	98.1	95.7	1.4	1.5	1.8	0.4	0.5	1.2

(table continues on the following page)

Table 2A.4 (continued)

Country	% female adults employed						% female adults unemployed						% male adults employed						% male adults unemployed					
	1	2	3	4	5	Total	1	2	3	4	5	Total	1	2	3	4	5	Total	1	2	3	4	5	Total
Jamaica 1999	54.7	63.3	66.8	80.5	83.6	69.6	9.3	12.7	8.5	1.7	3.7	7.3	91.7	93.2	91.3	96.3	99.3	95.0	0.0	2.7	3.1	0.8	0.7	1.5
Mexico 2000	36.0	38.9	43.9	54.1	46.8	39.9	0.0	0.0	0.0	0.0	0.0	0.0	91.6	91.5	89.5	94.2	95.9	91.8	0.7	0.4	2.2	0.5	0.0	0.8
Nicaragua 2001	25.0	32.7	41.3	52.3	45.1	36.1	3.8	6.7	2.6	2.3	2.6	3.9	92.4	92.3	90.9	88.3	92.8	91.5	3.9	5.2	5.5	4.0	2.1	4.3
Panama 2000	15.7	25.0	32.8	48.1	55.8	29.2	2.3	2.3	2.7	2.7	2.0	2.4	89.9	90.1	90.0	89.9	90.6	90.0	6.2	4.4	3.2	3.5	1.5	4.3
Paraguay 1999	41.6	49.6	60.2	61.2	67.4	52.2	0.7	1.8	0.5	0.8	0.0	0.9	95.0	94.2	93.9	94.7	97.3	94.9	1.2	1.8	1.3	0.7	2.0	1.4
Peru 2000	82.6	76.4	76.3	77.2	77.1	79.1	0.1	0.8	0.7	0.0	0.0	0.4	97.8	97.5	97.6	97.9	99.1	97.8	0.4	0.3	0.3	0.0	0.0	0.3
Venezuela 1998	37.0	40.4	49.5	58.0	66.6	50.6	7.3	6.5	4.6	4.3	3.2	5.1	78.5	85.0	87.4	89.3	94.2	87.4	14.0	9.6	7.2	4.9	1.9	7.1

Table 2A.5 Percentage of Female Adults by Education Level and per Capita Income Quintile

	Education level																	
	Low						*Medium*						*High*					
Country	*1*	*2*	*3*	*4*	*5*	*Total*	*1*	*2*	*3*	*4*	*5*	*Total*	*1*	*2*	*3*	*4*	*5*	*Total*
Argentina 2001	73.6	60.1	47.3	33.3	11.7	41.3	22.5	32.6	39.5	39.6	36.3	34.9	3.9	7.3	13.2	27.1	51.9	23.8
Bolivia 2002	78.3	73.3	70.1	55.1	30.0	53.3	19.0	21.4	23.1	31.1	29.0	26.7	2.7	5.3	6.8	13.8	41.0	20.0
Brazil 2001	91.1	84.2	76.4	62.9	31.8	63.6	8.8	15.3	22.0	31.9	38.1	26.2	0.2	0.6	1.6	5.2	30.1	10.2
Chile 2000	54.4	44.1	37.0	27.7	14.5	32.8	42.9	51.4	53.7	53.8	39.4	48.1	2.7	4.5	9.4	18.5	46.1	19.2
Colombia 1999	76.7	71.2	65.1	56.5	30.3	53.1	20.9	25.6	30.2	35.8	39.9	33.4	2.4	3.2	4.7	7.7	29.8	13.5
Costa Rica 2000	80.4	64.7	54.2	43.3	22.9	43.9	18.4	32.2	38.1	42.2	32.1	34.4	1.2	3.0	7.8	14.5	45.0	21.7
Dominican Republic 1997	79.8	69.2	62.8	53.5	42.1	56.8	16.9	26.9	27.7	30.2	29.4	27.6	3.3	3.9	9.5	16.3	28.4	15.6
Ecuador 1998	72.7	64.9	55.7	46.6	26.7	45.7	20.8	28.7	32.0	35.9	38.2	33.9	6.5	6.4	12.3	17.6	35.1	20.4
El Salvador 2000	55.4	69.4	66.0	58.2	43.8	56.2	31.4	22.8	25.3	31.5	37.7	31.2	13.2	7.8	8.7	10.3	18.4	12.6
Guatemala 2000	94.6	89.5	86.7	80.2	50.6	69.7	2.9	9.5	11.1	17.1	33.1	21.8	2.4	1.0	2.2	2.7	16.2	8.5

(table continues on the following page)

Table 2A.5 (continued)

Country	Low						Medium						High					
	1	2	3	4	5	Total	1	2	3	4	5	Total	1	2	3	4	5	Total
Honduras 1999	87.5	89.3	78.4	67.4	38.4	64.1	12.0	10.3	19.7	30.3	44.0	28.7	0.5	0.5	1.9	2.3	17.6	7.2
Jamaica 1999	48.9	47.2	15.3	32.2	18.8	29.6	45.0	52.8	83.3	59.8	60.7	60.5	6.1	0.0	1.4	8.0	20.5	9.9
Mexico 2000	84.2	72.2	59.2	49.3	23.2	50.3	12.7	25.7	37.1	43.3	43.9	37.0	3.1	2.1	3.8	7.5	32.9	12.8
Nicaragua 2001	90.6	88.1	74.3	65.0	49.0	67.0	7.1	7.5	20.4	27.4	30.7	22.6	2.3	4.5	5.4	7.6	20.3	10.4
Panama 2000	52.6	42.4	35.6	30.8	11.7	28.0	42.7	50.9	51.8	46.2	36.3	44.2	4.7	6.7	12.6	22.9	52.0	27.7
Paraguay 1999	93.5	81.9	71.1	58.8	33.5	56.9	5.5	16.3	25.3	31.7	38.9	29.7	0.9	1.8	3.6	9.5	27.5	13.4
Peru 2000	62.1	52.5	41.4	33.0	18.3	34.0	30.7	37.1	42.9	42.0	38.9	39.9	7.2	10.5	15.7	25.0	42.8	26.1
Uruguay 2000	70.7	58.5	50.3	36.6	18.7	44.5	26.9	35.4	40.2	43.3	39.6	37.8	2.3	6.1	9.5	20.1	41.7	17.7
Venezuela 1998	60.4	68.2	62.5	49.2	20.2	39.5	26.8	25.3	29.8	39.3	37.1	35.0	12.8	6.6	7.6	11.5	42.7	25.4

Table 2A.6 Percentage of Male Adults by Education Level and per Capita Income Quintile

Country	Low						Medium						High					
	1	2	3	4	5	Total	1	2	3	4	5	Total	1	2	3	4	5	Total
Argentina 2001	76.7	60.4	48.7	35.2	13.0	42.6	20.9	33.1	42.8	46.5	36.4	37.0	2.4	6.6	8.5	18.3	50.6	20.4
Bolivia 2002	71.3	61.1	50.5	38.8	21.6	39.3	24.0	32.5	39.9	43.6	31.6	36.3	4.7	6.5	9.6	17.6	46.8	24.3
Brazil 2001	92.9	87.4	79.3	66.9	33.0	65.5	6.9	12.1	19.5	29.2	39.0	25.0	0.3	0.5	1.2	3.9	28.1	9.5
Chile 2000	52.3	43.6	32.9	24.7	9.5	29.2	44.4	50.9	56.1	54.2	35.9	47.8	3.3	5.4	10.9	21.0	54.6	23.0
Colombia 1999	76.4	69.8	63.4	54.0	25.1	49.9	19.3	25.5	31.5	37.3	36.6	32.8	4.3	4.7	5.1	8.7	38.3	17.3
Costa Rica 2000	73.9	61.1	54.6	43.5	23.5	41.5	22.8	35.2	36.3	40.2	33.7	35.3	3.2	3.7	9.1	16.3	42.8	23.1
Dominican Republic 1997	78.1	67.3	67.5	56.9	41.9	56.8	17.8	29.7	26.7	29.7	30.3	28.4	4.1	3.0	5.8	13.4	27.8	14.8
Ecuador 1998	65.3	69.8	50.6	48.2	26.0	44.3	28.1	22.7	36.7	32.2	31.3	31.2	6.6	7.5	12.7	19.6	42.7	24.5
El Salvador 2000	45.6	61.6	58.5	53.5	35.0	47.8	35.5	28.1	34.0	37.2	41.0	36.7	18.9	10.4	7.5	9.3	24.0	15.5
Guatemala 2000	95.0	85.4	78.2	71.4	39.0	59.8	4.4	7.3	20.4	23.0	29.6	23.2	0.6	7.4	1.4	5.6	31.5	17.0

(table continues on the following page)

77

Table 2A.6 (continued)

Country	Education level																	
	Low						Medium						High					
	1	2	3	4	5	Total	1	2	3	4	5	Total	1	2	3	4	5	Total
Honduras 1999	91.7	86.8	80.4	69.8	39.7	63.6	7.2	13.0	17.8	26.9	31.4	23.9	1.2	0.1	1.8	3.2	28.8	12.4
Jamaica 1999	41.7	43.2	37.4	31.9	21.5	30.1	58.3	54.3	62.6	64.9	65.8	63.3	0.0	2.6	0.0	3.2	12.7	6.6
Mexico 2000	78.4	65.8	53.7	39.5	19.9	42.9	17.1	31.4	39.5	43.4	31.8	35.3	4.6	2.8	6.8	17.2	48.3	21.8
Nicaragua 2001	88.2	85.5	82.4	66.4	46.8	65.7	8.9	11.0	15.5	26.5	30.6	22.9	2.9	3.4	2.2	7.0	22.6	11.4
Panama 2000	55.9	47.8	38.7	30.3	11.9	28.8	40.6	47.2	52.7	53.4	38.8	46.4	3.6	5.0	8.6	16.4	49.3	24.7
Paraguay 1999	86.3	74.3	65.5	51.4	30.2	50.3	10.5	25.3	29.6	41.1	43.0	36.4	3.3	0.4	5.0	7.5	26.8	13.3
Peru 2000	46.0	42.7	28.7	23.3	13.2	24.5	45.5	43.8	51.5	50.7	37.2	45.1	8.5	13.5	19.8	26.0	49.6	30.4
Uruguay 2000	70.0	58.7	49.6	37.8	18.3	44.6	27.3	37.0	42.8	47.6	45.7	41.0	2.7	4.3	7.6	14.6	36.0	14.4
Venezuela 1998	57.1	74.0	63.4	50.5	21.7	40.0	33.0	15.7	32.7	37.2	34.6	33.5	9.9	10.3	3.9	12.3	43.7	26.5

Table 2A.7 Percentage of Employed Adults and Youth by Education Level

Country	National Adult			National Youth			Urban Adult			Urban Youth			Rural Adult			Rural Youth		
	Low	Medium	High	Low	Medium	High	Low	Medium	High	Low	Medium	High	Low	Medium	High	Low	Medium	High
Argentina 2001	54.0	62.6	79.3	37.7	27.8	45.3	54.0	62.6	79.3	37.7	27.8	45.3	—	—	—	—	—	—
Bolivia 2002	79.9	81.1	80.1	63.3	43.4	38.9	74.7	79.6	79.5	47.6	38.2	37.2	85.3	91.8	92.1	76.3	67.1	83.2
Brazil 2001	67.2	75.1	84.7	49.9	56.4	70.8	63.7	74.8	84.6	45.3	55.8	70.7	81.3	81.0	88.6	66.5	64.7	—
Chile 2000	52.9	64.9	79.6	37.5	28.0	28.3	53.1	65.2	79.6	34.0	28.1	28.4	52.5	60.3	77.5	44.2	27.2	23.9
Colombia 1999	61.3	69.0	82.4	44.4	33.1	48.7	60.0	68.6	81.9	40.1	33.2	48.0	62.8	71.3	86.3	48.5	33.1	55.8
Costa Rica 2000	57.4	69.0	80.0	52.8	36.7	59.1	58.8	68.6	80.9	51.3	37.2	56.9	56.6	69.7	77.2	53.6	36.0	64.4
Dominican Republic 1997	59.5	67.8	80.3	42.8	38.0	55.9	59.6	68.7	79.3	42.4	38.9	56.2	59.4	65.0	88.0	43.2	35.9	53.4
Ecuador 1998	75.8	76.3	86.1	69.3	54.0	65.5	72.6	74.8	85.9	59.6	50.8	64.8	78.5	82.5	88.1	76.3	63.6	69.8
El Salvador 2000	66.2	76.3	81.2	47.6	42.6	39.9	69.3	76.4	81.4	43.1	41.2	40.0	62.6	75.1	75.9	51.1	47.5	38.5
Guatemala 2000	63.5	73.7	83.0	54.5	51.5	72.6	65.5	73.5	82.9	57.9	52.2	72.4	62.3	74.8	84.4	52.9	49.1	73.9

(table continues on the following page)

Table 2A.7 (continued)

| | National | | | | | | Urban | | | | | | Rural | | | | | |
| | Adult | | | Youth | | | Adult | | | Youth | | | Adult | | | Youth | | |
Country	Low	Medium	High	Low	Medium	High	Low	Medium	High	Low	Medium	High	Low	Medium	High	Low	Medium	High
Honduras 1999	68.4	78.6	85.5	55.0	49.3	42.4	71.7	78.6	84.8	52.9	48.1	41.9	65.7	78.2	94.7	56.8	53.8	—
Jamaica 1999	79.8	85.7	90.5	55.0	39.6	73.7	78.9	87.3	—	47.8	43.1	—	80.4	84.4	—	58.0	37.0	—
Mexico 2000	63.1	72.2	83.4	56.2	45.1	48.5	62.3	72.1	83.2	57.8	43.9	47.9	64.7	73.2	89.5	53.8	51.6	63.5
Nicaragua 2001	64.3	72.5	80.3	50.7	37.4	48.8	65.2	72.5	80.6	46.3	36.4	47.7	63.4	72.8	76.9	54.7	42.7	63.4
Panama 2000	57.5	64.4	80.6	40.3	31.8	54.4	55.4	64.4	81.0	32.3	32.3	54.4	59.3	64.4	77.2	46.8	30.5	54.7
Paraguay 1999	69.1	78.9	87.4	52.1	45.0	68.8	65.8	78.4	86.8	49.0	44.7	69.5	72.4	82.0	92.3	54.9	45.9	64.0
Peru 2000	76.0	73.5	77.9	62.6	48.3	57.1	64.2	69.3	77.1	42.7	41.6	56.2	87.6	91.4	88.0	77.3	69.8	62.9
Uruguay 2000	60.1	74.9	82.4	42.9	47.3	34.6	60.1	74.9	82.4	42.9	47.3	34.6	—	—	—	—	—	—
Venezuela 1998	64.5	74.6	82.5	47.2	37.2	44.2	70.0	75.6	84.2	41.3	43.8	49.1	63.8	74.3	81.8	47.8	35.9	42.8

Note: — = not available.

Table 2A.8 Percentage of Urban Adults Employed in the Informal Sector or Self-Employed, by per Capita Income Quintile

Country	% adults employed in the informal sector						% adults self-employed					
	1	2	3	4	5	Total	1	2	3	4	5	Total
Argentina 2001	70.5	55.0	49.0	37.0	22.2	40.6	39.0	26.3	22.9	20.7	17.0	22.7
Bolivia 2002	86.5	82.3	71.7	63.6	41.9	60.4	66.0	56.1	49.2	43.8	33.1	43.4
Brazil 2001	73.6	59.2	51.2	43.3	27.3	44.3	45.3	37.6	32.3	28.6	22.8	30.3
Chile 2000	45.4	39.8	37.9	34.4	24.8	33.7	17.6	17.6	19.0	21.5	18.9	19.2
Costa Rica 2000	61.8	53.0	42.7	34.8	25.1	35.0	35.5	28.0	23.6	20.9	16.7	21.0
Dominican Republic 1997	71.8	58.7	47.3	43.7	35.6	44.4	59.5	45.5	35.5	35.0	30.4	35.8
Ecuador 1998	86.2	62.2	59.1	46.2	33.9	47.5	57.6	33.4	35.4	30.7	21.4	29.6
El Salvador 2000	35.8	53.3	52.6	50.2	40.6	46.0	24.6	36.3	35.3	34.8	30.6	32.5
Guatemala 2000	84.0	66.2	58.0	53.9	36.6	48.3	55.9	36.1	34.5	37.1	26.6	32.6
Honduras 1999	81.4	62.7	57.2	49.9	29.6	46.3	58.5	37.0	37.4	35.7	23.7	32.7

(table continues on the following page)

Table 2A.8 (continued)

Country	% adults employed in the informal sector						% adults self-employed					
	1	2	3	4	5	Total	1	2	3	4	5	Total
Jamaica 1999	59.0	63.7	61.4	63.7	63.6	62.7	25.5	33.0	38.2	30.2	22.4	27.7
Mexico 2000	81.2	60.6	51.8	35.6	21.5	40.7	45.1	26.1	22.0	17.6	13.5	20.1
Nicaragua 2001	80.1	69.7	60.9	48.6	43.7	53.0	45.3	40.3	33.5	29.0	28.5	31.8
Panama 2000	74.2	52.1	41.8	32.4	17.0	31.3	50.7	37.1	26.6	20.8	12.3	21.1
Paraguay 1999	86.4	74.3	58.9	48.3	32.9	47.3	50.2	43.6	37.0	29.8	24.1	30.7
Peru 2000	82.3	73.6	65.7	55.2	37.8	54.6	51.8	50.5	48.2	38.4	33.2	40.6
Uruguay 2000	65.9	51.3	40.6	33.0	21.7	38.8	35.8	28.0	22.6	19.5	17.6	23.1
Venezuela 1998	35.1	40.3	42.9	40.0	24.6	32.3	29.5	35.2	37.2	33.9	31.9	33.3

Table 2A.9 Percentage of Rural Adults Employed in the Informal Sector or Self-Employed, by per Capita Income Quintile

Country	% adults employed in the informal sector						% adults self-employed					
	1	2	3	4	5	Total	1	2	3	4	5	Total
Bolivia 2002	92.9	86.7	80.0	71.9	62.4	85.7	51.7	51.1	50.9	42.5	39.3	49.8
Brazil 2001	93.1	82.4	77.0	73.0	58.1	82.3	39.7	34.8	33.1	36.1	33.6	36.4
Chile 2000	58.7	53.9	52.7	56.3	52.8	55.2	29.0	25.0	30.0	36.9	37.1	30.2
Costa Rica 2000	73.2	57.7	46.7	43.3	31.2	50.4	37.5	25.5	24.6	24.1	22.1	26.7
Dominican Republic 1997	79.2	62.9	58.9	52.9	52.0	60.4	64.8	52.4	44.7	44.6	42.9	49.3
Ecuador 1998	93.6	82.2	69.5	67.0	51.0	78.1	51.6	43.1	37.8	34.7	31.6	42.4
El Salvador 2000	71.9	65.3	57.5	55.1	50.5	61.5	53.5	42.1	36.6	38.7	39.2	42.9
Guatemala 2000	80.3	65.8	59.1	59.8	53.7	64.8	57.5	42.2	35.9	42.0	41.1	44.6
Honduras 1999	85.7	79.7	70.2	67.4	61.8	73.7	56.2	56.4	54.9	51.3	53.6	54.6
Jamaica 1999	75.2	71.5	63.5	75.8	58.8	68.4	58.0	49.8	44.5	47.5	34.7	45.6

(table continues on the following page)

Table 2A.9 (continued)

Country	% adults employed in the informal sector						% adults self-employed					
	1	2	3	4	5	Total	1	2	3	4	5	Total
Mexico 2000	83.0	73.4	61.0	54.3	41.7	72.0	47.5	40.4	37.9	33.8	27.8	41.8
Nicaragua 2001	87.3	71.1	67.0	56.1	49.7	70.0	60.4	41.1	38.7	27.1	29.9	42.5
Panama 2000	86.5	65.0	53.7	43.0	34.8	61.8	63.9	39.2	35.2	29.0	27.1	42.5
Paraguay 1999	95.8	84.1	77.6	67.1	50.8	80.0	77.3	60.0	52.6	44.6	35.5	58.5
Peru 2000	89.0	80.4	74.8	66.7	57.9	80.9	43.6	45.8	45.1	50.5	44.8	45.2
Venezuela 1998	60.9	51.6	48.7	41.4	30.8	44.9	45.2	38.7	36.1	33.8	28.8	35.6

Endnotes

1. Sample sizes in other countries do not allow for meaningful statistics to be computed at this level of disaggregation.

2. The informal sector refers to the sector in which employment is not regulated and entails no social benefits, unemployment protection, or compliance with occupational safety regulations.

3. The OECD Program for International Student Assessment (PISA) study of 15-year-old students in 41 countries found poor performance in most Latin American countries. Argentina, the top-ranked country in the region, ranked 33rd, Mexico ranked 35th, Chile 37th, Brazil 38th, and Peru 41st (author calculation based on PISA data set, available at http://www.pisa.oecd.org/).

4. Quality of schooling could also help explain the divergence between the two income profiles for higher levels of education.

5. Participation by older workers also rose, partly as a result of the aging of the population: within 20 years, the elderly will represent more than 15 percent of the total population in half the countries in Latin America (Attanasio and Székely 2002).

6. In contrast, single mothers, whose participation in the labor force is generally much higher than that of married women, are less likely to increase their labor market participation following shocks.

7. Bosch Mossi and Maloney (2003) hint at the role of household responsibilities for women. They find that in Argentina, Brazil, and Mexico, women have different mobility patterns between jobs status, with higher rates of entry into and exit out of self-employment and inactivity.

8. On average self-employment accounts for 30 percent of employment in urban areas (40 percent in rural areas). Among the urban poor, 44 percent are self-employed, compared with 24 percent among the richest quintile. In most countries, self-employment decreases by income quintile; urban areas in Chile, El Salvador Jamaica, and Venezuela represent exceptions. The lowest rate of self-employment among the lowest income quintile is in Chile (17.6 percent); the highest is in Bolivia (66.0 percent).

9. In line with this finding, Calderon-Madrid (2000) suggests that in Mexico the likelihood of not staying on in employment in the formal sector increases if salaried workers work in firms with fewer than 15 workers, pointing to the differential ease of enforcing regulations across different types of firms.

10. The relation between income shock and household labor supply may also be difficult to identify if the increase in labor supply takes place abroad through migration of some household member. This type of coping response appears to have been underresearched for the urban poor in Latin America; no quantitative estimate of its magnitude is currently available.

11. Similar strategies may be put in place when households face idiosyncratic rather than covariant shocks.

12. Grade mismatch is correlated with dropout rates, possibly because of social pressures.

13. The focus here is on micro demand or supply side policies as opposed to macro policies, such as trade and exchange rate measures, that may affect job creation and overall economic growth.

14. See the introduction to Freeman and Gottschalk (1998) for a discussion.

15. An interesting contrast exists between the United States, where the wages of low-skilled workers have been falling, and Germany, where they have improved. The phenomenon is arguably due to the fact that the German school system brings all pupils to a minimum level of skills, so that the educational skills of low-skilled workers are much closer to the average than in the United States (Nickell 1998).

16. Freeman and Gottschalk (1998) mention a fourth approach, which consists of policies that affect the modality of pay (profit sharing and mandated wages and benefits). These options appear less relevant for the Latin American labor market, where the informal sector dominates.

17. For case studies and a discussion of how to design a local economic development strategy, see http://www.worldbank.org/urban/led/index.html.

References

Arias, Omar. 2001. "Are Men Benefiting from the New Economy? Male Economic Marginalization in Argentina, Brazil, and Costa Rica." World Bank, Washington, DC.

Arias, Omar, G. Yamada, and L. Tejerína. 2004. "Education, Family Background, and Racial Earnings Inequality in Brazil." *International Journal of Manpower* 25 (3): 355–74.

Attanasio, Orazio, and M. Székely. 2002. "A Dynamic Analysis of Household Decision-Making in Latin America: Changes in Household Structure, Female Labor Force Participation, Human Capital, and Its Returns." Working Paper R-452, Inter-American Development Bank, Washington, DC.

Barone, Márcia, and J. Rebelo. 2003. "Potential Impact of Metro's Line 4 on Poverty in the São Paulo Metropolitan Region (SPMR)." World Bank, Washington, DC.

Bartik, Timothy J. 1993. "The Effects of Local Labor Demand on Individual Labor Market Outcomes for Different Demographic Groups and the Poor." Staff Working Paper 93-23, W.E. Upjohn Institute for Employment Research, Kalamazoo, MI.

Bosch Mossi, Mariano, and W.F. Maloney. 2003. "Comparative Labor Market Analysis Using Continuous Time Markov Processes." World Bank, Washington, DC.

Calderón-Madrid, Angel. 2000. "Job Stability and Labor Mobility in Urban Mexico: A Study Based on Duration Models and Transition Analysis." Working Paper R-419, Inter-American Development Bank, Washington, DC.

Cardoso, Adalberto, Peter Elias, and Valéria Pero. 2003. "Urban Regeneration and Spatial Discrimination: The Case of Rio's *Favelas*." Proceedings of the 31st Brazilian Economics Meeting from ANPEC (Brazilian Association of Graduate Programs in Economics). Available at: www.anpec.org.br/encontro2003/artigos/F41.pdf.

Conning, Jonathan, P. Olinto, and A. Trigueros. 2001. "Managing Economic Insecurity in Rural El Salvador: the Role of Asset Ownership, and Labor Market
Adjustments." BASIS Collaborative Research Support Program, Department
of Agriculture and Applied Economics, University of Wisconsin, Madison.

Contreras, Dante, and Osvaldo Larrañaga. 1999. "Los activos y recursos de la
población pobre en America Latina: El caso de Chile." Working Paper No.
R-358. Inter-American Development Bank, Washington DC.

Cunningham, Wendy. 2001a. "Breadwinner or Caregiver? How Household Role
Affects Labor Choices in Mexico." Policy Research Working Paper No. 2743,
World Bank, Washington, DC.

————. 2001b. "Sectoral Allocation by Gender of Latin American Workers over the
Liberalization Period of the 1990s." Policy Research Working Paper No.
2742, World Bank, Washington, DC.

de Ferranti, David, Guillermo Perry, Francisco H.G. Ferreira, and Michael Walton.
2004. *Inequality in Latin America and the Caribbean: Breaking with History?*
Washington, DC: World Bank.

de Ferranti, David, Guillermo E. Perry, Indermit S. Gill, and Luis Servén, with
Francisco H.G. Ferreira, Nadeem Ilahi, William F. Maloney, and Martin
Rama. 2000. *Securing Our Future in the Global Economy.* Washington, DC:
World Bank.

de Ferranti, David, Guillermo E. Perry, Daniel Lederman, and William F. Maloney.
2003. *From Natural Resources to the Knowledge Economy: Trade and Job Quality.*
Washington, DC: World Bank.

Deutsch, Ruthanne. 1998. "Does Child Care Pay?: Labor Force Participation and
Earnings Effects of Access to Child Care in the Favelas of Rio de Janeiro."
Working Paper 384, Inter-American Development Bank, Washington, DC.

Duryea, Suzanne, and M. Arends-Kuenning. 2003. "School Attendance, Child
Labor, and Local Labor Market Fluctuations in Urban Brazil." *World Development* 31 (7): 1165–78.

Duryea, Suzanne, and A.C. Edwards. 2001. "Women in the LAC Labor Market:
The Remarkable 1990s." Working Paper 500, William Davidson Institute,
University of Michigan Business School, Ann Arbor, MI.

European Commission. 2003. *Employment in Europe 2003: Recent Development and
Prospects.* Employment Analysis Unit, Employment and Social Affairs DG,
Brussels.

Fallon, Peter R., and Robert E.B. Lucas. 2002. "The Impact of Financial Crises on
Labor Markets, Household Incomes, and Poverty: A Review of Evidence."
World Bank Research Observer 17 (1): 21–45.

Ferreira, Francisco H.G., and R. Paes de Barros. 1999. "The Slippery Slope: Ex-
plaining the Increase in Extreme Poverty in Urban Brazil, 1976–1996."
Working Paper 2210, World Bank, Washington, DC.

Fiszbein, Ariel, I. Adúriz, and P.I. Giovagnoli. 2002. "Argentina's Crisis and its
Impact on Household Welfare." Working Paper No. 1/02, World Bank,
Office for Argentina, Chile, Paraguay, and Uruguay, Washington, DC.

Flug, Karnit, A. Spilimbergo, and E. Wachtenheim. 1998. "Investment in Education:
Do Economic Volatility and Credit Constraints Matter?" *Journal of Development Economics* 55 (2): 465–81.

Freeman, Richard B., and Peter Gottschalk, eds. 1998. *Generating Jobs: How to Increase Demand for Less-Skilled Workers*. New York: Russell Sage Foundation.

Fuchs, Martina. 2001. "The Effects of the Crisis of 1994/95 on the Mexican Labour Market: The Case of the City of Puebla." *Urban Studies* 38 (10): 1801–1818.

Gilbert, Alan. 1997. "Employment and Poverty during Economic Restructuring: The Case of Bogotá, Colombia." *Urban Studies* 34 (7): 1047–1070.

Gottschalk, Peter. 1998. "The Impact of Changes in Public Employment on Low-Wage Labor Markets." In *Generating Jobs: How to Increase Demand for Less-Skilled Workers*, ed. Richard B. Freeman and Peter Gottschalk, 73–102. New York: Russell Sage Foundation.

Gramlich, Edward M., and Colleen M. Heflin. 1998. "The Spatial Dimension: Should Worker Assistance Be Given to Poor People or Poor Places?" In *Generating Jobs: How to Increase Demand for Less-Skilled Workers*, ed. Richard B. Freeman and Peter Gottschalk, 54–71 New York: Russell Sage Foundation.

Hallman, Kelly, A. Quisumbing, Marie Ruel, and Benedicte de la Briere. 2002. "Childcare, Mothers' Work, and Earnings: Findings from Urban Slums of Guatemala City." Working Paper No. 165, Population Council, Policy Research Division, New York, NY.

Katz, Lawrence. 1998. "Wage Subsidies for the Disadvantaged." In *Generating Jobs: How to Increase Demand for Less-Skilled Workers*, ed. Richard B. Freeman and Peter Gottschalk, 21–53. New York: Russell Sage Foundation.

Lay, Jann, and M. Wiebelt. 2001. "Towards a Dual Education System: A Labour Market Perspective on Poverty Reduction in Bolivia." Working Paper 1073, Kiel Institute for World Economics, Germany.

Maloney, William F. 1999. "Does Informality Imply Segmentation in Urban Labor Markets? Evidence from Sectoral Transitions in Mexico." *World Bank Economic Review* 13 (2): 275–302.

———. 2002. "Informality Revisited." Policy Research Working Paper No. 2965, World Bank, Washington, DC.

Maloney, William F., Mariano Bosch, Jorge Moreno, and Monica Tinajero. 2003. "Notes on Income, and Consumption Shocks." Background paper commissioned for the Mexico Poverty Assessment, World Bank, Washington, DC.

Martin, John P. 1998. "What Worked among Active Labour Market Policies: Evidence From OECD Countries' Experiences." Labour Market and Social Policy Occasional Papers No. 35, OECD, Paris.

Mckenzie, David J. 2003. "How Do Households Cope with Aggregate Shocks? Evidence from the Mexican Peso Crisis." *World Development* 31 (7): 1179–99.

Montes, Gabriel, and Mauricio Santamaría. 2004. "Poverty and Labor Markets in Urban Mexico." World Bank, Washington, DC.

Murrugarra, Edmundo, and M. Valdivia. 2000. "The Returns to Health for Peruvian Urban Adults by Gender, Age, and across the Wage Distribution." In *Wealth from Health: Linking Social Investments to Earnings in Latin America*, ed. William D. Savedoff and T. Paul Schultz, 151–88. Washington, DC: Inter-American Development Bank.

Nickell, Stephen. 1998. "The Collapse in Demand for the Unskilled: What Can Be Done?" In *Generating Jobs: How to Increase Demand for Less-Skilled Workers*, ed.

Richard B. Freeman and Peter Gottschalk, pp. 297–320. New York: Russell Sage Foundation.

Nopo, Hugo, J. Saavedra, and M. Torero. 2002. "Ethnicity and Earnings in Urban Peru." Grupo de Análisis para el Desarrollo (GRADE), Lima.

Perlman, Janice. 2003. "Marginality: From Myth to Reality in the *Favelas* of Rio de Janeiro, 1969–2002." In *Urban Informality: Transnational Perspectives from the Middle East, Latin America, and South Asia,* ed. Ananya Roy, 105–46. Lanham, MD: Lexington Books.

Pessino, Carola, and L. Andres. 2003. "Job Creation and Job Destruction in Argentina." Latin America Research Network Project for the Labor Market and Globalization Conference, held October 2003. Inter-American Development Bank, Washington, DC.

Ridao-Cano, Cristobal. 2003. "Household Welfare and Coping Strategies in the Face of Economic Crisis: Evidence from Uruguay, 2002." Background paper for the Uruguay Poverty Update, World Bank, Washington, DC.

Saavedra, Jaime. 2003. "Labor Markets During the 1990s." In *After the Washington Consensus: Restarting Growth, and Reform in Latin America,* ed. Pedro Kuczynski and J. Williamson, 213–63. Washington, DC: Institute for International Economics.

Saavedra, Jaime, and J. Chacaltana. 2001. *Exclusion and Opportunity.* Grupo de Análisis para el Desarrollo (GRADE), Lima.

Schady, Norbert. 2002. "The (Positive) Effect of Macroeconomic Crises on the Schooling and Employment Decisions of Children in a Middle-Income Country." World Bank Policy Research Paper No. 2762, Washington DC.

Stoll, Michael A., H.J. Holzer, and K.R. Ihlanfeldt. 1999. "Within Cities and Suburbs: Racial Residential Concentration and the Spatial Distribution of Employment Opportunities across Submetropolitan Areas." Discussion Paper 1189–99, Institute for Research on Poverty, Madison, WI.

Székely Pardo, Miguel. 2003. "Lo que dicen los pobres." Secretaría de Desarrollo Social (SEDESOL). Mexico D.F. www.sedesol.gob.mx/publicaciones/libros/Cuad13.pdf.

Trejos, Juan Diego, and N. Montiel. 1999. "El capital de los pobres en Costa Rica: Acceso, utilización y rendimiento." Working Paper R-360, Inter-American Development Bank, Washington, DC.

Urani, Andre. 2003. "Urban Poverty and Labor Markets in Latin America: Challenges, and Policy Recommendations." Background paper commissioned for this report. Instituto de Estudos do Trabalho e Sociedade, Rio de Janeiro.

3

Keeping a Roof over One's Head: Improving Access to Safe and Decent Shelter

Marianne Fay and Anna Wellenstein

Gaining access to housing that provides adequate shelter and physical safety is one of the greatest challenges confronting the urban poor. Most poor people live in informal housing, often located in marginal areas that are vulnerable to natural disasters and poorly served by public services or utilities.

This chapter looks at how the poor obtain shelter and what this implies in terms of their living conditions. It then discusses what can be done to improve the often dismal living conditions of the urban poor through housing and land policies, infrastructure reform, and disaster management interventions.

How Do the Poor Access Shelter?

The poor are typically homeowners with insecure tenure who improve their houses over time. Access to services is relatively high, although poor quality and informal coverage cause serious environmental risks. The poor quality of housing and infrastructure, combined with the fact that informal settlements are often located in risky locations, implies that residents of informal settlements are frequently at risk for natural disasters.

Marianne Fay is Lead Economist and Anna Wellenstein Sector Leader at the World Bank. This chapter benefited from the comments and inputs of Maria Emilia Freire, Francis Ghesquiere, Sonia Hammam, Paavo Monkkonen, and Tova Solo.

High Rate of Homeownership

The rate of homeownership is high (73 percent) in Latin America and the Caribbean, comparable to that in Asia and substantially higher than in Eastern Europe, Africa, or high-income countries (table 3.1). Homeownership is even higher than in the United States (69 percent), with its well-developed real estate market and long tradition of promoting homeownership. Informal tenure is common, accounting for about a third of homeownership. Although high, the proportion of informal tenure is much lower than in Africa or Asia (table 3.1).

Homeownership increases somewhat with income, but the relationship is not monotonic. In Argentina and Ecuador, for example, homeownership is higher in the poorest quintile than in the second and third quintiles. It is generally high among the urban poor, among whom the rate exceeds 60 percent in most countries (table 3.2). Surveys of slums or poor neighborhoods often show homeownership rates of 70–80 percent.[1]

Perhaps because of the high rate of homeownership, remarkably little research has been done on low-income rental markets. The assumption appears to be that homeownership is generally accessible to all (even if by informal means) and desired by all. The limited research that has been done does confirm that homeownership is almost a universal desire of low-income people (Edwards 1982).[2]

Rentals tend to be a solution that becomes more common where land markets are more mature and property rights better enforced, so that land occupation and informal housing become less of an option, as it has in Colombia. The majority of renters occupy a room in a private home. Data from Central America suggest that some 8 percent of poor urban households share their house with others. Others settle in *vecindades* or *mesones*, old central city buildings in which entire families share a single

Table 3.1   Latin America has very high rates of homeownership

	Owners			
Region	All	Informal tenure	Tenants	Other
Asia (without China)	74	45	19	7
Latin America and the Caribbean	73	25	21	6
Eastern Europe and Central Asia	66	1	34	3
Africa	63	38	23	15
China	44	9	50	6
High-income countries	42	2	57	1
World	61	19	34	5

Note: Figures may not add to 100 percent due to rounding.

Table 3.2   Homeownership has been stagnant or fell in the 1990s for the poorest

Country	Income quintile					Whole sample
	Q1	Q2	Q3	Q4	Q5	
Early 1990s						
Argentina	82	76	78	81	78	79
Brazil	—	—	—	—	—	71
Chile	72	59	58	64	71	65
Colombia	38	57	65	68	69	59
Mexico	64	68	71	79	86	73
Peru	73	71	71	74	74	72
Late 1990s						
Argentina	78	72	73	79	83	77
Brazil	—	—	—	—	—	75
Chile	62	64	68	72	68	67
Colombia	30	44	54	58	58	49
Mexico	63	65	69	77	81	71
Peru	65	72	71	77	82	73

Source: Fay, Yepes, and Foster (2003), except for the Brazil data, which are from Reis and others (nd).

Note: — Not available. Data are for urban areas only. Countries in this sample account for three-quarters of Latin America's urban population.

room, typically living in precarious and unsanitary conditions. These central city tenements appear to have become much less common in the past 20 years. A third category of tenants are those renting unifamily dwellings or apartments. By some accounts, they are the only category of tenants that are virtually undistinguishable in terms of income, age, and family profile from low-income homeowners. Most are self-employed, with their savings invested in their businesses (Edwards 1982).

The large-scale exploitative landlord no longer represents the norm: most landlords own few properties and belong to a similar or only slightly higher socioeconomic class than their tenants. In Caracas, Mexico City, and Santiago, landlords have similar per capita incomes as their tenants, and more than two-thirds of landlords have only one tenant (Gilbert 2003). In addition, landlords often live on the property they rent, and many of these properties are or were originally of an informal nature. These are thus subsistence landlords, producing housing as a survival strategy rather than an investment (Kumar 1996). They are usually older than tenants or other owners (Gilbert 2003), often owning property as a form of pension (see chapter 5).

Most important, the choice between rental and homeownership is primarily a lifecycle decision. Younger families rent (or share a house with relatives); as they accumulate savings, they purchase a home. Newcomers also typically rent, particularly if they are alone or have young families. Data from a survey of 31 poor Mexican neighborhoods (one in each of Mexico's state capitals) confirms that renters are indeed younger and tend to be more recent arrivals in the neighborhood (Ruggeri Laderchi 2005). They also appear less stable, as they are more likely to have recently moved. Income appears to have no direct effect on the decision to rent or own.

In addition to renting, lending and sharing shelter are frequently used housing options among the poor. In fact, "lent" houses are almost as common as rented ones in low-income neighborhoods. In Guayaquil, Mexico, 16 percent of households rent, while 15 percent "borrow," occupying a home they do not own without any monetary payment (Lanjouw and Levy 2002). In Mexico's poor neighborhoods, renters account for about 10 percent of households and borrowers about 8 percent. One theory is that "home lending" occurs when the property is untitled or ownership claims are uncertain: owners who cannot occupy the property themselves get a trusted friend or relative to do so rather than risk renting it to a stranger or someone outside their sphere of authority or dominance. This theory is broadly supported by the Mexico data, in which the probability of occupying a lent house is greater among poorer and female-headed households, which may be less able to claim or enforce de facto ownership.[3] Lent houses are also more common among indigenous people, perhaps because of stronger ties or reciprocal obligations.

Shared housing is similar to lent housing in that it is most common among relatives. Although it is a second-best strategy, surveys in Mexico City indicate that 54 percent of sharers are content with the situation (Coulomb and Sanchez 1991, cited in Gilbert 2003). The distinction between renting and sharing is not always clear, as sharers often contribute significantly to household finances.

Low-income renting can be characterized as informal, as it operates without formal written contracts or observance of rental regulations. Rented homes tend to be significantly older than shared homes, suggesting a more established property claim by homeowners. Data from La Paz, Bolivia, and Ciudad Juarez, Mexico, demonstrate how sharing becomes much less important than renting as an urban area matures.

Informal Markets

Most low-income families in Latin America cannot afford formal sector housing and acquire housing through informal markets, whose main characteristic is to allow for a gradual improvement of housing (box 3.1). Indeed, the survey of poor Mexican neighborhoods shows that the quality of housing as well as the probability of a house having access to services such as water, sanitation, solid waste removal, and electricity increases linearly with the age of the house (Ruggeri Laderchi 2005).[4]

Informal housing is estimated to account for about a quarter of all urban homes in Latin America (Angel and others 2001), ranging from 10 percent in Buenos Aires to 44 percent in Caracas (CEPAL 2000).[5] The proportion of households that can afford formal sector housing in these countries is very small, as doing so requires an income level placing a household in about the 70th percentile in Brazil and Mexico (Hoek-Smit

---

Box 3.1   How the Poor Typically Acquire Housing: Progressive Housing

In the formal sector the production of housing involves four steps: acquiring a plot of land, planning, constructing, and selling. In the informal sector the process is different. "Progressive housing" starts with occupation of a piece of land, then moves to transition and consolidation. Occupation can start with a single person building a shack or setting up a tent and living in it, although it usually involves some kind of middleman. Progressive housing can occur through invasions, usually occurring through the purchase of a plot of land that is not zoned for urban residential use, fails to meet standards, or has an unclear property title. When occupation is not opposed by the authorities or landowners, the transition phase begins. During this phase more families arrive. They construct rudimentary houses and begin demanding basic services and utilities from state and local governments. Consolidation occurs when the families obtain all basic infrastructure and urban services and receive title to the land (Siembieda and Moreno 1997). In many countries, services and utilities cannot be provided until disputes over the land's status and ownership have been cleared.

Progressive housing tends to be substantially cheaper than formal housing, because it avoids cumbersome regulation and excessive standards. In Buenos Aires the cheapest formal sector house or apartment costs 2.7 times the median income; similar housing in an informal settlement costs about 0.8 times the median income (Angel and others 2001). Informal housing also offers the opportunity for progressive or self-built houses, which can be improved over time in a pay-as-you-go system that allows the resident to make adjustments based on the family's economic situation over time instead of requiring a mortgage with fixed payments over a long period. Finally, for many poor people, progressive housing is all equity. It can be lived in, sold, rented, or passed on as family patrimony, however modest and incomplete. A significant proportion of informal housing homeowners do borrow from friends, relatives, or informal financial institutions in order to acquire or improve their house.

and Diamond 2003). The norm among the poor is self-construction, typically with help from neighbors or family. Three-quarters of poor families in Tegucigalpa, 70 percent in Panama City, and 62 percent in San Salvador report constructing their home themselves in a progressive manner (World Bank 2002c).

Lack of Land Tenure

In Mexico's poor urban neighborhoods less than half of homeowners have title to their land (table 3.3). Even in Argentina, where the housing market is quite mature, 18 percent of all homeowners lack full title (Angel and others 2001). Combined with underdeveloped rental markets, this may explain why the home ownership rate of the poor is much higher than in Europe (40–50 percent) or the United States (50 percent).

Tenure security and titling issues are discussed in detail in chapter 5. Two points are worth making here in the context of shelter. First, as households increase tenure security (through titling or other means) and therefore their sense of permanence, they tend to increase investment in their homes. Following a massive regularization program in Peru that granted titles to 1.2 million households and 6,000 businesses, 17 percent of households invested in home improvements the year following titling, housing quality improved overall (with more titled homes made of durable materials), and access to services (notably water) rose. Crowding was reduced, as households enlarged their homes and increased the number of rooms, which also stimulated the rental market (Mosqueira 2003).

Several factors make regularization a difficult and often controversial process, even for governments willing to make progress in this area. First, public officers and public opinion may be reluctant (or refuse) to regularize illegal settlements, which often violate property rights the

Table 3.3   Only about half of poor homeowners have formal title to their homes or their property
(percent)

City	Share of poor homeowners with registered title
Metro San Salvador	55
Metro Tegucigalpa	65
Greater Panama City	64
Mexico (31 cities)	48

Source: World Bank 2002c; Ruggeri Laderchi 2005.

Note: In Mexico the sample is poor neighborhoods in 2003; in Central America it is poor people living throughout the metropolitan area in 2001.

public sector is meant to protect. Regularizing occupied lands could be interpreted as rewarding illegal behavior. This feeling is more acute when occupation or illegal settlement takes place on privately owned land. Second, the sites may be unsuited for human settlement. Sites on disaster-prone areas are more likely to be available and are less expensive when transacted through informal markets. Third, the complexity of regularization can be daunting and may require specific legislation or provision to make it manageable (box 3.2). Local governments may not have the human or financial resources needed for very complex court cases. Moreover, settlers may not always push for full tenure, which could result in additional costs, such as property tax payments (World Bank 1993). This is more likely to be the case in well-settled areas that provide a certain degree of security and services. Indeed, evidence shows that many of the benefits of secure tenure can be achieved through a wide range of measures that increase security without providing fully enforceable titles (Lanjouw and Levy 2002; Payne 2002).

Although informal housing is generally the solution of choice for low-income families, it is clearly a second-best solution. It is much more difficult for the informal sector to properly undertake the collective action role of the public sector, ensuring the provision of public goods such as well-defined rights of way, properly titled properties, and basic services. Failure to properly plan for these goods means greater capital outlays in the future to provide infrastructure, replot rights of way so that emergency vehicles and collective transport can access these communities, and untangle legal claims on property, which can take years or decades.[6] It also creates settlement patterns that place low-income families at greater risk of natural hazards—an issue that is made worse by the low quality of housing and infrastructure that is usually associated with informal

---

Box 3.2   The Central City Slum of Santo Domingo

The central city slum of Santo Domingo in the Dominican Republic is home to 11 percent of the city's population—300,000 people crowded into less than 1.6 percent of the city. About three decades ago, the area was at the outer edge of the city. As the city has grown, this area has become prime property, with easy access to the city. If this land could be developed and sold, its market value would be in the tens of billions of dollars. Several attempts by the government to regularize the area have failed. Except for a section in the extreme south, the land is owned by one family, which has engaged in an ongoing court battle for decades.

Source: Fay and others 2001.

housing. The issue of access to services is reviewed first, followed by a discussion of the vulnerability of the urban poor to natural disasters.

Inadequate Access to Infrastructure Services

In general, access to services is much higher among urban than rural populations. But urban averages can hide wide differences between rich and poor. In urban Paraguay, for example, only 30 percent of poor households—less than half the urban average—have access to water (table 3.4). Household-level data reveal significant inequalities in access between rich and poor (figure 3.1), although these differences have been declining over time and the higher the coverage, the lower the inequality (Estache, Foster, and Wodon 2002). Thus electricity coverage, which is about 98 percent in most urban areas, shows little variation across quintiles (although some of the poor may have access through illegal connections). Telephone and sewerage and drainage tend to be the most unequally distributed services.[7]

Service coverage for the poor tends to improve with time, as settlements become formalized or simply more organized. Regression analysis for Mexico's *barrios* reveals that the key determinants of a household's access to services are the age of the house and the maturity of the settlement (as measured by both the age of the settlement and the proportion of the population that has recently migrated to it). Income also matters, but its effect quickly decreases. There is also evidence that it takes longer for the

Table 3.4   High average access to water obfuscates the situation of the poor

Country	Quintile					Urban average
	1	2	3	4	5	
Bolivia	76	84	87	93	97	91
Brazil	63	85	90	97	98	90
Chile	97	98	99	99	100	99
Colombia	92	97	98	98	99	97
Ecuador	52	64	70	73	92	75
Nicaragua	57	75	83	89	93	84
Paraguay	30	50	61	72	83	67
Peru	57	75	87	90	94	85
Quintile average	65	79	84	89	94	86

Source: PAHO 2002.

Note: Data are for urban populations only.

Figure 3.1 Services with lower coverage are the most unequally distributed

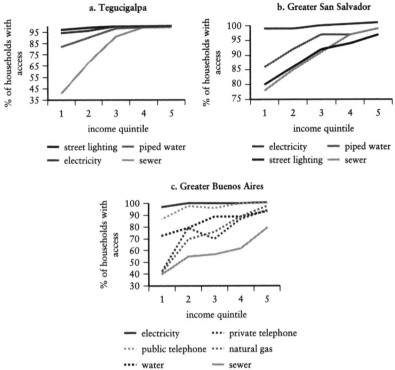

Sources: For Central America, World Bank (2002c); for Buenos Aires, Foster, CEER, and UADE (2003).

poor to obtain services: 22–30 percent of the population in the poorest quintile in San Salvador and Tegucigalpa had to wait five years or more to get water, while just 7 percent of households in the richest quintiles had to do so. In both cities about 60 percent of the poor report getting service through communal action. In contrast, three-quarters or more of the rich obtain access through a developer (World Bank 2002c).

These access figures do not take quality and reliability of service into account and may therefore overestimate effective access. In Tegucigalpa, for example, less than half of poor households but 78 percent of the richest quintile have water service more than 8 hours a day. In urban Mexico's poor neighborhoods, three-quarters of households have water service on their property (indoor or outdoor), but just 56 percent of them actually get water all day every day. This quality issue is most obvious in the case of water and solid waste, where it differentially affects the rich and the poor.[8] Electricity blackouts, where they occur, seem to affect all income quintiles almost equally (Ruggeri Laderchi 2005).

Unreliability of service and incomplete coverage cause serious environmental risks in urban areas. Demographic and Health Survey data show that the incidence of diarrhea and acute respiratory infections is higher among the urban poor than the rural poor in Latin America and infant mortality is about the same among the rural and urban poor, despite the urban poor's much higher access to health care (chapter 5).

A number of studies have documented the fact that the poor often pay more than the rich for services, particularly when they have to rely on alternative providers (Estache, Foster, and Wodon 2002). This is particularly true of nonnetwork provision (such as water tankers). It is also true of connections that are not managed by developers but acquired retroactively. Thus in San Salvador the reported cost of connection to the water utility's network in 2001 was $72 for the poorest but just $29 for the richest (World Bank 2002c).

In some cases the poor are served by alternative providers that are able to undercut the dominant firms by relying on networks but using lower cost and smaller scale technologies. This is the case of water provision in Asuncion, Paraguay; Barranquilla, Colombia; Cordoba, Argentina; and Guatemala City, Guatemala, where alternative providers account for 15–50 percent of the market (Estache, Foster, and Wodon 2002).

Utilities generally account for a substantial share of poor families' income or expenditures. In Argentina on average households in the poorest quintiles allocate 16 percent of their expenditures to utilities, while the richest quintiles spend just 11 percent (figure 3.2). As a share of household income, the contrast is even more dramatic: utilities absorb 22 percent of household income among the poorest quintile and only 7 percent for the richest.[9] In La Paz and El Alto, Bolivia, the poor spend about 10 percent of their income on water and electricity (Foster and Irusta 2001). Household expenditure shares vary across countries and utilities depending on pricing and subsidy schemes.

In addition to the cost of consumption, the connection cost can be a heavy burden on poor households, particularly if financing schemes are not available. In La Paz and El Alto, Bolivia, the water company allowed customers to spread the connection cost over time through monthly payments tied to the regular service bill. As a result, coverage expansion was very rapid. The electricity company's failure to offer a similar scheme resulted in much lower coverage expansion among poor households, even though the connection charge was very similar to that for water and sewer service (Foster and Irusta 2001).

Figure 3.2   Utilities represent a substantial share of household income or expenditures, especially for the poorest: The case of Argentina, 2002

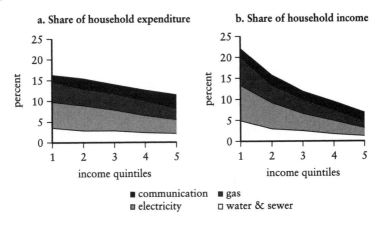

Source: Foster, CEER, and UADE 2003.

Note: Figures reflect the collapse in income and consumption that occurred in Argentina during the crisis of 2002. In 1997 infrastructure accounted for 11, 9, 8, 7, and 5 percent of expenditures for quintiles 1 through 5. Data on expenditures as a share of household income were not available for 1997.

Lack of affordability—whether because of connection or consumption cost—can be a strong deterrent to connecting to a service. These demand-side obstacles to universal coverage of basic services could be resolved without major investments in network expansion. In Guatemala, for example, the 20–40 percent coverage gap reflects households that choose not to take up a service, even though it is available in their neighborhood (Foster and Araujo 2001). Take-up increases dramatically with income: only half of Guatemalan households in the bottom two deciles choose to connect to electricity, even when it is locally available (Estache, Foster, and Wodon 2002).

Vulnerability to Natural Disasters

Natural disasters left 2.5 million people homeless in Latin America between 1990 and 1999.[10] The region has been plagued by about 90 disasters over the past three decades, causing an average 7,500 fatalities a year (Charvériat 2000). The frequency of natural disasters appears to be rising, partly as a result of rapid population growth leading to larger and denser human settlements, combined with environmental degradation.

The emergence of megacities, the concentration of populations in coastal areas that are particularly vulnerable to natural disasters, and persistent widespread poverty increase vulnerability to natural disasters. Indeed, if natural hazards are viewed as exogenous shocks, independent of human actions, natural disasters are at least partially controllable, being the result of concentrated human settlements and activities in disaster-prone areas. So vulnerability to natural disaster should be seen as a policy outcome.

Poor people are particularly vulnerable to disasters. In Mexico, which is particularly prone to natural disasters, 68 percent of people affected are poor or extremely poor (World Bank 2004). Among the poorest quintile of Honduran households affected by Hurricane Mitch, losses averaged 18 percent of total assets, compared with 3 percent among the richest quintile (Morris and others 2000). There are no general disaster statistics comparing the urban poor with other urban dwellers or the rural poor. But there is broad agreement in the natural disaster literature that cities are particularly vulnerable to natural hazards and that within the urban population the poor are generally (although not uniquely) at great risk (Charvériat 2000).

The vulnerability of cities is attributed to the high density of assets and people and to the poor quality of housing, urban planning, and urban infrastructure common in developing countries. In addition, the 20 largest cities in Latin America are in areas with steep slopes, swamps, floodable land, or seismic activity. As a result, many of the region's worst disasters have hit cities. Earthquakes hit Guatemala City, San Salvador, Lima, Managua, Mexico City, and Santiago, and landslides wreaked major destruction in Caracas and Rio de Janeiro.

The more hazardous location and poorer quality of their dwellings—which accounted for the 30,000 deaths caused by mudslides in Venezuela in 1999—puts the poor at particular risk from natural disasters. Poorly functioning land markets, urban sprawl, and poor public transportation push low-income households to settle in disaster-prone areas. In metropolitan San Salvador and Tegucigalpa, about one-fifth of the poor report having suffered damage from landslides in the past five years, and 10 percent of poor residents of San Salvador and 17 percent of the poor in Tegucigalpa report suffering from floods. These percentages are much higher than for richer groups (figure 3.3). As of 1993 at least 37 percent of Latin America's housing stock was estimated to provide inadequate protection against disaster and illness. There is also evidence that the low quality of infrastructure in poor communities contributes to vulnerability (World Bank 2000).

In addition, the poor tend to exhibit different risk behavior from higher income people. They are more risk averse in economic terms, because

Figure 3.3 Poor people are at greatest risk of suffering physical damage from a natural disaster

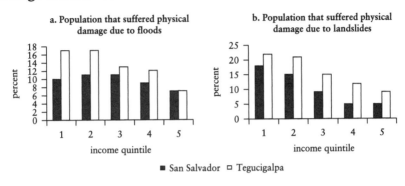

a. Population that suffered physical damage due to floods

b. Population that suffered physical damage due to landslides

■ San Salvador □ Tegucigalpa

Source: World Bank 2002c.

they lack savings or assets, but they are more risk inclined in terms of where they will live (Pantoja 2002). This could be because they are less informed of the risk or, more likely, because the advantages of risky locations (low cost, proximity to employment and therefore low transport cost) are perceived as outweighing the risks. In locations where catastrophic risk is recurrent and well understood, the low-income housing market clearly factors in this risk (box 3.3). Alternatively, the poor may not engage in risk-reduction strategies because they lack resources: resettlement, home retrofitting, and insurance coverage (seldom available for the poor) may be too costly relative to savings capacity and perceived benefits. As most of the poor's income is allocated to immediate survival, the

Box 3.3 Risk-Adjusted Housing Strategies in the Slums of Santo Domingo

Santo Domingo's central city slum spans several worlds, with varying vulnerability to flooding and landslides. When it rains, the risk of flooding ranges from 6 percent for households on higher, consolidated ground to 45 percent for households near the river or along the 11 main drainage systems and *cañadas* (gullies). Knowledge is common about which areas of the neighborhood are at risk of landslides. Rents (actual or imputed) reflect location safety and are almost twice as high in the safer areas than near the river or gullies. Housing quality also reflects risk perception, with simple wooden shacks in areas at risk for regular, catastrophic floods and multistory homes of durable materials in the consolidated part.

Source: Fay and others 2001.

low frequency of a natural disaster, however catastrophic its effects, may not justify a change in behavior.

The poor are also less able to recover from natural disasters, partly because of their lack of resources but also because of public policies. Four years after Hurricane Mitch, bridges linking poor neighborhoods in Tegucigalpa to the city center had still not been repaired, despite improvements in other parts of the city. In Venezuela eight months after the 1999 landslides, 33,000 people still lived in shelters or barracks in appalling conditions. Most lived in extreme poverty. Poor conditions in shelters and uncertainty over the future were linked to higher rates of rape, domestic violence, child prostitution, and drug abuse. The Venezuelan government was criticized for focusing on rebuilding roads and other economic infrastructure at the expense of social issues (International Federation of Red Cross and Red Crescent Societies 2001).

Women (especially household heads) are more likely to suffer long-term consequences after natural disasters. The proportion of women living in shelters in the immediate aftermath of Hurricane Mitch equaled their proportion in the general population in Central America. This percentage significantly increased over time, particularly for female household heads, possibly demonstrating their greater difficulty in accessing lodging and food-for-work programs. On the other hand, disasters can also create opportunities for empowerment of and leadership by women: nearly a third of shelters in Honduras were managed by women (World Bank 2001).

What Can Be Done to Improve Access to Shelter for the Urban Poor?

The current paradigm for public sector interventions in housing markets in general, and in low-income housing in particular, is an enabling one. The government is seen as the main guarantor of well-functioning markets through adequate housing and land legislation, rather than as a provider of housing. This is a striking evolution from previous approaches (box 3.4).

This approach focuses on homeownership rather than rental policies, because homeownership is perceived as a quasi-universal aspiration and presumed to be a desirable achievement, particularly for low-income households. As a result, there is very little discussion of policies to support rental housing for low-income populations. However, acknowledging and promoting rental housing as a shelter option is a logical expansion of the enabling paradigm in housing policy.[11] The little that is known is reviewed here.

Box 3.4   A Brief History of Housing Policies Since the 1950s

Starting in the 1950s and lasting through the 1970s, many governments built public housing for direct sale or rent. The construction followed Western standards and usually took the form of subsidized blocks of apartments built to high construction and infrastructure standards, often accompanied by the destruction of slum areas. Public housing usually failed to reach the poor, as the units were too expensive for the targeted households and required large subsidies, taxing fiscal resources and limiting the scale of programs. The buildings were typically in unattractive locations on the urban periphery, implying additional transportation costs. As a result, a high percentage of units were resold or rented to wealthier families.

In the 1970s and 1980s, governments began to recognize the value of squatters' gradual approach to housing and moved to support squatters' initiatives through upgrading of slums and sites and the provision of services. Slum upgrading involved improving the existing housing of the urban poor; site upgrading focused on providing vacant tracts of land for housing with only basic services or core houses for residents to improve. The lower costs of these approaches—through lower planning and engineering standards—boded well for scaling up. Nevertheless, sites and services projects generally suffered from the same problems as public housing—the apartments were too expensive for the poor, and they were located in unattractive locations, with plot sizes and layouts that poorly matched the needs of the beneficiaries. Upgrading projects suffered from a lack of fiscal resources and institutional capacity to expand the programs and maintain the services.

Public Policies for Low-Income Renters

Public policies for rental housing fall into three categories:

- *Policies on private sector rental housing.* Policies include rent control, regulation of the relationship between tenant and owner, and building and environmental health regulation. Rent control is problematic for a number of reasons. It discourages mobility and the production of affordable housing.[12] Although rent control depresses rents, countries with stricter rent control tend to have higher house prices (Rakodi 1995). However, simply removing rent control may not always be sufficient to stimulate the housing market; additional policies may be needed. In addition, reforms should be wary of eliminating embedded provisions that control the relationship between tenants and owners, although these tend to be ineffective for poor people, who seldom have contracts (usually a necessary condition for protection) and who lack the ability to resort to justice or arbitration. Promoting simple contracts and landlord-tenant arbitration could promote transparency in the rental sector. Bolivia's Office for Conflict in Renting and Bogotá's Chamber of Commerce, local governments, and faculties of law are examples of extrajudicial arbitration of rental disputes; their impact has not been evaluated. Building and environmental health regulations need to be applied with care in order not to displace poor people during upgrading. In most cases, regularization and upgrading of poor settlements tend to be accompanied by an increase in availability of rentals, particularly if accompanied by policies to increase density.

- *Policies on public sector rental housing.* Because it is generally in short supply, public housing tends to foster favoritism and bribery and not reach the very poor. In addition to this targeting problem, rent-setting is problematic. If it is too high or too low it will result in subletting. Maintenance is a common problem, although various countries have experimented successfully with alternative schemes, such as turning responsibility for maintenance to tenants associations. The problems and costs associated with public sector rental housing have led to the switch toward policies that support homeownership and the widespread sale of public sector rentals and to policies that encourage the private sector production of an adequate supply of rental accommodations.

- *Policies that increase the supply of rental accommodations.* Policies include the provision of land or credit on favorable terms and tax incentives. Because of the emphasis on homeownership, such policies are rare; exceptions include the Republic of Korea, Mexico, and Thailand (in the 1980s), with limited success in Korea and Mexico. More generally, if housing policy includes tax incentive and subsidy programs to purchase a home, an attempt should be made to extend the benefits to subsistence landlords and their tenants. The practical application of this idea has yet to emerge, as there are many obstacles to overcome, including the lack of institutional capacity. Most Latin American countries probably lack the administrative capacity to run a rental voucher program, such as the Section 8 program in the United States.[13]

The verdict on active policies for low-income rentals is not encouraging. It is important to keep in mind, however, that constraints on housing supply adversely affect urban households, particularly the poor, whether they rent or own. Thus it is possible that the best recommendations may be to improve the functioning of the overall housing market—preferably in a way that is tenure neutral. Making informal housing more secure, through tenure or other means, has an immediate positive impact on the supply of rental housing.

Box 3.5   Reforming the Rental Market in Colombia

In June 2003, the Colombian Congress passed a law that aimed to stimulate rental markets (Law 820; see http://www.secretariasenado.gov.co/leyes/ L0820003.HTM). The law seeks to simplify rental contracts in order to make them more effective and to streamline the law regarding tenant-landlord conflicts in the hope of speeding up the repossession process. In addition, the government lifted rent control and contemplated tax incentives and indirect subsidies for the development of rental housing. The results of this attempt to improve rental markets and attract investment in the rental sector will be closely watched.

Source: Gilbert 2003.

Because rental markets have not been part of housing policies in most countries, there is no evidence yet of its impact. Colombia appears to be the only country that is beginning to address the issue (box 3.5).

Public Policies for Low-Income Homeowners

Public housing policies aim for an integrated approach that supports demand (by strengthening property rights, developing mortgage financing, and rationalizing demand subsidies); helps organize supply (by providing infrastructure for residential land development, regulating land and housing development, and organizing the building industry); and promotes institutional development. Focusing on the poor, these policies seek to convert informal sector housing needs into effective demand for housing and increase the supply of land, infrastructure, and housing (Siembieda and Moreno 1997).

On the demand side, the objective is to ease the financial constraints of the poor. This includes alleviating liquidity constraints by providing access to microcredit and fostering household savings to allow the poor to better use their limited resources. It may also involve addressing solvency issues through the limited use of housing subsidies. Developing financing for low-income housing demand may stimulate the interest of private sector entrepreneurs for low-income development and construction.

MICROCREDIT
Commercial banks are out of reach for the majority of the population in the region, not only in terms of loans for home purchases but also in terms of savings and other banking services. Short-term successive microcredits for housing ($500–$5,000 payable over two to five years) are a powerful

---

Box 3.6   Using Housing Microfinance: The Micasa Program in Peru

Mibanco of Peru, one of the most successful microfinance agencies in the region, launched its home improvement program in mid-2000. Within 12 months, Micasa had 3,000 active clients and an outstanding portfolio of $2.6 million. Moreover, it was profitable, generating almost $16,000 a month in net income.

The program differs from Mibanco's successful microenterprise lending methodology, in that the loans carry a lower interest rate, allow for longer terms (up to 36 months), tend to be slightly larger in size, and are available not just to microentrepreneurs but also to low-income, salaried employees. Micasa loans average $916 over 11 months. Borrowers are not required to have legal title in order to obtain a loan, and the loans are often secured with household assets or guarantees by cosigners.

Source: Cities Alliance 2003.

---

tool for facilitating access to finance for low-income families (box 3.6). Unlike mortgage finance, which deals with complete units, housing microfinance is well suited to the incremental building process, as short-term loans can fund each progressive step at affordable market terms. Moreover, microcredit can be used by people who lack formal titles, income, or employment.

Housing microfinance is growing and looks very promising. But expansion will require tackling a number of challenges. First, in countries such as Mexico, interest rate subsidies and noncommercial origination and collection practices by public sector lenders crowd out private lenders. Second, legal and regulatory frameworks that are poorly adapted to non-bank financial institutions may either limit their expansion or make expansion financially risky. Third, there is a need for technical assistance in gradual construction processes to ensure the safety and stability of the structure, to follow construction standards, and so forth. Whether microfinance institutions should be providing this support is under debate. There have been many models for providing this assistance, from provision by lenders on a fee basis to involvement of the local government or a civil society organization.

SAVINGS AND SUBSIDY SCHEMES

Subsidized housing savings programs can ease financial constraints by enhancing households' capacity to make an initial investment in shelter and by building a credit history to allow households to leverage their savings through credit.[14] Perhaps the best known example of this type of scheme is Chile's Unified Subsidy and Basic House Program, which targets the lowest income groups, enrolling them in a savings program that eventually allows them to acquire a house by using their savings, a direct subsidy that varies with income, and an optional mortgage credit. A key to this program's success is that it allows participants to purchase an old or new housing unit or build a house if they already own land (World Bank 2002a). One of the weaknesses of the program has been its failure to attract private lending for the lowest income segments and the subsequent substitution of public lending and associated sustainability programs due to low levels of loan repayment. Costa Rica has also experienced some success with this type of scheme (box 3.7).

Residential savings programs, or mutual assistance programs, have also been used to leverage resources of very low-income communities for housing. The residents' savings are commonly pooled into a legal trust, often set up by an NGO or community association. The trust serves as a mechanism to leverage and attract additional sources of financing, to protect against default, and to receive and manage subsidies. The trust can provide the seed capital for community infrastructure and bridge loans and end-user finance.

A good example of a mutual assistance scheme is Mexico's Plan de Ayuda Mutua, a self-financing program for residents of informal settlements. Participants contribute a set amount every week over a savings cycle, generally less than a year, to maintain the interest of the participants. Funds are allotted every month (or week) based on a lottery, in which one participant receives benefits—in the form of construction materials, labor, or down payments on land—equivalent to the sum of his or her savings during the cycle (World Bank 2002a).

SUPPLY-SIDE ISSUES

Government agencies are without comparative advantage as land developers.[15] However, they can help reduce the cost of land and housing through several planning, regulatory, and fiscal mechanisms.

- *Land and urban regulations and standards.* Local governments can adjust standards for urbanization and construction to adapt to the effective demand of low-income populations. Reducing minimum plot size and increasing maximum floor and area ratios in poor neighborhoods can allow development of low-income housing that is profitable to the private sector yet affordable to low-income families. Different standards can also be considered for street design, basic services, community facilities, and pedestrian and bike streets. By lowering standards, the formal sector should be able to shift some of its housing production down market and legally produce subdivisions.

Box 3.7   Costa Rica's Direct Demand Housing Subsidy Program

The Costa Rican direct demand subsidy program, started in 1987, was modeled on the Chilean program. The program, which can be used for construction alone, land purchase and construction, or purchase or improvement of an existing unit, consists of the following elements:

- A subsidy voucher of an amount inversely related to household income, with a maximum value of about $4,000.
- The beneficiaries' down payment.
- A mortgage loan given by an "authorized entity," including government banks, nongovernmental organizations (NGOs), cooperative federations, and savings and loans. These entities have the authority to choose beneficiaries, deliver the direct subsidy, and extend a loan to complement the direct subsidy and the household's down payment. Households go to the authorized entities and ask them how much they can afford to pay for a housing solution. The authorities inform them of the maximum house price, the loan amount, and the required down payment. The household then seeks a housing solution that costs no more than this maximum price. The government housing bank then buys the authorized entities' social housing portfolio at below-market rates.

At its initiation, the program attempted to recapture the subsidy from the household when the house was sold. These efforts were abandoned in the early 1990s.

In contrast to Chile and most other countries that have adopted direct demand subsidies, Costa Rica has succeeded in attracting the private sector into the very low-income market. The main reason why it has been able to do so is that sophisticated NGOs experienced in housing development—a rarity in developing countries—have become the main developers under the program. When the direct subsidy program began, many for-profit developers used it. Most stopped participating in 1994, however, mainly because of increased political and economic risk. NGOs have stepped in to fill this gap. Some NGOs help households construct a unit on an existing lot by providing technical assistance. Others assemble groups of beneficiaries, extend credit, and develop units by contracting with for-profit construction firms.

Until recently, the program proved stable, delivering a significant number of direct subsidies each year from its inception in 1987 through the mid-1990s. Subsidies delivered between 1988 and 1998 (93,049) benefited 13 percent of households in Costa Rica. Authorized entities experienced few arrears on these loans.

Although the program has proved politically popular, fiscal constraints since the mid-1990s have caused a decline in resources available for subsidies. Various stop-gap measures—such as issuing bonds for funding the direct demand subsidy—have proved problematic and complicated the operations of the program.

Sources: Ferguson 2001; World Bank 2002b.

- *Permit processes.* Complicated and time-consuming procedures with unpredictable outcomes make it difficult for developers to quickly respond to changing housing demands and adequately gauge the cost of development. Streamlined procedures reduce uncertainty and help developers determine whether a project will be profitable.
- *Information.* Governments can play an important role in providing information in the form of data on available land, land characteristics, and urban trends, as well as examples of good practice and benchmarking. As part of the planning process, bringing various actors together and sharing perspectives can have a significant impact on policy outcomes (Prud'homme 2003).
- *Taxes and subsidies.* High taxes on undeveloped land can discourage the holding of such land, increasing the supply and thereby reducing the price of developed land.
- *Infrastructure investments.* By providing basic trunk infrastructure, governments can increase the supply of serviced urban land—reducing price, increasing affordability, and thereby reducing the probability of the continued formation of irregular settlements. Tertiary infrastructure and services can be built in a progressive manner, making land more affordable to the poor and providing some form of self-targeting, as only those who prefer partially serviced land would apply. A gradual strategy of urbanization may reduce many of the negative externalities of irregular development (such as unstructured neighborhood layout and construction in precarious areas), reducing the ex post cost of infrastructure provision. Governments can also play an important role in helping organize communities to help plan and construct local infrastructure. In finished formal housing, the housing unit is transferred with all supporting shelter amenities. In contrast, low-income housing, consolidated through a gradual construction process, is transferred with varying bundles of amenities. The gradual provision of infrastructure entails substantial transaction costs and as such requires a high level of technical assistance to households and community groups.

SLUM UPGRADING

Destruction of slums and the relocation of slum dwellers have proven costly in social and financial terms. In contrast, neighborhood upgrading provides residents with improved living environments without displacing them. It also costs about one-tenth as much as destruction and relocation (SIGUS 2001). The investment already made to properties remains, enhanced and stimulated. Regularization of land tenure results in significant private investment in these communities, with $1 of public funds typically generating about $7 in private investment (SIGUS 2001). In addition, upgrading projects can yield important social and economic benefits. In the upgraded area of El Mezquital, Guatemala, for example, infant mortality rates fell 90 percent and crime fell 43 percent (World Bank 2002a).

Neighborhood upgrading typically entails a set of geographically focused interventions. Traditionally, these interventions focused on physical improvements of living conditions—drainage, vehicular and pedestrian access, water supply and sanitation, public lighting and electricity, resettlement of houses living in areas vulnerable to natural disasters, and provision and land tenure. Experience has shown the need for additional attention to environmental and social issues. The Guarapiranga project in metropolitan São Paulo focused on water basin management; employment and job training were the focus of the *favela barrio* project in Rio de Janeiro.

Three decades of experience point to the following elements as essential for successful neighborhood upgrading:

• *Community and public sector involvement.* Upgrading requires extensive coordination by the public sector and community groups, notably in the provision of basic services (such as housing, water, and sewerage) and public goods (such as street lights and sidewalks). Utilities often ignore marginal neighborhoods, due to restrictions on providing services to areas without full tenure. These restrictions reflect the assumption that these areas are not profitable. But innovative community solutions and small-scale private providers have had success. In El Mezquital, Guatemala, the community formed a cooperative that manages sewerage services on a cost-recovery basis. In Asunción, Paraguay, *aguateros* (small private water suppliers) serve 30 percent of households, including most of the marginal peri-urban neighborhoods not covered by the main utility.

• *Appropriate standards.* Inappropriate development standards are partly responsible for the creation of informal neighborhoods. Lower levels of services or alternative technologies should be considered to increase affordability and accommodate physical limitations imposed by the generally irregular and dense layout of marginal neighborhoods. One of the best-known cases is the use of condominial sewerage, which allows provision of network sewer services through piping in the rear of lots, along sidewalks, or in front of lots to reduce costs in terms of in-house and secondary network investment, destruction and repavement of streets, and displacement of homes in cases of irregular, dense urban layouts.

• *Effective land regularization and layout improvement schemes.* Land regularization in upgrading projects aims to stimulate household investment by improving tenure security and adjusting the layout of the neighborhood to reduce vulnerability to natural disasters and allow for the provision of services and access ways. In terms of layout adjustment, various schemes—land sharing, land pooling, land reconstruction—have proven successful, but all require residents to work together and with the landowner to agree on physical reorganization of the neighborhood and division of the land parcel.

- *Financial sustainability and the feasibility of scaling up.* Cost recovery can also be a powerful tool to ensure that services and investments are in line with residents' interest and willingness to pay and allow government to design appropriate subsidy policies if necessary and feasible. Specific strategies need to be developed for public and private goods, with the understanding that subsidization of public goods may be justified while full cost recovery for private goods should be a goal. Involving residents in issues of cost recovery during the planning phases will help build the ownership necessary for future sustainability. Evidence from numerous cases throughout the region shows that the poor can and are willing to pay for services and frequently pay more in cash, time, and work loss than the cost of standard services (Estache, Foster, and Wodon 2002). Reducing the fiscal costs of upgrading through more appropriate standards, cost recovery, and tighter poverty targeting of subsidies would help reduce the financial barriers to scaling up.

Making Infrastructure Work for the Poor

Making infrastructure work for the poor requires promoting access and ensuring consumption affordability.[16] Promoting access can entail reducing connection costs, increasing the number and types of suppliers, and requiring operators to promote access. Promoting affordability can entail reducing actual bills, service cost, and facilitating payment.

Several actions can promote access:

- *Require operators to promote access.* This type of instrument is used mostly when the operator is a private one and increased access becomes an integral part of its service obligation. It takes one of two forms: a universal service obligation (USO), in which there is a legal obligation to bring service to all households, or connection targets. USOs tend to be defined in general terms and require complementary specifications of connection targets, access costs, and sources of subsidy to be operational. USOs can be bidirectional, in which case households are obliged to connect once the service is made available. When they are, affordability issues are particularly critical. Connection targets entail clear obligations (they typically include the exact number of households, their location, and the date at which they need to be connected.) Attaining the targets requires that customers pick up the service, however.

- *Reduce connection cost.* Connection costs can be reduced in several ways. One is to allow for a combination of technology choice and quality of service that allows for faster and cheaper service for the poor (condominial sewerage is one example). Financing arrangements should be designed that allow poor customers to spread out the connection cost over time (financing is usually provided by the operator, as in the La Paz/El Alto case discussed earlier). Cross-subsidies, in which the connected population contributes to a connection fund, tend to be well targeted toward the poor (who are typically the ones without connection). They are most suitable where the unconnected population is small relative to the connected one. Governments can also choose to provide connection subsidies, either general or targeted at specific components of the connection cost that customers find difficult to pay for. Connection subsidies are administratively more cost-effective than recurring subsidies for the use of a service, because they involve one-time rather than ongoing payments.
- *Increase the number and type of suppliers.* Alternative network suppliers can provide competition as well as tailor services to the needs of the poor. Supporting them in a way that is beneficial to the poor can entail providing a legitimate role for such suppliers, promoting cooperation between the dominant operator and alternative suppliers, and requiring the utility to provide various types of services.
- *Reduce the cost of the bill.* Targeted subsidies can be allocated on the basis of consumption levels, income, needs, or location. Subsidies issued on the basis of consumption do not target the poor effectively, given the weak correlation between income and consumption. Targeting based on income or needs requires a reliable poverty proxy and a relatively advanced administrative mechanism for screening individual households. Such a mechanism can be very costly if it does not already exist as part of a broader platform for social protection.[17] Finally, geographic subsidies tend to be poorly targeted given the income heterogeneity of most poor urban neighborhoods. Rebalancing fixed and variable tariffs, whereby most of the charges are recovered through the variable tariff, is more attractive to small consumers. Voucher programs are used in the United States and Europe but so far not in Latin America. They rely on some form of means testing and therefore suffer from the same types of advantages and inconvenience as means-based targeted subsidies.
- *Reduce the cost of service.* The cost of service can be reduced by letting consumers opt for lower quality service (choosing to be among the first to be rationed in time of energy scarcity, for example) or by placing physical limits on the volume of consumption (through telephone service that limits the volume of calls that can be made over a given period or

by allowing a minimum amount of energy to be consumed over a given period). Both approaches have been used in the United States and Europe with success.

- *Facilitate payment.* Poor households with little or no liquid savings often find it difficult to pay relatively infrequent and unpredictable bills or to cover them in periods of crisis (illness, loss of jobs). One approach is to allow for more frequent billings (although doing so increases administrative costs) or to install prepayment meters. Prepayment meters function best for telephones. They appear to be costly for water and electricity.

Estache, Foster, and Wodon (2002) discuss international experiences with all of these approaches and provide guidance on how best to choose among combinations of instruments. For the most part, all of these instruments can be used whether the operator is a private or public one. Regardless of who the operator is, a quasi-universal lesson of infrastructure reform is that where utilities are inefficient, the poor suffer most. Thus improving overall performance is a necessary—but not sufficient—prerequisite for making infrastructure work for the poor.

Reducing Vulnerability to Natural Disasters

The risk of disaster can be diminished by reducing either the hazard factor or the vulnerability factor. The risk of certain types of hazards, such as floods and landslides, can be mitigated through engineering solutions. The risk of others, such as earthquakes and hurricanes, cannot. Much can be done to reduce vulnerability to these events, however (Kreimer and others 1999). Land use planning can prevent settlements in dangerous areas. Infrastructure and housing quality can be improved to make it more disaster resistant—through building codes and the provision of hurricane shutters and better roofing. Insurance can help ensure faster recovery and limit long-term impacts.

Many of these recommendations are difficult for poor cities to implement and pose special difficulties for poor people, for several reasons. First, few Latin American cities have undertaken the hazard or vulnerability assessments needed to plan for development, evaluate options for mitigation or risk reduction investments, and prepare for a response in case a disaster hits.[18] Second, few cities in the region have the capacity to prevent settlement in disaster-prone areas. Rules and regulations, when they exist, are seldom enforced. Moreover, regulations that declare certain areas unsafe for habitation may make matters worse, by limiting the land available for safe settlement (in case of overly strict regulations) or reducing the price of unsafe land, making it attractive to those who cannot afford anything else. Third, improving or retrofitting infrastructure usually occurs in the richer parts of a town or city. Poor neighborhoods are typically characterized by low-quality infrastructure and are usually in need of basic repairs, let alone upgrading or retrofitting.

Despite the problems, some successes have been achieved, even in poor communities. Indeed, the case of Cuba shows that political will and good institutional organization can overcome the lack of wealth (box 3.8). A number of communities and cities in Cuba organized themselves and successfully averted major disasters. In the Dominican Republic a government organization and NGOs organized workshops to help communities come up with community emergency plans. During Hurricane George, in 1998, communities that had such plans successfully evacuated people, established shelters, organized clean-up brigades, and requested and distributed assistance. Participating communities were less affected than other communities by the hurricane (CGCED 2002). More generally, building social assets in a neighborhood can greatly contribute to minimizing the impact of a disaster. In Catuche, a neighborhood of Caracas, very few people died during the floods, reportedly due to community mobilization and mutual help efforts (Sanderson 2000).

Box 3.8   Minimizing Deaths from Natural Disasters through Good Planning: The Case of Cuba

Developing countries are more vulnerable than developed countries to natural disasters. The San Francisco earthquake of 1989, with a magnitude of 7.1, caused 63 deaths, while a 6.2 earthquake near Guatemala City in 1976 resulted in 22,780 fatalities. Countries with similar occurrences of natural disasters, such as Japan and Peru, have very different disaster-related deaths statistics: between 1970 and 1999 Peru had 2,420 fatalities, while Japan recorded 315.

However, the different outcomes seem to be related less to the wealth of a country than to its degree of preparedness. When Hurricane Michelle ripped through Cuba in November 2001, only five people were killed. In comparison, Hurricane Mitch, which was of similar strength, killed 20,000 people when it hit Central America. In Cuba successful civil defense and Red Cross planning ensured that 700,000 people were evacuated to emergency shelters in time; search and rescue and emergency health care plans were in place. In Havana electricity and water were turned off to avoid electrocution and sewage contamination. A UN report concluded that the government's high degree of preparedness was essential in preventing major loss of life.

Sources: Charvériat 2000; International Federation of Red Cross and Red Crescent Societies 2002.

A number of countries are experimenting with improving disaster preparedness by building stronger buildings. In the British Virgin Islands, 100 percent of new buildings are reportedly equipped with hurricane shutters, which are tax exempt. National development foundations in Antigua and Barbuda, Dominica, and St. Lucia have implemented hurricane-resistant home improvement programs for poor and vulnerable communities. These programs are designed to strengthen safer building practices in the informal housing sector by conducting workshops for builders and artisans and by providing access to loans for home retrofit and upgrade (CGED 2002).

While disaster insurance is fairly common in industrial countries, in large part thanks to government intervention, in developing countries it is mainly confined to wealthy individuals, large companies, and government organizations. Irregular settlements without titles or valuation and suboptimal housing are generally considered uninsurable. The model adopted by the city of Manizales, in Colombia, shows that this is not the case and that with innovative schemes and political will, even the very poorest can have access to catastrophic insurance (box 3.9).

Box 3.9   Providing Catastrophic Insurance to the Poor: The Experience of Manizales, Colombia

The city of Manizales has been at the forefront of disaster risk management in Latin America. Its insurance program covers buildings owned by the poorest strata of its population. Through an agreement with an insurance company, the city allows any resident to purchase insurance coverage through the municipal tax collection system. Once 30 percent of the insurable buildings in the metropolitan area participate in the plan, the insurance coverage extends to all properties that are exempt of property tax. These include some buildings hosting organizations dedicated to the provision of public good (NGOs, foundations, and nonprofit organizations), as well as all properties with cadastral value of less than 25 minimum monthly salaries (about $3,400), as established by the municipal council.

The insurance contract is priced competitively and designed so that the insurance company ends up with a direct contractual relationship with the individual taxpayer who decides to participate in the insurance plan. The municipal administration acts only as a premium collector and is not responsible for any claims under the plan, which remain the responsibility of the insurance company. The municipality retains 6 percent of the value of the premiums collected for handling the process, transferring the rest of the proceeds to the insurance company.

Source: Written by Francis Ghesquiere, Senior Urban Specialist at the World Bank.

An exhaustive study of the role of microfinance in disaster risk management suggests that microcredit can play a role in both prevention and recovery (Pantoja 2002). Housing loans promote the adoption of appropriate building technologies; microfinance institutions occasionally include some type of technical assistance. Access to a loan in the aftermath of a disaster can make a critical difference in a poor family's ability to recover. But microcredit is limited in what it can do. Microcredit institutions do not usually reach the poorest of the poor. And the fact that disasters are a covariant risk implies that microfinance institutions have to protect themselves, both to avoid serious financial reversals and to ensure that they can keep resources flowing after a disaster: to remain viable, microcredit institutions need to maintain financial discipline.

A 1997 USAID survey of disaster mitigation and response efforts of municipalities in seven South American countries found that most cities had limited roles, usually within the limited confines of existing legislation that established national civil defense legislation. Where municipalities do not have the capacity to carry out responsibilities designated to them in the decentralized civil defense system, the vulnerability of the population is very high.

Some cities in the region are taking action. Cali, Medellin, and Manizales, Colombia, have created municipal disaster prevention and relief systems that are models for the rest of Latin America (CGRTCA 1998). In the United States communities or municipalities tend not to organize on their own unless there is a federal incentive in place (CGRTCA 1998). Thus increased recognition of the importance of local initiatives should not come at the expense of a national framework.

Conclusion

The dismal shelter situation of the urban poor in Latin America and the Caribbean has important implications for their well-being and health, issues addressed in chapter 5. Improving housing for the poor is complex, but it is by no means beyond the scope of Latin America's governments. Slums are, to a large extent, the products of failed policies. Preventing the development of future slums and improving living conditions in existing ones therefore requires policy reform.

What might be the priorities for governments that seek to improve the housing situation of the poor? Clearly, priorities are context specific. Priority setting may also be guided by the fact that there is clearer knowledge on some interventions than others—and that many of the needed reforms depend on the institutional and political context.

Annex: Basic Principles of Housing Subsidy Schemes (Adapted from Hoek-Smit and Diamond 2003)

Well-designed and executed subsidies can help mitigate housing market failures and meet public policy goals. To do so, it is crucial to clearly identify the program's objectives and ensure that they are consistent with the country's overall housing goals (public health, social stability, overcoming market inefficiencies, and so forth). Subsidies should be used as a last resort, after relevant regulatory, policy, and macroeconomic reforms have been considered.

The following considerations should be taken into account in designing a subsidy that efficiently meets policy objectives:

- cost (directed, indirect, and administrative) relative to expected social and economic benefits
- expected displacement of investments or expenditures that would have occurred anyway
- equity issues (horizontal and vertical), including cliff effects resulting from subsidies with rigid income or housing price brackets and cut-off points
- portability and possible labor market effects due to reduced mobility
- administrative simplicity
- extent of market distortion (programs that specify housing type and price brackets will often drastically increase both the supply and the price of the type of housing specified)

In recent decades governments have favored demand-side subsidies to beneficiary households and, on a more limited basis, incentives to financial agents over public construction and ownership of social housing. Demand-side subsidies focus on increasing the willingness and ability of households to consume better housing or housing of a particular type. Such subsidies can be provided through housing allowances or vouchers for rental or owner-occupied housing or through up-front grants tied to savings or housing finance. The risk associated with demand-side lump-sum grants is that they are often tied to nonmarket (informal) new housing with questionable resale value, in undesirable locations. As a result, the private sector may not be interested in lending to the target group. In Chile, where the lump-sum demand-side subsidy was pioneered effectively in a scheme in which public grants to households are matched by loans from banks, the private sector could not be induced to service the lowest income market. As a result, the state had to sponsor lending for that segment of the market.

In contrast, supply-side subsidies reduce the opportunity costs and risks for private lenders and developers to deliver low-income housing. In general, supply-side subsidies are efficient only when input markets do not work well and do not respond to regulatory or policy incentives to deliver specific types of housing. For example, there may be high demand for new low-income housing and the construction sector may ready to deliver but lenders are reluctant because they perceive the market as too risky or unprofitable. In this case, a supply-side subsidy may be effectively used on a declining basis to provide incentives for private lenders to enter and gain experience in assessing the profitability and risks associated with lending to lower income borrowers. The risk of supply-side subsidies is that they distort markets, particularly when government takes on roles that could be performed more efficiently by the private sector.

Endnotes

1. Surveys from poor neighborhoods suggest home ownership is indeed high. It averages 81 percent across 31 poor neighborhoods distributed across all of Mexico's state capitals (excluding the Federal District). According to surveys, home ownership among the poor is 87 percent in Metropolitan San Salvador, 82 percent in Tegucigalpa, and 86 percent in greater Panama City (World Bank 2002c). In the central city slum of Santo Domingo, Dominican Republic, home ownership is 58 percent (Fay and others 2001).

2. It is unclear whether the high rate of home ownership springs from some innate desire to own one's roof, or because of the greater insecurity of rentals, from which one can be evicted at any point and which require generating a steady stream of income in order to pay the rent.

3. The Mexico survey of poor neighborhoods shows that households occupying lent houses are also more likely to have a relative or trusted friend living in the neighborhood (Ruggeri Laderchi 2005). However, they are less likely to have helped this person solve problems of money, transport, health, or lodgings over the past month, possibly because benefiting from lent housing is more likely to occur among people who are in a subordinate position in the patronage network. This is consistent with female-headed households being more likely to live in lent accommodation.

4. The results are less clear for the age of the settlement. Housing quality increases with age, reaching its highest level for settlements 6 to 10 years old and decreasing thereafter. For services, age of settlement seems to matter (positively) only for access to water.

5. It is estimated that more than 46 percent of the population of Recife, Brazil, and 40 percent of the population of Mexico City (CEPAL 2000) live in informal settlements.

6. For infrastructure provision, the rule of thumb among urban planners is that retrofitting costs three to six times more than providing the services ex ante.

7. For telephones this seems to remain true despite the extraordinary rise of cellular phones.

8. The poor in Tegucigalpa and San Salvador are substantially more likely to experience problems with solid waste management, such as pests and garbage accumulation (World Bank 2002c).

9. The difference between using income or expenditure as a denominator stems from the fact that the rich tend to save a much larger proportion of their income.

10. This section draws heavily on Charvériat (2000). For more information on disaster management, see http://worldbank.org/dmf/and http://www.iadb.org/.

11. This section draws on Rakodi (1995) unless otherwise specified. For a more Latin America–specific discussion, see Gilbert (1993) and Gilbert and Varley (1991).

12. Problems include patchy enforcement and uneven distribution of benefits; even if programs are designed so that they benefit low-income populations, they often favor long-term tenants over newcomers. Most important, rent control deters maintenance and inhibits investment in new housing, resulting in the entrapment of tenants in poor quality housing and the use of illegal payments, such as key money, which penalize new tenants and further discourage mobility.

13. Under the Section 8 rental voucher program, "the public housing authority (PHA) generally pays the landlord the difference between 30 percent of household income and the PHA–determined payment standard—about 80–100 percent of the fair market rent (FMR). The rent must be reasonable. The household may choose a unit with a higher rent than the FMR and pay the landlord the difference or choose a lower cost unit and keep the difference" (http://www.hud.gov/progdesc/voucher.cfm).

14. For subsidized schemes to work, they need to respect a number of principles (discussed in appendix C).

15. Public efforts to create land reserves for housing the poor have consistently been overtaken by a market-based approach of illegal sale and subsequent conversion.

16. This section is based on Estache, Foster, and Wodon (2002).

17. A recent article comparing Chile's individual means-tested subsidy and Colombia's geographic subsidy suggests that both suffer from large errors of inclusion (subsidizing households that should not be) but that errors of exclusion seem to be fewer in the Colombian scheme, which, overall, appears more cost-effective (Gómez-Lobo and Contreras 2000).

18. Hazard assessments identify hazard zones; vulnerability assessments evaluate the expected performance of structures, infrastructure, and institutions under the stress of a disaster.

References

Angel, Schlomo, N.A. Félix, C. de Hoz, M. Jiménez, S. Lebedinsky, L. Lucioni, N. Pazos, P.A. Pereyra, and M.B. Rudolfo. 2001. *El sector de vivienda y la política de vivienda en Argentina: Una evaluación expeditiva.* Washington, DC: Inter-American Development Bank.

CGCED (Caribbean Group for Cooperation in Economic Development). 2002. *Natural Hazard Risk Management in the Caribbean: Revisiting the Challenge.* Washington, DC: World Bank, Latin America and the Caribbean Region, Caribbean Country Management Unit.

Charvériat, Céline. 2000. "Natural Disaster in Latin America and the Caribbean: An Overview of Risk." Working Paper No. 434, Inter-American Development Bank, Research Department, Washington, DC.

Cities Alliance. 2003. "Shelter Finance for the Poor." *CIVIS* (April). www. citiesalliance.org/citiesalliancehomepage.nsf/.

CEPAL (Comisión Económica para América Latina y el Caribe). 2000. *From Rapid Urbanization to the Consolidation of Human Settlements in LAC: A Territorial Perspective.* Santiago, Chile.

CGRTCA (Consultative Group for the Reconstruction and Transformation of Central America). 1998. "Municipalities in the Reconstruction and Transformation of Central America and the Caribbean: Consultative Group Meeting." Inter-American Development Bank, Washington, DC.

Edwards, Michael. 1982. "Cities of Tenants: Renting among the Urban Poor in Latin America." In *Urbanization in Contemporary Latin America: Critical Approaches to the Analysis of Urban Issues,* ed. Alan Gilbert, J.E. Hardoy, and R. Ramirez, New York: John Wiley and Sons.

Estache, Antonio, V. Foster, and Q. Wodon. 2002. *Accounting for Poverty in Infrastructure Reform.* Washington, DC: World Bank Institute Development Studies, World Bank.

Fay, Marianne, J. Luis Guasch, Rosanna Nitti, and Soumya Chattopadhyay. 2001. "The Anatomy of a Slum: The Ozama *Barrios* in Santo Domingo." Background paper for the 2001 Poverty Assessment of the Dominican Republic, World Bank, Washington, DC.

Fay, Marianne, Tito Yepes, and Vivien Foster. 2003. *Asset Inequality in Developing Countries: The Case of Housing.* Washington, DC: World Bank.

Ferguson, Bruce. 2001. "Strategy and Design Option for a Low-Income Housing Program for Mexico." Paper prepared as a background study for *Mexico: Low-Income Housing: Issues and Options* (World Bank 2002b).

Foster, Vivien, and Caridad Araujo. 2001. *Does Infrastructure Reform Work for the Poor? A Case Study from Guatemala.* Washington, DC: World Bank.

Foster, Vivien, CEER, and UADE (Universidad Argentina de la Empresa). 2003. *Hacia una política social para los sectores de infraestructura en Argentina: Evaluando el pasado y simulando el futuro.* Washington, DC: World Bank.

Foster, Vivien, and O. Irusta. 2001. *Does Infrastructure Reform Work for the Poor? A Case Study on the Twin Cities of La Paz and El Alto.* Washington, DC: World Bank.

Gilbert, Alan. 1993. *In Search of a Home: Rental and Shared Housing in Latin America.* London: University College London Press.

———. 2003. *Rental Housing: An Essential Option for the Urban Poor in Developing Countries.* Nairobi: United Nations Human Settlements Programme.

Gilbert, Alan, and Ann Varley. 1991. *Landlord and Tenant: Housing the Poor in Urban Mexico.* London: Routledge.

Gómez-Lobo, Andrés, and D. Contreras. 2000. "Subsidy Policies for the Utility Industries: A Comparison of the Chilean and Colombian Water Subsidy Schemes." Department of Economics, University of Chile, Santiago.

Hoek-Smit, Marja C., and D. Diamond. 2003. "The Design and Implementation of Subsidies for Housing Finance." Paper prepared for the World Bank Seminar on Housing Finance, March 10–13. www.worldbank.org/wbi/banking/capmarkets/housing.

International Federation of Red Cross and Red Crescent Societies. 2001. *World Disasters Report 2001*. Geneva: International Federation of Red Cross and Red Crescent Societies.

———. 2002. *World Disasters Report 2002*. Geneva: International Federation of Red Cross and Red Crescent Societies.

Kreimer, Alcira, M. Arnold, C. Barham, P. Freeman, R. Gilbert, F. Krimgold, R. Lester, J. Pollner, and T. Vogt. 1999. *Managing Disaster Risk in Mexico: Market Incentives for Mitigation Investment*. Disaster Risk Management Series, Washington, DC: World Bank.

Kumar, Sunil. 1996. "Subsistence and Petty Capitalist Landlords: A Theoretical Framework for the Analysis of Landlordism in Third World Urban Low-Income Settlements." *International Journal of Urban and Regional Research* 20 (2): 317–29.

Lanjouw, Jean O., and Philip I. Levy. 2002. "Untitled: A Study of Formal and Informal Property Rights in Urban Ecuador." *Economic Journal* 112 (October): 986–1019.

Morris, Saul, Oscar Neidecker-Gonzales, Calogero Carletto, Marcial Mungui, and Quentin Wodon. 2000. *Hurricane Mitch and the Livelihoods of the Rural Poor in Honduras*. Washington, DC: World Bank, Latin America and the Caribbean Region, Poverty Reduction and Economic Management Department.

Mosqueira, Edgardo. 2003. "Land Titling: The Case of Peru." Paper presented at conference Mejores Practicas de Politica Social, Mexico City, May 7–9.

PAHO (Pan-American Health Organization). 2002. *Serie de informes técnicos: Desigualdades en el acceso, uso y gasto con el agua potable en América Latina y el Caribe*. Washington, DC. www.paho.org/Spanish/HDP/HDD/hdd-agua.htm.

Pantoja, Enrique. 2002. *Micro-Finance and Disaster Risk Management: Experiences and Lessons Learned*. Washington, DC: World Bank.

Payne, Geoffrey, ed. 2002. *Land Rights and Innovation: Improving Tenure Security for the Urban Poor*. London: Intermediate Technology Development Group.

Prud'homme, Rémy. 2003. *Urban Land Issues in Mexico*. Washington, DC: World Bank.

Rakodi, Carole. 1995. "Rental Tenure in the Cities of Developing Countries." *Urban Studies* 32 (4–5): 791–812.

Reis, Eustáquio J., Luis Otávo Reiff, and Paulo Tafner. n.d. *Distribuição de riqueza imobiliára e de renda no Brasil: 1992–99*. Rio de Janeiro: Instituto de Pesquisa Economica Aplicada.

Ruggeri Laderchi, Caterina. 2005 "Places of the Poor: Mexico's Poor Barrios." In *Urban Poverty in Mexico*. Washington, DC: World Bank.

Sanderson, David. 2000. "Cities, Disasters, and Livelihoods." *Environment and Urbanization* 12 (2): 93–102.

Siembieda, William J., and Eduardo López Moreno. 1997. "Expanding Housing Choices for the Sector Popular: Strategies for Mexico." *Housing Policy Debate* 8 (3): 651–77. http://www.fanniemaefoundation.org/programs/hpd/pdf/hpd_0803_siembieda.pdf.

SIGUS (Special Interest Group in Urban Settlement), and School of Architecture and Planning, MIT. 2001. *Upgrading Urban Communities: A Resource for Practitioners.* Cambridge, MA: Massachusetts Institute of Technology. web.mit.edu/urbanupgrading/upgrading/.

World Bank. 1993. *Housing: Enabling Markets to Work.* Washington, DC: World Bank.

———. 2000. *World Development Report 2000/01: Managing Economic Crises and Natural Disasters.* Washington, DC: World Bank.

———. 2001. *Hurricane Mitch: The Gender Effects of Coping and Crises.* Poverty Reduction and Economic Management Network Notes 56, Washington, DC.

———. 2002a. *Brazil: Progressive Low-Income Housing: Alternatives for the Poor.* Report No. 22032-BR, Washington, DC.

———. 2002b. *Mexico: Low-Income Housing: Issues and Options.* Report No. 22534-ME, Washington, DC.

———. 2002c. "Urban Service Delivery and the Poor: The Case of Three Central American Cities." Report No. 22590, Washington, DC.

———. 2004. *Poverty in Mexico.* Report No. 28612-ME. Washington, DC.

4
Violence, Fear, and Insecurity among the Urban Poor in Latin America

Caroline Moser, Ailsa Winton, and Annalise Moser

Over the past decade, accelerating rates of violence and crime in Latin American cities have transformed the problem of individual criminal pathology into a serious development constraint. The problem is not limited to urban areas—the region is one of the most violent of the world—but it is particularly problematic in urban areas, where the relationship between violence and poverty is neither unidirectional nor straightforward. In urban areas in Latin America and the Caribbean, the poor are the most likely to both be seriously affected by crime violence and be held responsible for the crime and violence committed. This presents challenges for identifying successful urban-focused violence reduction interventions.

This chapter first looks at categories of violence, introducing an urban violence roadmap. It then discusses the measurement, trends, and characteristics of urban violence. The third section examines the causes, costs, and consequences of the phenomenon, particularly among the urban poor. The last section reviews a range of current national and sector-level violence-reduction interventions, particularly those focusing on the urban poor.

A Roadmap of Categories and Manifestations of Urban Crime and Violence

The sheer scale of violence in the *barrios* (slums) of Latin American cities means that violence has become "routinized" or "normalized" into the

Caroline Moser is a visiting Fellow at the Brookings Institution in Washington DC, and Senior Research Associate at the Overseas Development Institute in London. Ailsa Winton is Lecturer in Human Geography at Queen Mary, University of London. Annalise Moser is a Programme Specialist with UNIFEM. Bernice Van Bronkhorst, Urban Social Specialist at the World Bank, edited this chapter and contributed new material on cross-sectoral urban interventions.

functional reality of daily life (Poppovic and Pinheiro 1995; Koonings 1999; Scheper-Hughes 1995.) Different "banal" or "ubiquitous" manifestations of violence overlap to form a complex layering of multiple practices (Schrijvers 1993; Pecaut 1999; Torres Rivas 1999). But what does violence actually mean? In its recent *Global Report on Violence*, the World Health Organization (WHO) defines it as "the intentional use of physical force or power, threatened or actual, against oneself, another person, or against a group or community, that either results in or has a high likelihood of resulting in injury, death, psychological harm, maldevelopment or deprivation" (WHO 2002, p. 5).[1] Most definitions recognize that violence involves the exercise of power that is invariably used to legitimate the use of force for specific gains (Keane 1996).

Definitions of violence overlap with definitions of conflict and crime, but there are important distinctions. While violence and conflict are both concerned with power, conflict-based power struggles do not necessarily inflict physical or mental harm on others, while violence by its very nature does.[2]

In recent years violent crime as a proportion of total crimes committed has increased in much of Latin America. For example, in 1995 violent crime accounted for almost half of all reported crime in Nicaragua, where crimes against life almost tripled in a single year, rising from 9,392 in 1997 to 25,804 in 1998 (Call 2000; Rodgers 1999). Crimes against property declined during 6 of the 11 years between 1985 and 1994, but homicides increased considerably over the same period (Briceño-León and Zubillaga 2002). It is thus not crime per se but the lethality associated with it that is the critical issue.

The range of types of urban violence and crime is both complex and context specific. In an urban community in Jamaica, local residents in a participatory assessment listed 19 types of violence, including political, gang, economic, interpersonal, and domestic disputes. Poor urban communities in Guatemala identified an average of 41 types of violence and crime; in Colombia the figure was 25 (Moser and Holland 1997; Moser and McIlwaine 2000, 2001).

It is therefore helpful to categorize types of violence, highlighting those that are overwhelmingly urban in nature. These vary by country and discipline. For instance, Colombian experts distinguish between geographically confined rural violence (*la violencia del monte*) and urban violence (*la violencia de la calle*) (Deas 1998), with intraurban differentiations between violence in private arenas (*violencia en la casa*) and violence in public arenas (*violencia en la calle*) (Jimeno and Roldán 1996). Other dichotomies include political and nonpolitical violence; political, criminal, and social violence (Chernick 1998); political, economic, and intrafamilial violence (Carrión 1994); and the Inter-American Development Bank's distinction between criminal and social violence at the individual, household, and community levels (Buvinić, Morrison, and Shifter 1999).

This chapter distinguishes between political, institutional, economic, and social violence, based on the primary motivation behind the violence identified.[3] Since any categorization is static, this typology is a continuum, with important reinforcing linkages between different types of violence. From the perspective of the social actors, the same act can be committed for different reasons. This categorization provides the framework for a roadmap of the predominant categories, types, and manifestations of everyday violence in Latin American cities (table 4.1).

An Urban Violence Profile: Trends, Similarities, and Differences

While violence is present in much of the daily reality of life in Latin America and the Caribbean, its nature and extent varies significantly, both between and within countries. This section reviews trends and discusses the different manifestations of urban violence.

Trends in Urban Violence

The level of violence is extraordinarily high in Latin America and the Caribbean. Worldwide the homicide rate is 5.1 per 100,000 inhabitants, and a rate of more than 10 is generally considered dangerously high (Call 2000). In Latin America in 2000 the homicide rate was 27.5, the highest for any region in the world (WHO 2002).

Within the region, the level of violence varies greatly. Overall, El Salvador, Guatemala, and Colombia consistently have the highest homicide rates in the region, while Argentina and Chile have rates far below the regional average, even below the worldwide average of 5.1. Chile's homicide rate in 1994 was 2.5, while the rate in El Salvador was 164. Although the annual homicide rate in El Salvador fell to about 80–90 per 100,000 by 1999, it still far exceeded the regional average (Call 2000). Over the same period Colombia's homicide rate was 50–60 per 100,000 (World Vision 2002).

Although high levels of violence are a relatively recent phenomenon— with notable exceptions, such as Colombia—violence is now firmly established among the top five causes of death in much of Latin America, and it is the leading cause of death in Brazil, Colombia, El Salvador, Mexico, and Venezuela. Violence caused more deaths in Colombia between 1986 and 1996 than HIV/AIDS did in all of Latin America (Briceño-León 1999).

Table 4.1 Urban violence in Latin America and the Caribbean takes many forms

Primary direction of violence continuum	Category of violence	Types of violence by perpetrators or victims	Manifestations	Secondary direction of violence continuum
↑ (arrow up)	Political	State and non-state violence in situations of political conflict	Guerrilla and paramilitary conflict Armed conflict between political parties Political assassinations	
	Institutional	Violence by the state and other "informal" institutions, including the private sector	Extrajudicial killings by security forces State- or community-directed social cleansing Lynching	State institutional violence resulting in lack of trust in police and judiciary system
Intrahousehold social violence results in youths leaving the home and at risk to variety of street violence	Economic/institutional	Organized crime Protection of business interests	Kidnapping Armed robbery Drug trafficking Car theft Small arms dealing Trafficking in prostitutes Intimidation and violence as means of resolving economic disputes	↓ (arrow down)
	Economic	Delinquency, robbery	Street theft and robbery	

Table 4.1 (continued)

Primary direction of violence continuum	Category of violence	Types of violence by perpetrators or victims	Manifestations	Secondary direction of violence continuum
	Economic/ social	Youth gangs	Collective "turf" violence Robbery and theft	
	Economic/ social	Street children (boys and girls)	Petty theft	
	Social	Domestic violence between adults	Physical, sexual, or psychological abuse	*State institutional violence resulting in lack of trust in police and judiciary system*
	Social	Child abuse	Physical and sexual abuse, particularly in the home	
	Social	Intergenerational conflict between parents and children (both young and adults)	Physical and psychological abuse	
Intrahousehold social violence results in youths leaving the home and at risk to variety of street violence	Social	Gratuitous and routine daily violence	Lack of citizenship in areas such as traffic, road rage, bar fights, and street confrontations	

Source: Adapted from Moser and Winton 2002.

Box 4.1   The Difficulty of Measuring Crime and Violence

Measuring crime and violence is difficult. Broad proxy measures of violence generally include mortality statistics; official crime statistics (generally police data); murder or intentional injury statistics, including death certificates (from hospitals and morticians); and judicial records, such as offender rates and surveys (Arriagada and Godoy 2000; Glaeser and Sacerdote 1999; see table 4A.2). These measures are limited by underreporting and difficulties in interpretation (Short 1997). In addition, national and regional differences in data collection methods, recall periods, and cultural definitions of crime and violence make it difficult to make valid cross-country comparisons. Only a fraction of victims of domestic and sexual violence report the crimes, and in some places distrust and the inefficiency of police and judicial systems discourage people from reporting nonfatal crimes, especially in poorer areas (Dammert 2000.) Looking at homicide figures alone is misleading, since they do not reflect the range of nonfatal violence.

Victimization survey data often offer a useful comparative tool with which to complement and balance official figures, although they rarely provide comparable regional level data. Two comparative surveys of Latin America are Latinobarometro, a public opinion survey of 17 Latin American countries, conducted annually since 1995, and the 1996 ACTIVA study, carried out by the Pan-American Health Organizations (PAHO) in eight cities of Latin America and Spain.

Within countries, violence today is usually most severe in large urban areas. Differences in urban homicide levels across the region are striking, however, with rates ranging from 6.4 per 100,000 in Buenos Aires to 248.0 per 100,000 in Medellín (Piquet Carneiro 2000). Caracas, Lima, Mexico City, and Rio de Janeiro and São Paulo account for more than half the total of their national homicides (Briceño-León 1999). Venezuela's homicide rate increased 226 percent between 1986 and 1997, but 478 percent in Caracas (Sanjuán 1998).

Latinobarometro data on the relationship between city size and crime rates show that a city's demographic growth rate is a stronger indicator of its crime rate than its size. Between 1979 and 1998 the homicide rate in metropolitan Rio de Janeiro rose a relatively modest 35 percent, while that of fast-growing metropolitan São Paulo rose 103 percent (Piquet Carneiro 2000). In Bogotá, Colombia, homicide levels have declined since the mid-1990s to levels that are relatively low in the national urban context, and homicides are now concentrated in a few small, very violent areas (Llorente and others 2001). While victimization increased overall with city size in Colombia, robbery was most common in Bogotá (the largest city); homicide and assaults were more common in mid-size cities, especially Cali and Medellín (Gaviria and Pagés 1999).

Differences in rural-urban violence levels are most marked in postconflict countries, where rural violence is often still more widespread than urban violence. In El Salvador 76 percent of homicides occur in rural areas (World Vision 2002; Cruz and Beltrán 2000). In Guatemala the homicide rate is 101.5 in Guatemala City, but more rural departments show still higher rates, with the highest rate of 165 recorded in the department of Escuintla (Rodríguez and de León 2000).

Within Latin American cities, disparities in violence levels are based on neighborhood income levels. More prosperous areas suffer from property-related violent crime, such as vehicle theft (Gaviria and Pagés 1999; IESA/FLACSO 1999), while severe violence is generally concentrated in lower income areas. Violent crime rates are particularly high in poor neighborhoods on the peripheries of cities (Briceño-Leon and Zubillaga 2002; Fundación Mexicana para la Salud/Centro de Economía y Salud 1998; Lira 2000; Reyna and Toche 1999; Zaluar 1999). However, increases in vehicle robbery, which sometimes includes murder, have heightened personal insecurity among wealthier populations (Piquet Carneiro 2000). Increases in violent robbery only partially account for the increase in the homicide rate, suggesting that in a significant proportion of homicides, the victim knows the aggressor (IESA/FLACSO 1999).

Violence rates also vary based on age and gender, with young men most likely to be both victims and perpetrators. Rates of violence were higher for men than for women in six of the seven cities in the ACTIVA study (Cruz 1999). In Brazil the estimated homicide rate in 1999 among men 15–24 was 86.7 per 100,000 inhabitants, while the rate for young women was 6.5 (PAHO n.d.). In Puerto Rico the homicide rate for men 15–29 was 101, while the rate for women the same age was 6.8 (WHO 2002).

The type of violence is an important predictor of victimization by gender. In Peru young women are more likely to be victims of robbery than young men, while the victims of physical aggression are predominantly young men (Instituto Apoyo 1999). In Argentina 47 percent of those accused of homicide in 1997 were between 18 and 29, and nearly 10 percent were under 18 (Arriagada and Godoy 1999). Thus even in countries with relatively low levels of violence, juvenile violence among boys and young men is both rising and growing in intensity (Dammert 2000).

Categories of Urban Violence

While homicide and victimization statistics illustrate the scale of violence, they say little about the differing characteristics of the phenomenon. Visibility is critical in shaping levels of tolerance, fear, and insecurity. In much of urban Latin America, drug-related and organized crime, as well as the robberies committed by juvenile delinquents and gangs, attract considerable media attention. In contrast, social violence, including gender-based domestic violence, child abuse, and intergenerational conflict, is less visible and therefore has a lower profile in terms of public opinion. Given the extensive range of types of violence, this chapter can provide only a brief overview of the categories of violence that particularly impact on the urban poor.

ECONOMIC VIOLENCE: ORGANIZED CRIME AND GANGS

With the increasing dominance and grip of the drug trade over Latin American cities, organized drug-related crime is the most worrisome phenomenon, particularly in large capital cities. While the "drug problem" is primarily viewed as a national or international drug production or trafficking problem, the escalation of drug-related violence in low-income urban areas is closely linked not only to trafficking but also to high levels of drug consumption. Brazil, for example, is now the second-largest consumer of cocaine and cocaine derivatives after the United States, and the poor have become the main consumers. Drugs are integral to a variety of forms of violence, including gang warfare (to control the drug market), robberies and assaults (to purchase drugs), constant (often violent) quarrels in the home among drug users and their families, and the murder of drug addicts by "social cleansing" groups (Moser and McIlwaine 2003). Of these forms of crime, gang warfare is most associated with the drug trade.

With killings shifting from kidnappings and disappearances in the mid-1990s to armed attacks in public areas throughout the city, both intended targets and innocent bystanders are now victims, and what was once a remote threat of drug-related violence has now become a real fear for the general population (U.S. State Department 2002). In Rio de Janeiro in 2002, the local government's attempt to intervene in gang activities resulted in the bombing of the city hall and the closing down of the city itself (Sives 2002; Leeds 1996). Increasingly local community dynamics can be entirely transformed by drug gangs (Rodgers 2003); in some cases drug groups have taken control of the local institutional structures of entire poor urban communities. In such contexts the state often increases its mechanisms of control in an attempt to counteract the growing power of drug barons. The targeting of low-income communities by state security forces in the fight against drugs highlights the fact that it is the low-level, not the high-level, actors who are vulnerable (Leeds 1996).

In the *favelas* of urban Brazil, drug groups impose their own systems of justice, with the presence of drug barons legitimized through complex reciprocal and, to a degree, mutually beneficial relationships. The drug lord is given anonymity and freedom to conduct business; in return the community receives internal security and often a range of services, such as money to pay for medical treatment, soup kitchens, and day care centers. The services provided are valuable only because the state does not provide them and because the state entities charged with providing essential security services act as a corrupt and repressive force.

In Colombia drug traffickers have played a distinct but indirect role in the escalation of violence (Gaviria 1998). Although only 10 percent of homicides are directly associated with drug trafficking, the trade indirectly generates high levels of everyday violence through various criminal externalities. These include congestion in law enforcement, the supply of weapons, and the creation of a culture that favors easy money and violent conflict resolution over more traditional values, particularly among urban youth.

Increasingly, youth gangs, long seen as the main source of urban Latin American violence, have become linked to drugs.[4] Youth gangs, some highly formalized, others very loosely structured, have been identified in Brazil, Colombia, Ecuador, El Salvador, Guatemala, Honduras, Mexico, Peru, and Venezuela. In Central America, where gangs known as *maras* have a distinct structure, the *maras* 18 and Salvatrucha operate throughout the region. In Guatemala City in 1997 the Prensa Libre identified 53 *maras* operating in 12 zones (UNDP 1998); another source put the figure at 330 *maras* in 1995 (PRODEN 1996). In Honduras a nationwide register lists 340 gangs, with a membership level of almost 15,000 young people between 11 and 30; people working with juvenile offenders estimate the number at close to 60,000 (Castellanos 2000). In Medellín, Colombia, there are reportedly about 200 gangs of young people between 12 and 22 (Arriagada and Godoy 1999). In Peru more than 1,000 youth gangs were reported to have committed 13,000 criminal offenses between 1996 and 1998 (Reyna and Toche 1999).

Traditionally, youth gangs have had both social functions (related to youth identity and exclusion and linked to territorial control or neighborhood protection) and economic functions (related to illicit economic gain from robbery). Increasingly however, the divide between youth gangs and organized narco-crime is disappearing. In Brazil, for example, children as young as six and seven are hired as lookouts and carriers, often paid in crack cocaine or other drugs.

Violent robbery has also increased dramatically across the region. This includes street crime such as mugging, armed robbery, and kidnapping, all of which are committed by organized groups as well as individual delinquents and robbers. In 1999, most robberies in Lima occurred in the street (62 percent); a significant number took place on public transport (15 percent) and in the market (12 percent) (Instituto Apoyo 1999).

Kidnapping is one of the most important activities undertaken by organized criminal gangs. In El Salvador reported kidnappings increased from 97 cases in 1998 to 179 in 1999, dropping to 114 in 2000, while they increased 200 percent in Ecuador between 2000 and 2001 (World Vision 2002).[5] Although victims are generally presumed to belong to higher socioeconomic groups, victimization has become more generalized in recent years in Guatemala, affecting different segments of the population (UNDP 1998).

The incidence of much organized violence is, in part, attributable to past civil conflict in the region. In some but not all cases, demobilized ex-combatants have formed armed bands. Guatemala is estimated to have some 600 organized crime gangs, with 20,000 members. Most of these gangs are headed by ex-army officials (UNDP 1998). In Nicaragua armed bands made up of former *contras* engage in kidnapping for ransom and armed robbery in the north and north-central regions of the country (U.S. Department of State 2001). In Jamaica armed gangs involved in the trafficking of narcotics and guns control many inner-city neighborhoods. Better equipped than the police, they have targeted security patrols, police officers, and their families (U.S. Department of State 2002).

Millions of predominantly urban poor people face daily violence on public transportation. Recent surveys of Brazil reveal that 45 percent of respondents in San José, Costa Rica; 66 percent in Santiago, Chile; and 91 percent in Salvador de Bahia, Brazil fear violence on public transportation. Their fears are not unfounded: assaults on buses are common, with robbers boarding buses to assault passengers and even murder the driver or anyone who resists.

INSTITUTIONAL VIOLENCE

In some contexts state security forces use extrajudicial systems of informal justice, commonly known as "social cleansing," to retain order and power. Levels of police brutality are high, and such institutional violence usually goes unpunished. Much police brutality occurs in urban areas, where it is often racially motivated. In Venezuela state and private security forces were responsible for 241 extrajudicial killings between October 2000 and September 2001. Such "social cleansing" is often targeted at "undesirable" groups, which include suspected criminals, members of youth gangs, street children, and homosexuals. In situations of seemingly uncontrollable violence, the populace increasingly supports such extralegal activities by the police (Briceño-León and Zubillaga 2002).

It is not just the police who are involved in the application of arbitrary justice. In the face of insufficient state protection or resources to enlist private security, many residents of marginal urban areas believe there is no option but to resort to rudimentary vigilantism (Arriagada and Godoy 1999). Established vigilante groups are a powerful presence in many low-income urban communities in Latin America. In Venezuela a vigilante group known as the *grupo exterminio* (extermination group) was reportedly responsible for up to 100 killings between mid-2000 and 2001 in the cities of Acarigua and Araure (U.S. Department of State 2002). In poor urban settings, these informal justice systems often result in collusion between nonstate and state social actors, particularly the police. With allegations difficult to prove, it is easy for such deaths to be passed off as the result of intergang rivalry or drug trafficking. This is a particular problem in the case of the murder of urban street children and other "undesirable" youth (see www.casa-alianza.org).

SOCIAL VIOLENCE, INCLUDING GENDER-BASED DOMESTIC VIOLENCE, RAPE, AND CHILD ABUSE

Most violence against women takes place in the home, as physical, psychological, or sexual abuse; violence against women also occurs outside the home, in the form of assaults and rape. Although reporting rates for domestic and sexual violence are extremely low, Arriagada and Godoy (1999) estimate that half of all Latin American women have been subjected to abuse at home at some point in their lives.

Given the reluctance to report such offenses, survey data are a more reliable source of comparative data than reported incidents. Survey data cited by the WHO (2002) suggest that Latin America has the highest rates of sexual assaults against women of any region in the South. A national survey in Peru found that at least 41 percent of women reported having been battered by their partner during 2000, with 16 percent of these women reporting being beaten regularly (U.S. Department of State 2002). Survey data from seven studies in Latin American cities show high rates of sexual assault by a partner, ranging from 10.1 percent of respondents in São Paulo to 46.7 percent in Cusco, Peru (WHO 2002; table 4A.3). Violence within the home can be deadly: a 1993 PAHO study found that 45–60 percent of homicides against women were carried out at home, the majority by partners (UNDP 1999).

Across the region important differences are evident between the levels of visibility and the levels of tolerance of domestic violence. In Nicaragua domestic violence has a very high profile, with child violence and sexual abuse also receiving widespread media coverage. In Chile public awareness campaigns and legal reform led to an impressive 75,559 cases being presented in the courts in 1999 (U.S. Department of State 2002). In countries without such high-profile campaigns, or inadequate judicial procedures, domestic violence is still often treated as a private issue. Indeed, although laws against domestic violence now exist in most of Latin America, many are deficient or inadequately implemented.

Two large Nicaraguan studies of intrafamily domestic violence show that wife abuse was associated with poverty, low education, having 4 or more children, and living in an urban area (Ellsberg 1997; INEC/MINSA 1998). The surveys show that in 50–60 percent of cases, children witness the violence, with significant repercussions. Children of abused mothers are twice as likely to suffer from emotional, learning, or behavioral problems and seven times more likely to be abused themselves.

Of all the types of sexual violence against women, rape is the most hidden. Reported levels vary from just 277 cases in El Salvador to 1,181 in Nicaragua and more than 3,600 in Venezuela (U.S. Department of State 2001, 2002). It is unlikely that such a vast disparity actually exists. According to the Permanent Commission of the Rights of Women and Children in Peru, there are 25,000 rapes in Peru a year (U.S. Department of State 2002). The United Nations Development Programme recorded a rate of 109.7 rapes per 100,000 women over the age of 15 in Nicaragua in 1994 (UNDP 2000). Sexual violence and rape are not solely directed at women, however. Men are also vulnerable to sexual assault, at home, in the street, during war, and in prison or police custody.

Children are vulnerable to a range of abuse, both inside and outside the home. In Mexico an estimated 300 children a year die as a result of domestic abuse. In Peru 70 percent of sexual assaults on children occur in the home by a relative or someone known to the victim and his or her family (U.S. Department of State 2002). In Honduras many urban street children have been sexually molested, and about 40 percent regularly engage in prostitution. This is reflected in the incidence of HIV/AIDS: 30 percent of street children in Tegucigalpa and San Pedro Sula, Honduras, are reported to be HIV-positive. Forty-seven percent of girls between 10 and 18 in nine Caribbean countries and 40 percent of 16- to 17-year-olds in Lima reported that their first sexual intercourse was forced (U.S. Department of State 2001).

The Causal Roots of Urban Violence in Latin America

The complex causes of violence imply that holistic approaches, rather than those focusing on a specific type of violence, are necessary. One of the most popular, the so-called "ecological model," identifies violence at the structural, institutional, interpersonal, and individual levels and demonstrates that no single cause determines or explains violence (Bronfenbrenner 1977; WHO 2002).[6] Another important distinction can be made between factors that cause violence and those that shape and facilitate it.[7] The discussion of causes of violence presented here is organized around economic, social, and political factors.

Economic Factors Related to Poverty: Inequality and Exclusion

The common stereotype is that poverty is the primary cause of violence. But the evidence clearly shows that in Latin America, inequality and exclusion, associated with the unequal distribution of economic, political, and social resources in urban contexts across the region, are more important (Fajnzylber, Lederman, and Loayza 1998, 2002; Londoño and Guerrero 1999; Bourguignon 2001). At the same time, in situations of widespread and severe inequality, the daily living conditions of the urban poor can heighten the potential for the emergence of conflict, crime, or violence (Vanderschueren 1996).

Links between inequality and violence relate not only to income disparities but also to unequal access to employment, education, health, and basic physical infrastructure. In addition, lack of or inadequate state security protection, policing, and judicial systems disproportionately affect the poor, who are unable to pay for their own services and are therefore more susceptible to the impunity, corruption, inefficiency, and even brutality associated with such institutions.

Globalization has been identified as a causal factor underlying the increasing prevalence of urban youth exclusion and the associated growth of gangs. Increasing social fragmentation is countered by the development of an alternative societal membership, in which the violence of gangs becomes a way to gain an acknowledged identity (Briceño-León and Zubillaga 2002). Precarious living conditions, excessive working hours of parents, the increased material and emotional responsibility of women, severe overcrowding, and the lack of recreational space all weaken the socialization function of the family (FLACSO n.d.; Kramer 2000). If the family cannot cover its basic necessities, it cannot carry out a protective and developmental function for its members (De Orrellana 1997). An oft-cited reason for joining gangs is to find what is not available at home (AVANCSO 1996; Smutt and Miranda 1998).

In Central America the exponential growth of youth gangs is also attributed to the deportation of young Salvadorans from the United States, with deported gang members from Los Angeles "bringing gang wars from the ghettos of Los Angeles to the streets of El Salvador" (De Cesare

1997, p. 38).[8] Migration within Central America has contributed to the regional dissemination of gang culture.

Political Factors Linked to the Legacy of Regional Conflict and Authoritarian Regimes

Recent Latin American political history has affected current patterns of violence, with implications for the urban poor. Political factors include the legacy of decades of protracted internal civil conflict in Central American countries such as El Salvador and Guatemala (and the continuing civil conflict in Colombia), as well as the heritage of brutality associated with totalitarian or authoritarian regimes in countries such as Argentina and Brazil. In both contexts, democratic governments have found it difficult to fight the culture of institutionalized and arbitrary violence (Kruijt and Koonings 1999). Few newly democratic states in Latin America have successfully reformed the police and judiciary (Pereira 2001). As a consequence, state security and judicial apparatuses are widely perceived as repressive, with police officers and other state actors viewed as complicit in organized crime, particularly drug trafficking and prostitution (Adorno 1997). Corruption makes attempts to reduce violence even more challenging and further reduces public confidence in state institutions.

A second historical legacy is the role that prolonged state conflict has played in the "normalization of violence," creating norms, values, and attitudes that reinforce or stimulate the use of violence to resolve conflicts (Kruijt and Koonings 1999). This is perpetuated in democratic contexts when state institutions are unable to maintain social order or uphold justice without recourse to violence as a legitimate means of exerting authority. For example, the judicial void left by institutional failure is a causal factor underlying the rise of violent informal institutions, such as vigilante and self-defense groups. A consequence of armed conflict has been the proliferation of firearms, contributing to the "mass production and consumption" of violence (Kruijt and Koonings 1999, p. 15). In El Salvador, for example, 1.5 million weapons are now believed to be in private hands, only a third of which are legally registered; in Guatemala some 2 million arms are estimated to be in the hands of 36 percent of the civilian population (World Vision 2002; Arriagada and Godoy 1999).

Urban violence has also intensified and changed in political contexts markedly different from those described above. Jamaica, for instance, has relatively low levels of inequality and a virtually homogenous ethnic population, and it has been democratic for many decades since independence. On closer inspection, however, Jamaica is neither cohesive nor democratic, with a political system based on violence-supporting social and political divisions.

Social Factors, Including Media Sensationalization of Violence, the Availability of Firearms, and the Consumption of Drugs and Alcohol

The Latin American media are partly to blame for creating an atmosphere of fear. Reporting on youth violence and youth gangs is often excessive. In Honduras, for instance, less than 5 percent of crime is committed by youths under the age of 18, yet media representation of this phenomenon is so great that it has created a perception that youths are responsible for a majority of crimes (Arriagada and Godoy 1999). The media have shaped perceptions of insecurity, leading to increases in the number of people who carry guns, increased support for the death penalty, illegal or violent police behavior, and support of the right to kill (Briceño-León 1999). In Chile the media have been noted as being partially responsible for the increase in perceptions of insecurity since the advent of democracy in the early 1990s, before which violence went unreported.[9]

Not all violence attracts equal press coverage. Violence in poor urban neighborhoods is often reported with aggregate figures and is thus depersonalized. In contrast, violence in middle-income areas is considered more headline worthy. It triggers long articles about individual events and is thus personalized. In this way the media construct some victims as more important than others (López Regonesi 2000).

Both drugs and alcohol play roles as risk factors and triggers rather than causes of urban violence, but they differ in their effects. While drug use is associated more with economic violence, alcohol consumption is related more to social violence, particularly gender-based domestic violence. In Nicaragua, for example, 54 percent of abused women indicate that their husbands were usually intoxicated during violence, and nearly one-third cited alcoholism as the major cause of violence (Ellsberg 1997).

The Costs and Consequences of Urban Violence

Monetary cost data provide the basis for comparing the costs of violence and other social ills and for analyzing the cost-benefit implications of different policy options (Macmillan 2000). But violence has a dramatic impact on poor people's well-being in terms of both livelihood security and the functioning of local social institutions, which these data do not capture. Indeed, it has been argued that the tendency to rely on data on the costs of violence has led to the neglect of the very factors that seem to be the principal consequences of violence, namely insecurity, fear, terror, and a deteriorating quality of life (Rubio 1998). Thus both macro-level costs as well as micro-level impacts of urban violence on various aspects of well-being need to be addressed.

Macro-level costs include both the direct and indirect costs of violence. The greatest advances have been made in measuring the direct economic costs of violence, the associated losses due to deaths and disabilities, and the income transfers from victims of property crime to the perpetrators, calculated as percentages of GNP or GDP (box 4.2). Constraints include the lack of access to information on violence-related expenditure assessments by the police, the judiciary, the penal system, and the armed forces (Arriagada and Godoy 2000). A further limitation is the difficulty of separating the costs of crime in general from those incurred by violent crime. Thus regional cost comparisons are difficult to make, especially at the urban level, where the data are even more limited. In addition, many of the components of indirect costs, both for individual victims and society as a whole, are intangible. Rubio (1998) argues that global measures and international comparisons of the costs of violence are of limited use, given the heterogeneous magnitude and composition of the phenomenon. Consequently, a capital assets framework that analyzes the multiple outcomes of violence in terms of their direct and indirect effects on physical, financial, human, social, and natural capital (see Chambers and Conway 1992; Carney 1998; Moser and Norton 2001) complements analysis of the quantitative data. Of particular concern are financial, human, and social capital.

Box 4.2   The Inter-American Development Bank's Approaches to Measuring the Costs of Violence

The Inter-American Development Bank includes four elements in its estimates of the costs of violence:

- Direct costs: Health system, police, justice system, housing, and social services.
- Indirect costs: Higher morbidity and mortality due to homicides, suicides, abuse of alcohol and drugs, and depressive disorders.
- Economic multiplier effects: Macroeconomic impacts and impacts on the labor market and intergenerational productivity.
- Social multiplier effects: Impact on interpersonal relations and the quality of life.

Source: IDB 2000b.

Violence and the Erosion of Financial Capital

The direct financial costs of violence include increased government expenditure on the police, judicial, and health care systems. Indirect macro-level costs include decreases in foreign and domestic investment and reductions in tourism. Violence in Latin America cost the region an estimated 14.2 percent of GDP, with the highest costs in the form of intangible losses (table 4.2).

There are significant national variations in the financial burden of violence, in terms of both the level and nature of costs. In Colombia the cost of violence is equivalent to almost 25 percent of the GDP. In Peru the figure is just over 5 percent (figure 4.1). Intracountry differences are also significant, often revealing an urban bias. The costs of violence in Caracas alone, for example, accounted for 3 percent of GDP in Venezuela (IESA/FLACSO 1999).

Security costs are high and borne disproportionately by individuals. This effective privatization of security not only delegitimizes the state as an institution of security and control, it also severely affects those unable to pay for their own security (Arriagada and Godoy 1999; Briceño-León and Zubillaga 2002). In Trinidad and Tobago, for instance, the costs incurred by citizens protecting themselves from crime are estimated to amount to $3,696 per household per lifetime in fixed costs (World Bank 2002). In Caracas the most significant cost of violence is private security (IESA/FLACSO 1999). Virtually all vehicle owners have security devices in their vehicles, 73 percent of the population has private security in their

Table 4.2 Violence imposes significant costs on Latin America
(percent of GDP)

Type of cost	Percent of GDP	
Health losses	1.9	
Medical attention		0.2
Healthy years lost		1.7
Material losses	3.0	
Public security		1.1
Private security		1.4
Justice		0.5
Intangible losses	7.1	
Deterioration in investment productivity		1.8
Deterioration in consumption and work		5.3
Income transfers	2.1	
Total	14.2	

Source: Londoño and Guerrero 1999.

Figure 4.1   The cost of violence varies significantly across countries but is high throughout Latin America

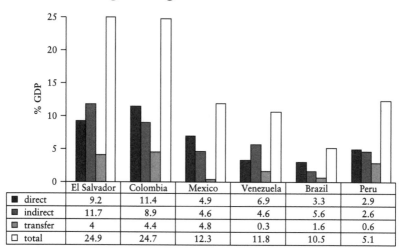

	El Salvador	Colombia	Mexico	Venezuela	Brazil	Peru
■ direct	9.2	11.4	4.9	6.9	3.3	2.9
■ indirect	11.7	8.9	4.6	4.6	5.6	2.6
▦ transfer	4	4.4	4.8	0.3	1.6	0.6
□ total	24.9	24.7	12.3	11.8	10.5	5.1

Source: Adapted from Londoño and Guerrero 1999.

homes, and 39 percent have contributed money or time to community initiatives to reduce crime (IESA/FLACSO 1999).

Health costs associated with violence account for 0.3 percent of GDP in Venezuela, 1.3 percent in Mexico, 1.5 percent in Peru, 1.9 percent in Brazil, 4.3 percent in El Salvador, and 5.0 percent in Colombia (Buvinić, Morrison and Shifter 1999). PAHO estimates that 30 percent of hospital admissions in the region are the result of violence (Briceño-León 1999). In El Salvador, the treatment of victims of violence accounts for 21 percent of the national hospital budget and 12 percent of the budget of the Ministry of Public Health and Social Services (IUDOP 1998).

The violence-related costs firms must incur inhibit domestic and international investment. Firms in Guatemala suffer average losses of about $5,500 a year due to crime (Moser and Winton 2002). Violence also affects access to the local labor supply, particularly the female labor force. Fear of violence also depresses sales and restricts output by limiting working hours when shift patterns are disrupted because staff can travel only at certain times due to fear of violence (Briceño-León and Zubillaga 2002). In Colombia, for example, 31 percent of respondents avoided nightshifts because of fear of violence (Rubio 1998; IESA/FLACSO 1999).

Tourism is severely affected by violence. For example, it was estimated that a decline in youth crime by 1 percentage point would increase the number of annual tourists by more than 45,000 in Jamaica and by 36,000 in the Bahamas, equivalent to a combined increase in revenue of more than $70 million (World Bank 2002).

Violence and the Erosion of Human Capital

The costs of violence in terms of human capital can be measured in terms of the loss in disability-adjusted life years (DALYs) resulting from violence (box 4.3). Violence reduces life expectancy significantly, since the young are most at risk from many types of violence. Almost 70 percent of homicide victims in Caracas, for example, are between 15 and 30 (Sanjuán 1998).

Violence also inhibits human capital formation by discouraging some individuals from investing in education, encouraging them instead to develop criminal skills. Violence also discourages some people from studying at night (Buvinić, Morrison, and Shifter 1999). Domestic violence has implications not just for the victims but also for future generations, since violence in the home reduces performance at school and therefore future productivity. Women who suffer domestic violence are less productive in the workplace and tend to earn less than women who do not suffer domestic abuse (Buvinić, Morrison, and Shifter 1999). Thus violence against women is not a "private problem but unquestionably a public problem

---

Box 4.3   The Health Costs of Violence in Latin American Cities

Violence in Latin American cities is having a devastating effect on health and life expectancy:

- In 1995 violent death resulted in the loss of 60,792 DALYs in Peru, 163,136 in Rio de Janeiro, and a staggering 178,000 in El Salvador (Buvinić, Morrison, and Shifter 1999).
- In Rio de Janeiro violence accounted for 19 percent of all DALYs lost, almost twice the 10.3 percent of DALYs lost to cancer (Briceño-León 1999).
- Violence caused the loss of 68,000 DALYs in Mexico City in 1995, 79 percent the result of homicide (Fundación Mexicana para la Salud/Centro de Economía y Salud 1998).
- Violence against women was the third most common source of lost DALYs in Mexico City, after diabetes and complications from childbirth (Buvinić, Morrison, and Shifter 1999).
- In Managua, Nicaragua, abused women use health services (surgery, hospitalization, and visits due to illness) about twice as frequently as nonabused women (Morrison and Orlando 1999).

because the whole of society pays monetarily, as well as nonmonetarily"
(Yodanis, Godenzi, and Stanko 2000, p. 273).

Violence and the Erosion of Social Capital

As Rubio (1998) has argued, to see the outcomes of violence, particularly
violent deaths, solely in terms of economic costs is to miss the point: there
are serious social and cultural consequences when a death is intentional
rather than accidental. The social costs of violence include fear and the
associated restrictions on community life (Sanjuán 1998). In reducing
social contact between members of the community and increasing mis-
trust, violence erodes social capital (Moser and Holland 1997; Moser and
McIlwaine 2003). In Cali, for example, 43 percent of survey respondents
reported greatly limiting their recreational activities due to fear of violence (PAHO n.d.); in Caracas the figure was 72 percent (IESA/FLACSO
1999). Almost one in five respondents in a survey of 10 state capitals in
Brazil reported that violence had a "very intense" impact on family life,
with withdrawal from community life associated with areas most affected
by violence (Cardia 1999). Overall, a large proportion of the urban poor in
Latin America live with unprecedented levels of violence and with the
associated range of consequences, all of which erode their well-being.

Innovative Interventions

Increased concern with violence across the region has meant that violence
prevention and reduction is now a growth industry. Given the wide range
of direct and indirect interventions, this section can provide only a brief
overview of current policy approaches to violence reduction and highlight some of the more relevant interventions.

The main policy approaches and their associated urban-focused interventions can be divided into two types: sector-specific approaches and
cross-sectoral approaches (table 4.3). Sector-specific approaches are dominated by the criminal justice approach, which seeks to control and treat
violence, and the public health (epidemiological) approach, which aims to
prevent violence.

Newer approaches, such as conflict transformation and human rights,
reflect increasing concern with political and institutional violence. Recent
recognition of the importance of more integrated, holistic approaches has
opened the door for cross-sectoral approaches, such as citizen security,
crime prevention through environmental design (CPTED), and urban renewal. Still being developed are community-based approaches to rebuild
trust and social capital. Such policies are essentially ideal types. Policymakers

Table 4.3 A variety of approaches and interventions are used to reduce urban violence

Policy approach	Objective	Types of violence	Innovative urban-focused interventions
Sector-specific approaches			
Criminal justice	Deter and control violence through higher arrest and conviction rates and more severe punishment	• Crime • Robbery • Corruption • Delinquency • Family violence	• Judicial reform • Alternative dispute resolution mechanisms • Police reform • Accessible justice systems • Mobile courts • Alternative sentencing • Community policing • All-women police stations
Public health	Prevent violence by reducing risk factors	• Youth violence	• Epidemiological and geographical mapping of crime and violence • Youth policies/social protection • Education reform • Entrepreneurship • Vocational skills training • Cultural and recreational activities • Promotion of behavioral change
Conflict transformation/ human rights	Achieve nonviolent resolution of conflict through negotiation and legal enforcement of human	• Political violence • Institutional violence • Human rights abuses • Arbitrary detention	• Traditional systems of justice • Government human rights advocates or ombudsmen • Civil society advocacy NGOs

(table continues on the following page)

Table 4.3   (continued)

Policy approach	Objective	Types of violence	Innovative urban-focused interventions
Sector-specific approaches			
	rights by states and other social actors		
Cross-sectoral approaches			
Crime prevention through environmental design/urban renewal	Reduce violence opportunities by focusing on settings of crime rather than perpetrators	• Economic violence • Social violence	• Municipal-level programs
Citizen/ public/ community security	Prevent or reduce violence through cross-sectoral measures	• Economic violence • Social violence	• National level programs • Municipal level programs
Community-driven development/ social capital	"Rebuild" social capital, trust, and cohesion in informal and formal social institutions	• Youth gangs and *maras* • Domestic violence	• Community-based solutions • Crisis services for victims • Ongoing support and prevention • Communication campaigns • School programs • Programs for perpetrators

Sources: Adapted and updated from Moser and others 2000; Moser and Winton 2002.

have shifted from sector-specific menu-like checklist interventions toward more integrated approaches that combine established policies with more innovative ones.

There are no magic bullets or one-off solutions to reducing violence, although some appear more promising than others. Unfortunately, little rigorous evaluation of violence reduction interventions over time has been conducted, this review of sector-specific and cross-sectoral approaches is primarily descriptive.[10] Where sufficient evidence is available, prescriptive recommendations are provided.

Sector-Level Interventions with Strong Urban Focus

THE CRIMINAL JUSTICE APPROACH

Criminal justice is the most established approach to urban violence reduction. It focuses on deterring and controlling violence through higher rates of arrest and conviction and harsher punishment. The approach, which involves a combination of judicial, police, and penal reform, is particularly popular with politicians seeking "quick-fix" solutions to the problem of violence.

Judicial reform is a crucial institution-level intervention given the limited access to justice in many Latin American countries and the lack of transparency, predictability, or independence of the judiciary and of alternative resolution mechanisms. Judicial reform is particularly significant for the urban poor, who lack the means to secure their own protection or hire legal counsel, routinely face unequal access to justice, distrust the justice system, and lack information on alternative channels through which to contest matters of rights and justice (Vanderschueren and Oviedo 1995). Reform measures that bring justice into local communities are far more effective than those that reform the overall system. At the urban level, therefore, justice projects in Argentina, Brazil, Chile, Colombia, Peru, and Venezuela have increasingly focused on access to justice in community-focused interventions that include alternative dispute resolution mechanisms, reduction of court costs, legal aid, the creation of small claims courts, and attention to gender issues (Dakolias 1996).

Police reform is another important institutional issue given the widespread lack of trust in the police in poor urban communities, which is closely linked to corruption and human rights abuses. In postconflict settings police demilitarization has been a crucial first step in allowing elected officials to exercise political power. It is essential to the democratic delivery of protection, order, and justice. Local-level interventions are considered particularly effective. One, community policing, is increasingly popular. Its philosophy is to broaden the role of police from maintaining order and preventing criminality to involving the community in the design and implementation of strategies to reduce and prevent violence. A growing number of countries, including Brazil, Colombia, and many countries in Central America, have implemented programs based

Box 4.4   Community Policing in Hatillo, Costa Rica

In 1996 a community policing experiment was initiated in Hatillo, Costa Rica, an area with a high level of insecurity. Its objective was to identify and resolve problems of delinquency and public safety, to reduce the public's feeling of insecurity, to enhance the public's perception of the police, and to incorporate the community in action plans targeting public safety. One hundred and twenty police officers received training in legal and interpersonal skills, and police units were installed to decentralize the police force. New forms of patrols—notably foot and motorcycle patrols—were introduced to patrol Hatillo's narrow streets. Special programs were developed on intrafamily violence, youth delinquency, alternative forms of conflict resolution, and drug prevention. A Monitoring and Communitarian Security Council was established as a permanent consultation body for the planning and execution of police actions.

One year after implementation, the program had achieved the following outcomes:

- The city's biggest problem, assaults, decreased.
- The percentage of the population that felt insecure decreased from 36 percent to 19 percent.
- The proportion of the population that did not trust the police decreased from 49 percent to 29 percent.
- Rates of delinquency and armed and unarmed robbery decreased very little, and rates of burglaries and motor vehicle theft actually increased slightly.

Source: Chinchilla 1999.

on these principles. Costa Rica has adopted a particularly innovative approach (box 4.4).

A comparison of four community policing programs in urban areas in Brazil, Colombia, and Guatemala (sponsored by the Military Police in Brazil, the National Police in Colombia, and the Inter-American Institute for Human Rights in Guatemala) reveals that the primary components were institutional change, training strategies for police personnel, community participation, and coordination with other public agencies (Frühling n.d.).

Community policing also includes a growing number of women's police stations. These were pioneered in the mid-1980s in São Paulo, Brazil, as a means of responding to intrafamily and sexual violence. Notable for their primarily female staff trained in handling women victims of violence, Brazil's women's police stations provide services such as counseling and conflict mediation, and they encourage women to file complaints.

The criminal justice approach has its limitations. It focuses on addressing the problem after a crime or violent act has been committed. It usually involves "toughening up" the legal and justice system, increasing policing resources and capacities, and introducing harsher penalties in an effort to deter and repress crime and violence. In this approach, crime and violence are seen as the responsibility of the police and the courts.

Most countries battling high levels of crime and violence find that the criminal justice approach is not sufficient and usually fails to adequately deal with crime and violence. This can result in a loss of confidence in the criminal justice system. In addition, high-profile *"mano dura"* approaches, such as those currently in place in El Salvador and Honduras, have raised human and civil rights concerns.

THE PUBLIC HEALTH APPROACH

The public health approach to urban violence focuses primarily on youth violence from a prevention and risk-reduction perspective. Its major contribution has been to bring epidemiological analysis—meaning the "mapping" of crime and violence, and the identification of risk factors—to the policy debate. Much of the work on the control of alcohol and firearms (risk factors) is a result of the public health approach, pioneered in the region in Cali, Medellín, and Bogotá, Colombia. The implementation of social preventative youth policies is undertaken mostly through local government and community-level NGOs. Interventions include training and skills development, particularly in vocational skills; sports and sporting facilities; and recreational, artistic, and cultural activities to engage youth and promote positive behavior. Organizations such as Casa Alianza, an NGO working in Central America, provide street children shelter, drug counseling, and vocational training while using a "life plan" approach to rehabilitation. That approach sets attainable goals to foster self-respect and hope, qualities often lacking in children who have experienced prolonged violence on the streets.

THE HUMAN RIGHTS AND CONFLICT TRANSFORMATION APPROACHES

The human rights and conflict transformation approaches include a broad range of strategies for peacefully resolving conflicts. In Latin America the approach has focused mainly on political violence in Central America, with top-down legal or military enforcement reinforced by negotiation among conflicting parties and space for popular participation. These approaches are not specifically urban but can be applied successfully in urban settings.

A human rights–based approach to reducing political violence focuses on the state's role in protecting citizens' rights to be free from victimization and the threat of violence. Such interventions involve collaboration between civil society and local advocacy NGOs. One effective effort is the Peruvian "In the Name of the Innocents" campaign, run during the 1990s by Peruvian human rights NGOs in response to the country's draconian antiterrorism legislation (Yamin 1999). Examples from Brazil include the NGOs Viva Rio and Sou da Paz (São Paulo), which have campaigned against police brutality and "social cleansing."

Cross-Sectoral Urban Interventions

Cross-sectoral interventions have received growing attention in the past decade. Three interventions that are of particular importance in the cities of Latin America are examined here.

CRIME PREVENTION THROUGH ENVIRONMENTAL DESIGN

A key cross-sectoral approach to urban violence reduction is Crime Prevention through Environmental Design (CPTED). The fundamental concept is that the physical environment affects criminal behavior and can be changed in a way that will reduce the incidence and fear of crime (Cooke 2003). Focusing on the settings of crime rather than the perpetrators, the approach is concerned not only with the criminal justice system but also with private and public organizations and agencies, such as schools, hospitals, transport systems, shops, telephone companies, public parks, and entertainment facilities (Clarke n.d.). CPTED techniques have been particularly popular in North American and European cities, where they have achieved some success. Recently they have also been adapted to African and Latin American contexts (see, for example, the work piloted in Chile by Rau and others 2003). The World Bank is also starting to integrate CPTED principles into its urban operations in Brazil and Honduras.

CPTED provides practical recommendations on how to plan, design, and manage the physical environment to reduce urban crime. Planning and design measures can help enhance feelings of safety in areas where people feel vulnerable, through a comprehensive framework of action for planners, urban designers, and architects:

- *Planning:* Dealing with vacant land, encouraging 24-hour land use, promoting safe pedestrian infrastructure, ensuring equitable provision of facilities, and sustaining urban renewal.
- *Design:* Designing appropriate lighting, landscaping, and signage in each of the following areas: soft open spaces (vacant land, parks); movement networks (intersections, taxi ranks, train stations); hard open spaces (pedestrian subways, open parking lots, informal trading); public facilities (communal areas, emergency contact points); and site layout and building design (facades, alleys, garages, toilets, shopping centers).

- *Management:* Establishing institutional arrangements to ensure effective management of the strategy, the support structures and vehicles for implementation, and the environment to ensure ongoing effectiveness (Kruger, Landman, and Liebermann 2001; Rau and others 2003).

South Africa has adopted a modified CPTED framework (table 4.4). Responding to the extreme levels of violence in the Cape Town township of Khayelitsha, the German Bank for Reconstruction and Development (KfW) together with the city of Cape Town designed an innovative "Violence Prevention through Urban Upgrading" project. The project uses urban renewal as the entry point to address violence through urban renewal strategies for better environmental arrangements to reduce opportunities for violence, criminal justice measures to discourage potential violators, and public health and conflict resolution interventions to support victims of violence. The range of solutions includes offender deterrence, victim support, and urban renewal strategies (table 4.5). One of the advantages of spatial solutions is that physical infrastructure initiatives are relatively straightforward to implement and can increase perceptions of safety and well-being.

Despite success stories, the CPTED approach has its limitations, since it focuses only on reducing criminal opportunities and may have a limited impact on the level of crime if carried out in isolation (Aurora and others 1999; Kruger, Landman, and Liebermann 2001). To address this concern, "second-generation CPTED" stresses the need to implement the approach as part of a coordinated and participatory crime-prevention strategy, including effective policing and social prevention.

CITIZEN, PUBLIC, AND COMMUNITY SECURITY

Another cross-sectoral approach is citizen, public, or community security (the terms are used interchangeably in different projects and contexts), developed at both the national and municipal level. Since the late 1990s, the Inter-American Development Bank has taken the lead in Latin America and the Caribbean in developing an extensive lending portfolio of national programs to promote "peace and citizen security/coexistence." The underlying policy approach links public health (violence prevention) and criminal justice (violence control). Projects in Colombia, El Salvador, Honduras, and Jamaica share similar objectives (table 4A.5). Although none of the projects frames its analyses in terms of the importance of urban violence per se, each of the projects targets urban areas.

The Inter-American Development Bank's approach is a blueprint approach, with similar project components across countries. These include

Table 4.4   The Khayelitsha Violence Prevention through Urban Upgrading Project includes many components

Location	Types of violence and manifestations	Spatial and nonspatial violence prevention or reduction interventions
Shebeens (bars)	• Assault • Murder • Rape • Drug- and alcohol-related violence • Murder; domestic and child abuse	• Relocate shebeens to sites where social and police control is more efficient. • Provide alternative opportunities for socializing where alcohol is controlled. • Establish business code of conduct by shebeen owners association.
Domestic spaces	• Assault • Rape • Child abuse • Emotional abuse	• Provide more houses of refuge and counseling facilities. • Equip police stations with trauma facilities and female officers. • Establish facilities for conflict resolution. • Train police in handling domestic violence cases. • Launch awareness-raising campaigns on domestic rights.
Open public space Open fields Narrow lanes Empty stalls	• Rape • Robbery • Assault • Murder	• Improve street lighting and visibility. • Expand and increase functionality of the telephone system. • Establish rape-relief centers and offer self-defense training. • Create safe walkways.

Table 4.4   (continued)

Location	Types of violence and manifestations	Spatial and nonspatial violence prevention or reduction interventions
		• Lock vegetable stalls at night. • Operate a 24-hour-a-day public transportation system in the neighborhood. • Increase the visibility of police patrols and neighborhood watches.
Banks and automatic teller machines (ATMs)	• Robbery along routes to and from banks and ATMs	• Increase access to banking and safe deposit places. • Increase the visibility of police patrols and neighborhood watches. • Improve income generation opportunities.
Informal housing	• Burglary in unsecured homes	• Improve income generation opportunities. • Expand and increase visibility of police patrols and neighborhood watches.
Sanitary facilities	• Rape on narrow paths to and from outside sanitary facilities	• Install sewers and phase out outside toilets. • Provide smaller lids for refuse containers so that bodies cannot be dumped. • Supervise communal sanitary facilities.

(table continues on the following page)

Table 4.4   (continued)

Location	Types of violence and manifestations	Spatial and nonspatial violence prevention or reduction interventions
Schools	• Theft • Vandalism and gangsterism • Physical violence • Possession of drugs and weapons • Gang rape	• Declare schools gun-free zones. • Protect schools against theft and keep out guns by installing better fencing, metal detectors, and guard dogs. • Use guarded schools as safe off-street playgrounds after hours.
Roads and transportation	• Deaths and injuries related to taxi violence • Robbery • Assault • Sexual harassment and assault by drivers	• Declare stations gun-free zones; install metal detectors and lockers. • Bring jobs and services closer to residents to reduce transportation needs. • Place police on trains. • Provide conflict management and development programs to reduce taxi violence by drivers.

Source: Adapted from KfW and City of Cape Town 2002.

creation of information systems, strengthening of institutions, prevention of juvenile violence, development of community-police relations programs, and establishment of social awareness and rehabilitation programs.[11] Budget allocations vary across countries. In all countries the greatest proportion (38–52 percent) is spent on community and other actions to prevent juvenile violence and delinquency, and 23–31 percent goes to institutional strengthening (table 4.5). Community police programs and strengthening the criminal justice system receive about 30 percent of the budget in Colombia but only 4 percent in Honduras. The size of the project loans suggests that these countries are seriously investing in

Table 4.5   Budget allocations in violence reduction projects funded by the Inter-American Development Bank vary

Component	Colombia		El Salvador		Honduras		Jamaica	
	Millions of dollars	Percent	Millions of dollars	Percent	Millions of dollars	Percent	Millions of dollars	Percent
Institutional strengthening	27.9	29	8.4	24	6.8	31	5.2	26
Community and other actions to prevent juvenile violence and delinquency	19.7	20	13.8	39	11.4	51	7.6	38
Social awareness and communication	8.8	9	4.1	11	0.5	2	0.6	3
Community policing and criminal justice	28.5	30	3.3	9	0.9	4	2.8	14
Total	95.6	100	35.4	100	22.2	100	20	100

Source: Authors' calculations based on project documents (IDB 1998, 2001, 2002, 2003.)
Note: Totals may not add up to 100 percent because of rounding errors. Differences in the ways in which countries assign activities across project components make cross-project comparison difficult. Colombia, the earliest project, divides all activities between national and municipal levels rather than by component type. The other three projects divide activities by component type. Due to these mixed categories of component activities, the data have been recategorized to enable useful comparison across projects.

violence reduction. Whether the outcomes will be commensurate with the investment made remains to be seen.

Citizen security projects are also being developed at the municipal level. Key players include local government leaders, law enforcement and criminal justice agencies, human and social services agencies, civil society, business owners, schools, and neighborhood associations.

Four main elements form the basis of the municipal-authority approach to citizen security (Shaw 2000; CSIR 2000):

- *Diagnosis*: Identifying the crime problems and key local partners involved in crime prevention in a community and analyzing the primary challenges and risk factors related to crime.
- *Action plan*: Developing a local plan of action with short- and long-term goals, selecting the most suitable solutions, and addressing the causes of crime and victimization, not just the symptoms.
- *Management and implementation*: Developing timelines, budgets, and benchmarks.
- *Monitoring and evaluation*: Identifying project objectives and establishing and implementing methods of evaluating project performance.

This approach recognizes that primary responsibility falls not only with the police but with local governments as well, with a crucial role for municipal leaders (Shaw 2000). It considers the strengths and assets of individuals and communities, rather than just their problems. Prevention is cost-effective compared with criminal justice solutions (Shaw 2000).

Like CPTED, the municipal authority approach to crime prevention has been implemented mainly in Europe and North America. Manuals and pilot projects have been developed to assist in planning and implementation in South Africa (CSIR 2000) and Latin America (World Bank 2003), and the approach forms the basis of the strategy of the UN-HABITAT Safer Cities Program (www.unchs.org/programmes/safercities/). Colombia has achieved extraordinary results with a version of the approach (box 4.5). Other successful experiences come from Diadema in the suburbs of São Paulo and the Fica Vivo Program in Belo Horizonte, Brazil (Beato 2005).

There are limits to the extent to which local municipalities can be successful in preventing crime. Rowland (1990) analyzes the challenges faced by a neighborhood policing strategy and a police professionalization strategy in the Mexican municipality of Naucalpan. She finds that the main constraints to public security are its nonexclusive nature, the need for public subsidies to finance it, the potential for spatial externalities, and the lack of municipal capacity. Further constraints in municipal crime prevention exist where drug traffickers control local communities, as they do in Brazil's large cities. In these settings, the limited ability of government

---

Box 4.5   Reducing Crime and Violence in Bogotá

Championed largely by mayors Mockus and Peñalosa, the city of Bogotá has transformed itself through an approach combining public health, reclaiming of public space, and criminal justice. Crime and violence had steadily increased in the city during the 1980s and early 1990s, with a cumulative negative effect on citizens' sense of security. The increase in insecurity was attributed to a loss of values and traditions of social order, high consumption of alcohol, access to fire arms, impunity, lack of credibility of justice and police institutions, attitudes favoring violent forms of conflict resolution, inappropriate treatment of violence in the media, and the presence of gangs and other armed groups (Castro and Salazar 1998).

Against this context, in 1994 the district administration began implementing a comprehensive program that included improving access to justice; controlling alcohol consumption and traffic accidents; aiding vulnerable groups, such as at-risk youth; and recovering public spaces, such as parks. In terms of public security, efforts were made to strengthen the police force, reduce crime and homicide, and reform the judicial system. Much media attention was given to the *ley zanahoria* (the "carrot law"), which imposed a 1 a.m. closing time for bars and restaurants, and to the rush hour restrictions on private cars.

The results of these interventions have been extraordinary. Homicide rates decreased 50 percent over six years, and the number of deaths from traffic accidents fell from 1,387 in 1995 to 824 in 2000 (Mockus 2001).

---

institutions to work collaboratively with local community institutions can make the types of municipal crime prevention programs outlined above difficult to implement.

The Community-Driven Development/Social Capital Approach

The community-driven development/social capital approach focuses on rebuilding social cohesion in informal and formal institutions. Using bottom-up, participatory processes, this approach aims to create trust by building on the strengths and assets of poor communities affected by violence and to strengthen the organizational capacity of local communities. This approach has been used to fight gang and domestic violence (box 4.6).

The importance of addressing violence interventions that the poor prioritize is a crucial aspect of the community-driven development/social capital approach. Using participatory methodologies, studies of violence in poor urban communities in Colombia, Guatemala, and Jamaica documented community members' interest in identifying solutions, even though they often felt powerless to effect change (Moser and McIlwaine 2000, 2001; Moser and Holland 1997). The most striking aspect of these results was

---

Box 4.6   Preventing Gang Violence in El Salvador: The Homies Unidos Program

Homies Unidos is a nonprofit gang violence prevention and intervention organization in San Salvador. Run by former gang members, its goal is to create a productive and peaceful future for young people who are surrounded by violence. The program is committed to developing creative alternatives to violence through leadership development, self-esteem building, peer counseling, health education programs, and access to vocational training and income opportunities. Members perform rap music as a way of reaching other gang members. The program stresses the need for members to have ownership and a sense of responsibility in the project. It considers dialogue and peaceful mediation the keys to creative conflict resolution.

Magdaleno Rose Avila, founder of the project, comments, "We're the only organization that is run by gangs and by active gang members. We don't pull people out of the gangs... because we think that the gangs are not all negative. If you have a dysfunctional government and a dysfunctional family, the only family [you] have is the gang structure.... So we say that we're going to build a positive role model for gang members... to find a way to reach youth and excite them about a vision that is bigger than the violence they see right now— to make them see beyond the obstacles."

Sources: www.homiesunidos.org; www.changemakers.net.

---

that more than half of the violence reduction interventions suggested focused on increasing social capital (table 4.6).

Community-driven development/social capital approaches to domestic violence are designed to empower local victims of abuse. Typically, local women's NGOs provide victim crisis services, short-term accommodation facilities for female victims of domestic abuse, counseling, and

Table 4.6   Colombia and Guatemala have tried to reduce violence by increasing capital
(percentage of all solutions)

Intervention	Colombia	Guatemala	Total
Increase social capital	48	58	53
Productive	35	35	35
Perverse	13	23	18
Increase human capital	31	31	31
Increase physical capital	21	11	16

Source: Moser and McIlwaine 2000, 2001.
Note: Figures may not sum to 100 percent because of rounding.

legal advice and support. Ongoing support and prevention programs for both victims and perpetrators provide longer term community-driven services.

By their very design, community-driven development projects are small and demand driven. They are essential if the needs of communities are to be identified. In the case of victims of domestic violence, a growing number of municipal projects have complemented and scaled up the community-driven development models originally developed by NGOs, providing more extensive support and prevention programs than can be done at the local level (Larraín 1999). Municipalities often offer psychological counseling and therapy services, and they form part of an institutional network to provide referrals to other sectors, such as health, justice, and the police.

Conclusion: Toward an Integrated Framework for Urban Intervention

Urban violence is now widely recognized as a serious development problem, and an increasing number of interventions have been designed to address it. Nevertheless, this is still a new area of inquiry and intervention. As a result, data constraints are severe, as there is very little systematization of information, either analytically or in operational terms.

This chapter shows how social and economic factors affect crime and violence. Too little attention has been paid in the literature to the impact of political and institutional factors at the urban level. The evidence suggests that poor urban communities, particularly in large cities, are caught between the formal institutional violence perpetuated by the state and the arbitrary control of local-level informal institutions. Organized crime, drug dealers, and gangs affect, and sometimes dominate, the governance of local communities. This has critically important implications for the design, implementation, and likely success of local violence reduction interventions.

No adequate assessment (or baseline indicators) has been conducted of the plethora of violence reduction interventions or the institutional capacity of many of the implementing institutions. Despite the vast number and wide range of initiatives addressing youth violence in the region, little data analysis or monitoring of their impact on violence has been conducted (World Bank 2002).

While there is no "silver bullet" to the problem of urban crime and violence, the experiences of different policy approaches suggest that an integrated framework combining each approach's strengths can reduce urban crime and violence. This framework for local action should be based on a participatory and comprehensive diagnostic. It should include some elements of each of the following types of reform:

- *Judicial/policing reform*: Ensuring that order, fairness, and access to due process are maintained in the day-to-day activities of the community and reducing the public fear of crime.[12]
- *Social prevention*: Establishing targeted multiagency and community-driven development programs that address the causes of and risk factors for crime and violence.
- *Situational prevention*: Adopting measures that reduce opportunities for particular crime and violence problems through urban spatial interventions, such as CPTED and urban renewal.

Preventing and reducing crime and violence require a shared local vision, strong leadership, commitment, and an action plan for the short, medium, and long terms.

One of the most effective entry points for crime and violence prevention is the municipal level. It is the level of government closest to the people, the level at which projects can be designed to target the specific needs of the community. The municipal level is also where the day-to-day delivery of services takes place. These services improve the quality of people's life and help build better living environments. Many of these services are also the basic elements of crime and violence prevention. Effective local government action requires that all municipal services work together rather than in isolation. It requires support from the different sectors in the community, including justice, health, education, the media, the police, social services, the private sector, and NGOs. It also requires support from higher levels of government and links between the national level and state, regional, and provincial governments.

Annex

Table 4A.1   Categories of Violence

Category	Definition	Manifestation
Political	The commission of violent acts motivated by the desire, conscious or unconscious, to obtain or maintain political power.	Guerrilla conflict, paramilitary conflict, political assassinations, armed conflict between political parties
Institutional	The commission of violent acts motivated by the desire, conscious or unconscious, to exercise collective social or political power over other groups and individuals.	Violence perpetrated by state political institutions, such as the army and police; social cleansing by civil vigilante groups; lynching of suspected criminals by community members
Economic	The commission of violent acts motivated by the desire, conscious or unconscious, for economic gain or to obtain or maintain economic power.	Street crime; carjacking; robbery/theft; drug trafficking; kidnapping; assaults, including killing and rape committed during the perpetration of economic crimes
Social	The commission of violent acts motivated by a desire, conscious or unconscious, for social gain or to obtain or maintain social power.	Interpersonal violence, such as spouse and child abuse; sexual assault of women and children; arguments that get out of control

Source: Adapted from Moser and Clarke 2001; Moser and McIlwaine 2003.

Table 4A.2   Types and Sources of Violence Data

Type of data	Data sources	Examples of information collected
Mortality	Death certificates; vital statistics registries; reports from medical examiners, coroners, and mortuaries	Characteristics of the deceased; cause, location, time, and manner of death
Morbidity and other health data	Hospital, clinic, and other medical records	Information on disease; injury; physical, mental, and reproductive health
Self-reported	Surveys, special studies, focus groups, media	Attitudes, beliefs, behaviors, cultural practices, victimization and perpetration, exposure to violence in the home or community
Community	Population records, local government records, other institutional records	Population counts and density, levels of income and education, unemployment rates, divorce rates
Crime	Police records, judiciary records, crime laboratories	Type of offense, characteristics of offender, relationship between victim and offender, circumstances of event
Economic	Program, institutional, and agency records; special studies	Expenditures on health, housing, and social services; costs of treating violence-related injuries; use of services
Policy or legislative	Government or legislative records	Laws, institutional policies, and practices

Source: WHO 2002.

Table 4A.3   Incidence of Sexual Abuse of Women in Selected Latin American Cities

Country	City	Year	Sample size	Percentage of respondents
Adult women ever sexually assaulted by an intimate partner[a]				
Brazil	São Paulo	2000	941	10.1
	Pernambuco	2000	1,188	14.3
Mexico	Durango	1996	384	42.0
	Guadalajara	1996	650	23.0
Nicaragua	León	1993	360	21.7
Peru	Lima	2000	1,086	22.5
	Cusco	2000	1,534	46.7
Women 16 or older sexually assaulted in the past five years				
Argentina	Buenos Aires	1996	1,000	5.8
Bolivia	La Paz	1996	999	1.4
Brazil	Rio de Janeiro	1996	1,000	8.0
Colombia	Bogotá	1997	1,000	5.0
Costa Rica	San José	1996	587	2.7
Paraguay	Asunción	1996	587	2.7

Source: WHO 2002.
a. Defined as attempted or completed forced sex.

Table 4A.4   Preventing Crime: What Works, What Doesn't, What's Promising

What works	What doesn't	What's promising
• Frequent home visits by nurses for infants (reduces child abuse)	• Gun buyback programs	• Proactive drunk driving arrests
• Weekly home visits by teachers for preschoolers	• Community mobilization against crime in high-crime poverty areas	• Community policing with meetings to set priorities
• Family therapy and parent training on delinquent and at-risk preadolescents	• Police home visits to couples after domestic violence incidents	• Police showing greater respect to arrested offenders
• Organizational development for innovation in schools	• Individual and peer counseling of students in schools	• Police field interrogations of suspicious persons
• Clarifying and communicating consistent norms in schools	• Drug abuse resistance education	• Mailing arrest warrants to domestic violence suspects who leave the scene before the police arrive
• Teaching social competency skills in schools	• Drug prevention classes focused on fear and other emotional appeals	• More police officers in cities
• Training high-risk youth in thinking skills	• School-based leisure time enrichment programs	• Gang monitoring by community workers and probation and police officers
• Vocational training for male ex-offenders	• Summer jobs or subsidized work programs for at-risk youth	• Community-based mentoring
• Nuisance abatement action against owners of rental housing used to sell drugs	• Short-term, nonresidential training programs for at-risk youth	• Community-based after school recreation programs
• Extra police patrols in high-crime hotspots	• Diversion from court to job training as a condition of case dismissal	• shelters for battered women
• Monitoring high-risk repeat offenders by specialized police units	• Neighborhood watch programs organized with police	• Schools that group students into smaller units
		• Training at-risk youth in thinking skills
		• Building school capacity through organizational development

Table 4A.4 (continued)

What works	What doesn't	What's promising
• Incarcerating high-risk repeat offenders • On-scene arrest of unemployed domestic abusers • Rehabilitation programs with risk-focused treatments for convicted offenders • Therapeutic community treatment programs for drug users in prison	• Arrests of juveniles for minor offenses • Arrests of unemployed suspects for domestic violence • Increased arrests or raids on drug market locations • Storefront police officers • Police newsletters with local crime information • Correctional boot camps using military basic training • Visits by minor juvenile to adult prisons • Shock probation, shock parole, and split sentences • Intensive supervision on parole or probation • Rehabilitation programs using unstructured counseling	• Improved classroom management techniques • Prison-based vocational training for adults • Moving urban public housing residents to suburban homes • Establishment of enterprise zones • Redesigned layout of retail stores • Target hardening • Metal detectors • Street closures, barricades, and rerouting of traffic • Intensive supervision and aftercare of juvenile offenders • Problem solving analysis at each crime location • Fines for criminal acts • Drug courts

Source: Sherman and others 1998.

Table 4A.5 Features of Inter-American Development Bank Projects to Reduce Violence in Four Latin American Countries

Item	Colombia	Jamaica	El Salvador	Honduras
Project	Peaceful Coexistence and Citizen Security Support	Citizen Security and Justice Program	Social Peace Program Support Project	Peace and Citizen Coexistence Project
Disbursement period	4½ years beginning in 1998	4 years beginning in 2001	4½ years beginning in 2002	3–5 years beginning in 2003
Budget	IDB: $57 million Local: $38.6 million Total: $95.6 million	IDB: $16 million Local: $4.0 million Total: $20 million	IDB: $27.9 million Local: $7.5 million Total: $35.4 million	IDB: $20.0 million Local: $2.2 million Total: $22.2 million
Executing agencies	National Development Project Fund, National Planning Dept, Capital District; municipalities	Ministry of National Security and Justice	Ministry of the Interior	Municipality of San Pedro Sulas
Target population	Bogotá, Cali, and Medellín municipalities	Kingston Metropolitan Area	San Salvador and high-population municipalities	Sula Valley municipalities

Objective	Reduce violence and insecurity by strengthening efforts to prevent, counteract, and control criminal acts and violence	Enhance citizen security and justice by reducing violence, strengthening crime management, and improving judicial services	Improve citizen security and reduce rates of juvenile crime and violence	Improve levels of peace, coexistence, and citizen security by preventing violence and strengthening institutions
Components	1. National Subprogram ($34.0) • Create national crime database ($6.0) • Assist Ministry of Justice and develop alternative methods of justice ($2.6) • Conduct research on legal action and justice and gender ($1.5) • Develop national communications strategy ($0.3)	1. Capacity building of the Ministry of National Security and Justice ($4.6) • Strategic planning and project execution ($0.3) • Technical assistance ($4.3) 2. Community action ($7.6) • Violence prevention services ($5.2) • Community action committees ($0.6) • Community-based multipurpose facilities ($1.5)	1. Institutional strengthening ($8.4) • Project coordination and execution ($2.9) • Information technology and interconnectivity ($3.4) • Technical assistance ($0.2) • Monitoring and evaluation ($0.8) 2. Prevention of juvenile violence and delinquency ($19.6)	1. Institutional strengthening ($6.8) • Institutional support to municipalities, police, and public prosecutors • Integrated citizen security information system (SISC) • Monitoring and evolution 2. Social prevention of violence and juvenile delinquency ($11.4)

(table continues on the following page)

Table 4A.5 (continued)

Item	Colombia	Jamaica	El Salvador	Honduras
	• Educate police to improve relations with communities ($4.0)	• Improved community-police relations ($0.3)	• Social prevention of violence and delinquency in municipalities ($9.6)	• Positive development for vulnerable and at-risk youths
	• Provide technical assistance to promote exchange of experiences ($2.6)	3. Strengthening the criminal justice system ($2.8)	• Prevention of domestic violence and victim services ($0.5)	• Prevention of violence and delinquency in schools
	• Extend line of credit ($13.05)	• Assistance and training to Victim Support Program and Boards of Visitors ($0.4)	• Strategic plan for the national police ($3.3)	• Youth community center
	• Promote, administer, and monitor project ($1.0)	• Assistance and training to police complaints authority and information campaign ($0.2)	• Promotion of youth employment ($0.9)	• Job training and youth employment program
	2. Municipal Subprogram ($61.6)	• Support to a rehabilitation, vocational training, and transformation center for youths ($1.5)	• National social awareness strategy ($4.1)	• At-risk youth assistance
	• Crime report stations ($5.2)		• Innovative projects from civil society ($1.3)	• Prevention of domestic violence and victim assistance
	• Programs to improve access to justice ($14.4)		3. Rehabilitation and reintegration of juvenile offenders ($1.6)	3. Community police/crime prevention ($0.9)
	• At-risk youth and rehabilitation ($16.9)			• Support of community police
	• Citizen education ($8.8)			

- Police/community relations ($4.9)
- Citizen watch ($2.8)
- Institutional strengthening of government ($1.9)

- Technical assistance and training for courts ($0.7)
4. Social marketing ($0.6)
5. National crime and violence prevention strategy ($0.6)
- Study on costs of violence
- Technical assistance

- Reintegration of juvenile offenders ($0.2)
- Reintegration of young adult offenders ($1.4)

- Support of a regional family protection services division
- Support of a system for police oversight and accountability
4. Communication and social awareness ($0.5)
- Communication campaign
- Media awareness

Source: IDB 1998, 2001, 2002, and 2003.
Note: Figures in parentheses are in millions and do not include costs for financing and contingencies.

Endnotes

1. The WHO (2002) divides violence into three broad categories. *Self-directed violence* is physical harm inflicted by oneself. This category is subdivided into suicidal behavior and self-abuse. *Interpersonal violence* includes injury or harm caused by a relative (domestic violence) or an unrelated person (community violence). *Collective violence* includes harmful acts committed by a group. These acts can be politically, economically, or socially motivated.

2. Conflict can be peacefully resolved through negotiation without recourse to force; it becomes violent when it includes fighting and killing. By definition crime is an act (usually a grave offense) punishable by law; *violent crime* is defined as any act that causes a physical or psychological wound or damage that is against the law (Vanderschueren 1996).

3. This section draws on the work of experts on violence in Latin America and the Caribbean as well as on previous work by the authors (see Moser and others 2000; Moser and Winton 2002; Moser and McIlwaine 2003). Table 4A.1 summarizes some of the common types of violence for each category.

4. For detailed descriptions of the nature of youth gangs, see Moser and McIlwaine (2003) on Colombia and Guatemala, Rodgers (2003) on Colombia and Nicaragua, and Smutt and Miranda (1998) on El Salvador.

5. Reported statistics may not be meaningful, as the majority of kidnappings are believed to go unreported, because of fear of reprisals.

6. First used to explain human development (Bronfenbrenner 1977), the ecological model has been used by violence researchers to elucidate the complex causes of child abuse (Belsky 1980), sexual coercion (Brown 1995), and domestic violence (Heise 1998). The model is a multilevel framework that incorporates both individual-level factors—biophysical, psychological, and social—and external factors that act upon the individual.

7. Briceño-León (1999) identifies social inequality and the breakdown of traditional controls such as the family as factors that generate violence; the absence of mechanisms of conflict resolution as factors that promote violence; and easy access to firearms, alcohol and drug consumption, and media sensationalization as factors that facilitate urban violence (see also Arriagada and Godoy 1999).

8. The two main gangs in Central America, the maras 18 and Salvatrucha, use the same names as the two main Latino gangs in Los Angeles.

9. Reports of corruption and impunity, which did not occur under the previous regime, have also become everyday news.

10. The difficulty of evaluating programs is illustrated by a congressionally mandated evaluation of state and local crime prevention programs funded by the U.S. Department of Justice. A review of more than 500 crime prevention programs meeting certain standards, with special attention to youth violence, found only minimally adequate evidence to establish a provisional list of "what works, what doesn't, and what's promising" (Sherman and others 1998). This list is reproduced in table 4A.4.

11. Honduras has a distinct emphasis on positive development and community facilities for at-risk youth.

12. While the World Bank cannot be directly involved in policing issues, such as police reform, it can recognize the importance of the role of police and the judicial system, work on judicial reform, and encourage crime and violence prevention partnerships that include the police.

References

Adorno, S. 1997. "La criminalidad violenta urbana en Brasil: tendencias y características." Paper presented at the conference "El Desafío de la Violencia Criminal Urbana," Interamerican Development Bank, Rio de Janeiro, March 2–4.

Arriagada, I., and L. Godoy, 2000. "Prevention or Repression? The False Dilemma of Citizen Security." CEPAL Review 70: 111–36.

————. 1999. "Seguridad ciudadana y violencia en América Latina: Diagnóstico y políticas en los años noventa." Social Policy Series No. 32, CEPAL (Comisión Economica para America Latina), Santiago, Chile.

Aurora, N., C. Bartman, M. Druffel, and B. DeMuynck. 1999. "Defensibility: Research." East St. Louis Action Research Project, University of Illinois, Urbana-Champaign.

AVANCSO (Asociación para el Avance de las Ciencias Sociales en Guatemala). 1996. Por sí mismos: un estudio preliminar de las "maras" en la ciudad de Guatemala. 3rd ed. Cuaderno de Investigación No. 4. Guatemala City: AVANCSO.

Beato, Claudio. 2005. "Case Study: Fica Vivo." Course on Municipal Capacity Building on Crime and Violence Prevention, World Bank, Washington DC.

Belsky, J. 1980. "Child Maltreatment: An Ecological Integration." American Psychologist 35 (4): 320–35.

Bourguignon, F. 2001. "Crime as a Social Cost of Poverty and Inequality: A Review Focusing on Developing Countries." In Facets of Globalization: International and Local Dimensions of Development, World Bank Discussion Paper No. 415, pp. 171–91, Washington, DC.

Briceño-León, R. 1999. "Violence and the Right to Kill: Public Perceptions from Latin America." Paper presented at the conference "Rising Violence and the Criminal Justice Response in Latin America: Towards an Agenda for Collaborative Research in the 21st Century," University of Texas, Austin, May 6–9.

Briceño-León, R., and V. Zubillaga. 2002. "Violence and Globalization in Latin America." Current Sociology 50 (1): 19–37.

Bronfenbrenner, U. 1977. "Toward an Experimental Ecology of Human Development." American Psychologist 32 (5): 13–31.

Brown, S. 1995. "Gender Stereotypes and Sexual Coercion." In Sexual Coercion, and Reproductive Health, ed. L. Heise, K. Moore, and N. Toubi, pp. 28–30. New York: Population Council.

Buvinić, M., A.R. Morrison, and M. Shifter. 1999. "Violence in the Americas: A Framework for Action." In Too Close to Home: Domestic Violence in the Americas, ed. A.R. Morrison and M.L. Biehl, 3–34. Washington, DC: Inter-American Development Bank.

Call, C. 1998. "Police Reform, Human Rights, and Democratization in Post-Conflict Settings: Lessons from El Salvador." Paper presented at the seminar Convivencia y Seguridad Ciudadana en el Itsmo Centroamericano y la Isla de Española, Inter-American Development Bank, San Salvador, June 2–4.

———. 2000. "Sustainable Development in Central America: The Challenges of Violence, Injustice and Insecurity." Working Paper No. 8. CA 2020. Institut für Iberoamerika-Kunde, Hamburg, Germany.

Cardia, N. 1999. "Beliefs about Violence: Values and Behaviours of the Urban Population in 10 Brazilian Cities." Paper presented at the conference "Rising Violence and the Criminal Justice Response in Latin America: Towards an Agenda for Collaborative Research in the 21st Century," University of Texas, Austin, May 6–9.

Carney, D. 1998. "Implementing the Sustainable Rural Livelihood Approach." In *Sustainable Rural Livelihoods: What Contributions Can We Make?* ed. D. Carney, 3–23. London: Department for International Development.

Carrión, F. 1994. "De la violencia urbana a la convivencia ciudadana." In *Ciudad y violencias en América Latina,* ed. A. Concha Eastman, F. Carrión, and G. Cobo, 5–22. Quito: Programa de Gestión Urbana.

Castellanos, J. 2000. "Honduras: armamentismo y violencia." Paper presented at the First Central American Forum on the Proliferation of Light Arms, Antigua, Guatemala, July 26–29.

Castro, M.F., and M. Salazar. 1998. "La respuesta a la criminalidad y la violencia en Colombia: Acciones del estado para promover la convivencia y la seguridad en las ciudades." Paper presented at the conference "Violence in Latin America: Policy Implications from Studies on the Attitudes and Costs of Violence," Harvard University, Cambridge, MA, February 19–20.

Cervantes, F. 1999. "Helping Men to Overcome Violent Behavior toward Women." In *Too Close to Home: Domestic Violence in the Americas,* ed. A.R. Morrison and M. Loreto Biehl, 143–147. Washington, DC: Inter-American Development Bank.

Chambers, R., and G. Conway. 1992. "Sustainable Rural Livelihoods: Practical Concepts for the 21st Century." IDS Discussion Paper No. 296. Institute for Development Studies, Brighton, UK.

Chernick, M. 1998. "The Paramilitarization of the War in Colombia." *NACLA Report on the Americas* 31 (5): 28–33.

Chinchilla, L. 1999. "Policía de orientación comunitaria: una adecuada alianza entre policia y comunidad para revertir la inseguridad." Paper presented at the seminar "Dialogos sobre Convivencia Ciudadana," Santiago, Chile, October 13–15.

Clarke, R. n.d. "Aspects Taken from 'Situational Crime Prevention: Successful Case Studies.'" Summary prepared by the Surrey Community Safety Unit, Surrey, United Kingdom.

Cooke, G.R. 2003. "CPTED Makes a Comeback." www.vcnet.com/expert/library/cpted_gc.html.

Correa, J., and M.A. Jiménez. 1995. "Acceso de los pobres a la justicia en Argentina." In *Acceso de los pobres a la justicia en países de Latinoamerica,* ed. F. Vanderschueren and E. Oviedo, 21–48. Santiago, Chile: Ediciones SUR.

Cruz, J.M. 1999. "La victimización por violencia urbana: Niveles y factores asociados en ciudades de América Latina y España." Special Issue on Violence. *Pan American Journal of Public Health* 5 (4/5): 259–67.

Cruz, J.M., and M.A. Beltrán. 2000. "Las armas en El Salvador: Diagnóstico sobre su situación y su impacto." Paper presented at the First Central American Forum on the Proliferation of Light Weapons, Antigua, Guatemala, July 26–29.

CSIR (Council for Scientific and Industrial Research). 2000. *A Manual for Community-Based Crime Prevention*. Pretoria.

Dakolias, M. 1996. "The Judicial Sector in Latin America and the Caribbean: Elements of Reform." World Bank Technical Paper No. 319, Washington, DC.

Dammert, L. 2000. "Violencia criminal y seguridad pública en America Latina: La situación en Argentina." Serie Políticas Sociales No. 43, CEPAL, Santiago, Chile.

Deas, M. 1998 "Violence Reduction in Colombia: Lessons from Government Policies over the Last Decade." World Bank, Washington, DC.

De Cesare, D. 1997. "De la guerra civil a la guerra de pandillas: Crecimiento de las pandillas de Los Angeles en El Salvador." In *Proceedings of the PAHO Adolescent and Youth Gang Violence Prevention Workshop*, 38–40. Washington, DC: Pan-American Health Organization.

De Orrellana, S. 1997. "Situación de la violencia juvenil en El Salvador." In *Proceedings of the PAHO Adolescent and Youth Gang Violence Prevention Workshop*, 72–75. Washington, DC: Pan-American Health Organization.

Duncan, I., and M. Woolcock. 2003. "Arrested Development: The Political Origins and Socio-Economic Foundations of Common Violence in Jamaica." World Bank, Washington, DC. Processed.

Ellsberg, M. 1997. "Candies in Hell: Domestic Violence against Women in Nicaragua." Department of Epidemiology and Public Health, Umea University, Umea, Sweden.

Fajnzylber, P., D. Lederman, and N. Loayza. 1998. *Determinants of Crime Rates in Latin America and the World*. Washington, DC: World Bank.

———. 2002. "Inequality and Violent Crime." *Journal of Law and Economics* 45 (1):1–40.

FLACSO (Facultad Latinoamericana de Ciencias Sociales). n.d. *Programas para la prevención de la violencia y delincuencia juvenil*. Document ES-0116, prepared for the Inter-American Development Bank. Quito, Ecuador.

Frühling, H. n.d. "La policía comunitaria en America Latina: Un analisis basado en cuatro estudios de caso." Centro de Estudios en Seguridad Ciudadana de la Universidad de Chile, Santiago, Chile.

Fundación Mexicana para la Salud/Centro de Economía y Salud 1998. "Análisis de la magnitud y costos de la violencia en la Ciudad de México." Working Paper R-331, Inter-American Development Bank, Washington, DC.

Gaviria, A. 1998. "Increasing Returns and the Evolution of Violent Crime: The Case of Colombia." Discussion Paper 98-14, University of California, Department of Economics, San Diego.

Gaviria, A., and A. Pagés. 1999. "Patterns of Crime and Victimization in Latin America." Working Paper No. 408, Inter-American Development Bank, Washington, DC.

Glaeser, E., and B. Sacerdote. 1999. "Why Is There More Crime in Cities?" *Journal of Political Economy* 124 (4): 719–20.

Heise, L. 1998. "Violence against Women: An Integrated Ecological Model." *Violence against Women* 4 (3): 262–90.

IDB (Inter-American Development Bank). 1998. "Colombia: Proposal for Financing in Support of Peaceful Coexistence and Citizen Security." Washington, DC.

———. 2000a. "Boletin de la red de alcaldes contra la violencia." Programa de prevención de la violencia, División de Desarrollo Social, Bulletin No. 2, Washington, DC.

———. 2000b. "Economic and Social Consequences of Violence. " *Technical notes on Violence Prevention,* Note No. 4, Social Development Division. Washington, DC.

———. 2001. "Jamaica: Proposal for a Loan and Nonreimbursable Technical Cooperation Funding for a Citizen Security and Justice Program." Washington, DC.

———. 2002. "El Salvador: Proposal for a Project to Support the Social Peace Program." Washington, DC.

———. 2003. "Honduras: Proposal for a Loan for a Peace and Citizen Security Project for the Municipalities of the Sula Valley." Washington, DC.

IESA (Instituto de Estudios Superiores de Administracion)/FLACSO (Facultad Latinoamericana de Ciencias Sociales). 1999. "La violencia en Venezuela: Dimensionamiento y políticas de control." Working Paper R-373, Inter-American Development Bank, Washington, DC.

INEC/MINSA (Instituto Nacional de Estadisticas y Censos/Ministerio de Salud). 1998. *Encuesta Nicaragüense de demografía y salud 1998.* Bethesda, Maryland: Macro International.

Instituto Apoyo. 1999. *Criminal Violence: Study in the Cities of Latin America: The Case of Peru.* wbln0018.worldbank.org/LAC/lacinfoclient.nsf/ d29684951174975c85256735007fef12/8d7bc9307b31f5998525688100517866/ $FILE/exesum.pdf.

IUDOP (Instituto Universitario de Opinión Pública). 1998. "La violencia en El Salvador en los años noventa: Magnitud, costos y factores posibilitadores." Working Paper R-338, Inter-American Development Bank, Washington, DC.

Jimeno, M., and I. Roldán. 1996. *Las sombras arbitrarias.* Santa Fé de Bogotá Colombia: Editorial Universidad Nacional.

Keane, J. 1996. *Reflections on Violence.* London: Verso.

KfW (Kreditanstalt für Wiederaufbau), and City of Cape Town. 2002. "Violence Prevention through Urban Upgrading: Feasibility Study." KfW and City of Cape Town, Cape Town, South Africa.

Kramer, R.C. 2000. "Poverty, Inequality, and Youth Violence." *Annals of the American Academy of Political and Social Science* 567(1): 123–39.

Kruger, T., K. Landman, and S. Liebermann 2001. *Designing Safer Places: A Manual for Crime Prevention through Planning, and Design.* Pretoria: CSIR (Council for Scientific and Social Research).

Koonings, K. 1999. "Shadows of Violence and Political Transformation in Brazil: From Military Rule to Democratic Governance." In *Societies of Fear: The Legacy of Civil War, Violence and Terror in Latin America,* ed. K. Koonings and D. Kruijt, 197–234. London: Zed.

Kruijt, D., and K. Koonings. 1999. "Introduction: Violence and Fear in Latin America." In *Societies of Fear: The Legacy of Civil War, Violence and Terror in Latin America*, ed. K. Koonings, and D. Kruijt, 1–30. London: Zed.

Larraín, S. 1999. "Curbing Domestic Violence: Two Decades of Action." In *Too Close to Home: Domestic Violence in the Americas*, ed. A.R. Morrison and M. Loreto Biehl, 106–29. Washington, DC: Inter-American Development Bank.

Leeds, E. 1996. "Cocaine and Parallel Politics in the Brazilian Urban Periphery: Constraints on Local-Level Democratization." *Latin American Research Review* 31 (3): 47–85.

Lira, I. S. 2000. "Costo económico de los delitos: Niveles de vigilancia y políticas de seguridad ciudadana en las comunes del gran Santiago." Serie Gestión Publica No. 2, CEPAL (Comisión Económica para America Latina) Santiago, Chile.

Llorente, M.V., R. Escobedo, C. Echandía, and M. Rubio 2001. *Violencia homicida en Bogotá: Mas que intolerancia*. Bogota, Colombia: Centro de Estudios para el Desarrollo (CEDE), Universidad de los Andes.

Londoño, J.L., and R. Guerrero. 1999. "Violencia en América Latina: Epidemiología y costos." Working Paper R-375, Inter-American Development Bank, Washington, DC.

López Regonesi, Eduardo. 2000. "Reflexiones acerca de la seguridad ciudadana en Chile: Visiones y propuestas para el diseño de una política." Serie Políticas Sociales No. 44, CEPAL (Comisión Económica para America Latina), Santiago, Chile.

Macmillan, R. 2000. "Adolescent Victimization and Income Deficits in Early Adulthood: Rethinking the Costs of Criminal Violence from a Life Course Perspective." *Criminology* 31 (1): 553–87.

Mehrotra, A. n.d. "AIDS: An Expression of Gender Based Violence." United Nations Development Programme. www.undp.org/rblac/gender/aidsgender.htm.

Mesquita de Rocha, M. 1997. "Women's Police Stations: Rio de Janeiro, Brazil." Paper presented at the conference "Domestic Violence in Latin America and the Caribbean: Costs, Programs, and Policies," Washington, DC, October 20–21.

Mockus, A. 2001. "Seguridad y convivencia en Bogotá: Logros y retos 1995–2001." Alcaldía Mayor de Bogotá, Bogota.

Montoya, O. 2000. *Swimming Upstream: Looking for Clues to Prevent Male Violence in Couple Relationships*. Managua, Nicaragua: Puntos de Encuentro.

Morrison, A.R., and M.B. Orlando. 1999. "Social and Economic Costs of Domestic Violence: Chile and Nicaragua." In *Too Close to Home: Domestic Violence in the Americas*, ed. A.R. Morrison, and M.L. Biehl, 51–67. Washington, DC: Inter-American Development Bank.

Moser, C., and J. Holland. 1997. *Urban Poverty and Violence in Jamaica*. Washington, DC: World Bank.

Moser, C., S. Lister, C. McIlwaine, E. Shrader, and A. Tornqvist. 2000. *Violence in Colombia: Building Sustainable Peace and Social Capital*. Report No. 18652-CO. Washington, DC: World Bank, Environmentally and Socially Sustainable Development Sector Management Unit.

Moser, C., and C. McIlwaine. 1999. "Participatory Urban Appraisal and its Application for Research on Violence." *Environment and Urbanization* 11 (2): 203–26.

————. 2000. *Urban Poor Perceptions of Violence and Exclusion in Colombia*. Washington, DC: World Bank.

————. 2001. *Violence in a Post-Conflict Context: Urban Poor Perceptions from Guatemala*. Washington, DC: World Bank.

————. 2003. *Encounter with Violence: Urban Community Perceptions from Colombia, and Guatemala*. London: Routledge.

Moser, C. and F.C. Clarke. 2001. *Latin American Experiences of Gender, Conflict and Building Sustainable Peace: Challenges for Colombia*. Report of a conference held in Bogota, Colombia in May 2000. Bogota: Tercer Mundo Editores.

Moser, C., and A. Norton. 2001. *To Claim Our Rights: Livelihood Security, Human Rights and Sustainable Development*: London: Overseas Development Institute.

Moser, C., and A. Winton. 2002. *Violence in the Central American Region: Towards an Integrated Framework for Violence Reduction*. ODI Working Paper No. 171, Overseas Development Institute, London.

National Crime Prevention Council. 1999. *Six Safer Cities: On the Crest of the Crime Prevention Wave*. Washington, DC: National Crime Prevention Council.

Ocampo, J.G. 2001. "Red de escuelas y bandas de música de Medellín: Semillero de paz." In *Educar en medio del conflicto: Experiencias y testimonios, retos de esperanza*, 55–59. Bogota: World Bank and Gobernación de Antioquia.

PAHO (Pan American Health Organization). n.d. "ACTIVA Project: Cultural Norms and Attitudes towards Violence in Selected Cities in Latin America and Spain." www.paho.org/English/HCP/HCN/VIO/activa-project.htm.

————. n.d. "Statistics on Homicides, Suicides, Accidents, Injuries and Attitudes towards Violence." www.paho.org/English/HCP/HCN/VIO/violence-graphs.htm#homicides-n-sa.

Pecaut, D. 1999. "From the Banality of Violence to Real Terror: The Case of Colombia." In *Societies of Fear: The Legacy of Civil War, Violence, and Terror in Latin America*, ed. K. Koonings, and D. Kruijt, 141–67. London: Zed.

Pereira, A.W. 2001. "Virtual Legality: Authoritarian Legacies and the Reform of Military Justice in Brazil, the Southern Cone, and Mexico." *Comparative Political Studies* 34 (5): 555–74.

Piquet Carneiro, Leandro. 2000. "Violent Crime in Latin American Cities: Rio de Janeiro and São Paulo." Department of Political Science, University of São Paulo.

Poppovic, M., and P.S. Pinheiro. 1995. "How to Consolidate Democracy? A Human Rights Approach." *International Social Science Journal* 143 March: 75–89.

PRODEN Promoción de los Derechos de la Niñez 1996. *Entre el olvido y la esperanza: La niñez de Guatemala*. Guatemala City, Guatemala: PRODEN.

Rau, M., G. Cuadros, C. Gutierrez, C. Mertz, and C. Gonzalez. 2003. *Espacios urbanos seguros: Recomendaciones de diseño y gestión comunitaria para la obtención de espacios urbanos seguros*. Ministerio de Vivienda y Urbanismo, Santiago, Chile.

Reyna, C., and E. Toche. 1999. "La inseguridad en el Perú." Serie Políticas Sociales No. 29, CEPAL (Comisión Económica para America Latina), Santiago, Chile.

Rico, M.N. 1996. "Violencia de genero: Un problema de derechos humanos." Serie Mujer y Desarrollo No. 16, CEPAL (Comisión Económica para America Latina), Santiago, Chile.

Rodgers, D. 2003. "Youth Gangs in Colombia, and Nicaragua: New Forms of Violence, New Theoretical Directions?" Outlook on Development Series, Collegium for Development Studies, Uppsala, Sweden.

———. 1999. "Youth Gangs and Violence in Latin America and the Caribbean: A Literature Survey." Sustainable Development Working Paper No. 4, World Bank, Latin America and Caribbean Region, Washington, DC.

Rodríguez, M., and M. de León. 2000. "Diagnóstico sobre la situación Actual de las armas ligeras y la violencia en Guatemala." Paper presented at the First Central American Forum on the Proliferation of Armas Livianas, Antigua, Guatemala, July 26–29.

Rowland, A. 1990. "Local Public Security in Mexico: Bases for Analysis, and Reform." Documento de Trabajo No. 75, Centro de Investigación y Docencia Económicas, Mexico D.F., Mexico.

Rubio, M. 1998. "Los costos de la violencia en América Latina." Paper presented at the conference "Convivencia y Seguridad en el Istmo Centroamericano, Haití y República Dominicana," Interamerican Development Bank, San Salvador, June 2–4.

Salazar, A. 1994. "Young Assassins of the Drug Trade." *NACLA* 27 (6): 24–28.

Sanjuán, A.M. 1998. "Dimensionamiento y caracterización de las violencias en Caracas." Paper presented at the seminar "Convivencia y Seguridad Diudadana en el Etsmo Centroamericano y la Isla de Española." Inter-American Development Bank, San Salvador, June 2–4.

Scheper-Hughes, N. 1995. "Everyday Violence: Bodies, Death, and Silence." In *Development Studies: A Reader*, ed. S. Corbridge, 438–47. London: Arnold.

Schrijvers, J. 1993. *The Violence of Development*. Utrecht: Institute for Development Research Amsterdam and International Books.

Shaw, M. 2000. *The Role of Local Government in Community Safety*. Montreal: International Centre for the Prevention of Crime.

Sherman, L.W., D.C. Gottfredson, D.L. MacKenzie, J. Eck, P. Reuter, and S.D. Bushway. 1998. "Preventing Crime: What Works, What Doesn't, What's Promising." *Research in Brief* (July). Washington, DC: National Institute of Justice.

Short, J.F. 1997. *Poverty, Ethnicity, and Violence Crime*. Boulder, CO: Westview.

Sives, A. 2002. "Changing Patrons from Politician to Drug Don." *Latin American Perspectives* 29 (5): 66–89.

Smutt, M., and J.L.E. Miranda. 1998. "El fenómeno de las pandillas en El Salvador." San Salvador: UNICEF/FLACSO.

Torres-Rivas, E. 1999. "Epilogue: Notes on Terror, Violence, Fear and Democracy." In *Societies of Fear: The Legacy of Civil War, Violence and Terror in Latin America*, ed. K. Koonings and D. Kruijt, 285–300. London: Zed.

Tudela, Poblete, P. 1999. "Seguridad ciudadana y policía comunitaria: un desafío pendiente." Paper presented at the seminar "Dialogos sobre Convivencia Ciudadana," Santiago, Chile, October 13–15.

UNDP (United Nations Development Programme). 1998. *Guatemala: los contrastes del desarrollo humano 1998*. Guatemala City: UNDP.

———. 1999. "La justicia puede cambiar." *Boletín Informativo del Sistema de las Naciones Unidas en Guatemala*, No.2, Guatemala City.

———. 2000. *Informe sobre desarrollo humano: Nicaragua 2000*. Managua, Nicaragua: UNDP.

UN-HABITAT. 2002. Safer Cities Program.

U.S. Department of State. 2001. *2000 Country Report on Human Rights Practices.* Bureau of Democracy, Human Rights, and Labor. www.state.gov/g/drl/ rls/hrrpt/2000/wha/.

———. 2002. *2001 Country Report on Human Rights Practices.* Bureau of Democracy, Human Rights, and Labor. www.state.gov/g/drl/rls/hrrpt/2001/wha/.

Vanderschueren, F. 1996 "From Violence to Justice and Security in Cities." *Environment and Urbanization* 8 (1): 93–112.

Vanderschueren, F., and E. Oviedo. 1995. "Presentación." In *Acceso de los pobres a la justicia en países de Latinoamerica*, ed. F. Vanderschueren and E. Oviedo, 7–19. Santiago, Chile: Ediciones SUR.

WHO (World Health Organization). 2002. *World Report on Violence and Health.* Geneva: WHO.

World Bank 2002. "Caribbean Youth Development: Issues and Policy Directions." Draft for discussion. Washington, DC.

———. 2003. *A Resource Guide for Municipalities: Community-Based Crime and Violence Prevention in Urban Latin America.* Washington, DC: World Bank.

World Vision. 2002. *Faces of Violence in Latin America and the Caribbean.* San José Costa Rica: World Vision International.

Yamin, A. 1999. *Facing the 21st Century: Challenges and Strategies for the Latin American Human Rights Community.* Washington, DC: Washington Office on Latin America and Lima: Instituto de Defensa Legal.

Yodanis, C.L., A. Godenzi, and E.A. Stanko. 2000. "The Benefits of Studying Costs: A Review and Agenda for Studies on the Economic Costs of Violence against Women." *Policy Studies* 21 (3): 263–76.

Zaluar, A. 1999. "Violence Related to Illegal Drugs, Youth, and Masculinity Ethos." Paper presented at the conference "Rising Violence and the Criminal Justice Response in Latin America: Towards an Agenda for Collaborative Research in the 21st Century," University of Texas, Austin, May 6–9.

5
Keeping Healthy in an Urban Environment: Public Health Challenges for the Urban Poor

Ricardo Bitrán, Ursula Giedion, Rubi Valenzuela,
and Paavo Monkkonen

Access to health care and infrastructure services is generally much higher in urban than rural areas, even for the poor. Yet there is increasing evidence of an "urban penalty"[1]: in many countries key health indicators for poor children are as weak in urban areas as they are in rural areas, despite the much wider availability of services. This is presumably due to the very different public health challenges that arise from living in higher density areas.

The urbanization of Latin America has contributed to a dramatic change in its epidemiological profile, as communicable diseases have been replaced by chronic, degenerative, and cardiovascular diseases and violence as the leading causes of death (figure 5.1). This epidemiological transition, which is typical as a society becomes more urbanized, is due to a combination of a changing lifestyle (more sedentary, with a greater proportion of processed foods); lower incidence of poverty; and better access to health care, infrastructure, and education.

This chapter draws on the limited literature on the topic to compare rural and urban health challenges and examine intraurban differences in health outcomes. The first section compares health indicators in rural and urban areas, particularly among the poor. The second section addresses the variations in health indicators within urban areas and assesses their potential causes, including inadequate access to infrastructure, health services, and education. The last section concludes with a call for more systematic research on a topic that appears seriously understudied.

Ricardo Bitrán is President, Ursula Giedion is Senior Associate, and Rubi Valenzuela is Senior Consultant with Bitrán g Asociados in Santiago, Chile; Paavo Monkkonen worked on this chapter while working as a Consultant for the World Bank. This chapter is based largely on material contained in a background paper written for this report by Bitrán, Giedion, and Valenzuela (2003). The chapter benefited from the comments and suggestions of Isabela Danel and Marianne Fay.

Figure 5.1   Noncommunicable diseases represent an increasing share of the disease burden in Latin America and the Caribbean

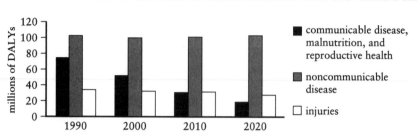

Source: PAHO Web site (http://www.paho.org/english/ad/dpc/nc/nc-unit-page.htm).
Note: Disability-adjusted life years (DALYs) are a summary measure that combines the impact of illness, disability, and mortality on population health. They combine years of life lost from premature death (relative to life expectancy at that age in a low-mortality population) and an adjustment for years of healthy life lost from disability. For more information on the concept see WRI 1998.

There is ample literature from both the health and economic fields on the determinants of health outcomes in populations. Excluding genetic makeup and biology, five sets of factors are considered important:

* *Socioeconomic status.* Higher income is positively correlated with better health, with the direction of causality clearly established from wealthier to healthier (Pritchett and Summers 1996). In addition, sickness and poverty often create a vicious cycle, in which health shocks can send households into poverty as debts are incurred for treatment or breadwinners are no longer able to work (WHO/UNICEF 2004).
* *Access to health services.* Surprisingly, there is no consensus in the literature on the extent to which consumption of health services improves health outcomes (Bitrán, Giedion, Valenzuela, and Monkkonen 2003). Studies have shown public expenditure on health services to have a limited impact, possibly due to variations in the quality of expenditure and the importance of individuals' health-seeking behavior (Filmer, Hammer, and Pritchett 1997).
* *Physical environment.* A person's physical environment, including access to water and sanitation, exposure to environmental contamination, the level of cleanliness, and protection from the elements, is a key determinant of health outcomes (Bitrán, Giedion, Valenzuela, and Monkkonen 2003).
* *Personal behavior.* Personal hygiene, nutrition, sexual habits, substance abuse, and choice of physical activities and employment can have an extremely important effect on health, affecting the probability of suffering from obesity, heart disease, cancer, sexually transmitted diseases, and

mental health problems (Bitrán, Giedion, Valenzuela, and Monkkonen 2003).

- *Social environment.* The relationship between a person's social environment—the level of community integration, stability, diversity, and security—and his or her health is not completely understood. But since the early twentieth century, research has demonstrated the beneficial effects of social integration on health. And a study conducted in the United States demonstrates an inverse relationship between membership in social groups and mortality (Kawachi and Kennedy 1997).

Of these five sets of factors, the first three are clearly different in rural and urban areas. The last two may be as well, although with the exception of security issues, addressed in chapter 4, and social capital, addressed in chapter 6, no analysis was found on the topic that distinguishes between rural and urban areas.

Differences in Urban and Rural Health Profiles

Urban and rural populations differ with respect to many health indicators, with the urban population typically better off. However, the picture is more varied when disaggregated by income categories: on some health indicators in some countries, the urban poor are worse off than their rural counterparts, and the health status of the urban population varies widely across countries and city sizes. In addition, urban populations are more susceptible to certain pathologies, although it is difficult to determine whether these pathologies have a greater incidence among lower income quintiles.

How different is the health of urban populations from that of rural populations? If we use the health of children as an overall health indicator, most evidence points toward much better health in urban areas. In Colombia child malnutrition and infant mortality are much more prevalent in rural areas (Flores 2000). In Peru health indicators are two to four times better in urban areas than in rural areas (table 5.1). This comes as no surprise given the higher incomes and better access to services of urban dwellers.

Distribution of Health Outcomes in Urban Areas

The superior performance of urban areas in terms of health indicators masks an important fact: the urban poor fare as badly as or worse than the rural poor in a number of countries and for many indicators. In nine countries in Latin America and the Caribbean, the urban poor perform consistently worse on almost all indicators measured than the urban nonpoor (figure 5.2). Child mortality rates are almost twice those of nonpoor

Table 5.1   Health indicators in rural and urban areas of Peru,
1997
(percent, except where otherwise indicated)

Indicator	Urban	Rural	Rural/urban ratio
Infant mortality rate (under 1 year)	30	62	2.1
Child mortality rate (under 5 years)	40	86	2.1
Children under 5 with average weight at least 1 standard deviation below the mean	16	40	2.5
Net birth rate (per 1,000 people)	24.2	33.5	1.4
Pregnancies without prenatal attention	18.6	53.2	2.9
Births without professional assistance	19.4	78.5	4.0
Female illiteracy	6	24	4.0
Households without drinkable water connection	28.3	74.5	2.6
Households without toilet	33.4	96.6	2.9
Overcrowding (more than five people per room)	13.9	27.8	2.0

Source: Cotlear and Javier 1999.

children, and the percentage of chronically malnourished children is three times as high. Infant and child mortality are higher among the urban poor than their rural counterparts in Brazil, Colombia, the Dominican Republic, and Paraguay. The percentage of chronic child malnutrition is higher among the urban poor than the rural poor in Colombia, Nicaragua, and Paraguay.

Pathologies in Urban and Rural Areas

Urban and rural populations have different incidences of pathologies. Certain pathologies, such as obesity; nutritional problems; sexually transmitted diseases, including HIV/AIDS; injuries from accidents; violence; drug addiction; and mental health problems seem to be more prevalent in urban areas.[2] These pathologies also seem to hit the poor harder.

OBESITY, SEDENTARISM, AND UNHEALTHY DIET
Urban children have a better variety and quality of food and less incidence of malnutrition than rural children, according to Ruel and Menon (2000). But the combination of a sedentary lifestyle and unhealthy diets associated with urban areas can lead to health problems. One of these problems, obesity, is associated with diabetes, hypertension, and heart disease, which increase morbidity and mortality.

Figure 5.2 The urban poor fare as badly as or worse than the rural poor in many countries

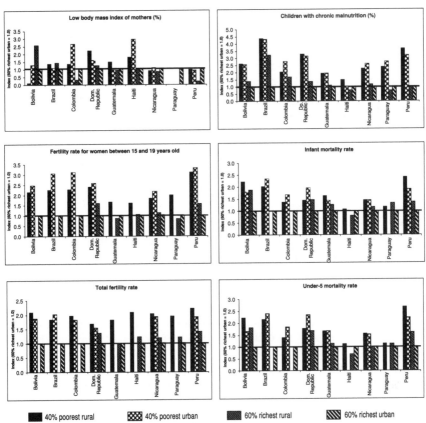

Source: Bitrán, Giedion, Valenzuela, and Monkkonen (2003) based on Demographic and Health Survey data (various years).

Note: Poverty line is based on an asset index comprising variables such as having vehicles and furniture.

Obesity is more prevalent in more urbanized areas in some Latin American countries, including Argentina; among lower income populations; and among women (O'Donnell and Carmuega 1998). The higher prevalence among lower income populations may reflect the relatively low price of unhealthy food.

The urban poor face additional nutritional problems due to the monetized economy of urban areas. Musgrove's study on income, family size, and the price of food (1991) shows that nutrition is more sensitive to changes in income and the price of food among poor urban families than among poor rural families (who are more affected by changes in family size).

SEXUALLY TRANSMITTED DISEASES, INCLUDING HIV/AIDS
A study analyzing data from 20 Latin American and Caribbean countries finds that the level of urbanization has a statistically significant positive correlation with the number of cases of HIV/AIDS (Stillwagon 2000). These results support the contention that HIV/AIDS is a greater problem in urban areas than in rural areas. In El Salvador, where 46 percent of the population lives in urban areas, 75 percent of the new cases of HIV reported between 1984 and 2002 occurred in urban areas (Mendoza 2000; Aguilar, Chacón, and Romero 1998). This despite the fact that it is easier to target at-risk populations in urban areas for sexually transmitted disease prevention programs (RCAP 1997).

TRAFFIC INJURIES
There is little concrete evidence on traffic injuries in Latin America and much need for research. Worldwide road injuries tend to be more prevalent in urban areas, due to higher population density, and to affect the poor disproportionately (WHO 2004b). Pedestrians, cyclists, and motorcyclists are particularly vulnerable in urban settings, given the growing presence of faster and heavier cars, buses, and trucks. In contrast to the trend in high-income countries, in low- and middle-income countries, annual road deaths are expected to rise 80 percent in the next 20 years (WHO 2004b).

TOBACCO, ALCOHOLISM, DRUG ADDICTION, AND MENTAL HEALTH PROBLEMS
The urban poor in Latin America may suffer disproportionately from tobacco-related illnesses, alcoholism, drug addiction, and mental health problems, although more research is needed to confirm this. In a study of the relationship between health and habitat in Buenos Aires and Santiago de Chile, Bazzani (1995) finds that the main problems of residents of poor neighborhoods include mental disorders (anxiety and depression) and drug addiction. The World Health Organization (WHO 2004b) finds evidence of a disproportionate effect of tobacco and alcoholism on poor people. Whether these effects are greater in urban areas is not clear.

Intraurban Differences in Health Outcomes

The variation in health indicators between income groups in urban areas appears to be significant. In Colombia, health inequality appears to be more pronounced in urban areas than in rural areas (Florez and Tono 2002). Although there is no completely conclusive evidence on the cause of this variation, differences in education, infrastructure, and access to medical services across income groups have a large impact.

Intraurban Variation in Health Indicators

The variation in health indicators within urban populations is significant, and is associated with both wealth and access to basic needs (figure 5.3). The countries with the most consistently unequal distribution of health indicators are Brazil and Peru.

Figure 5.3 Health indicators in urban areas vary widely across income groups
(concentration coefficients)

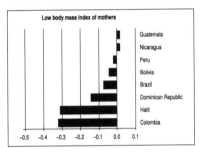

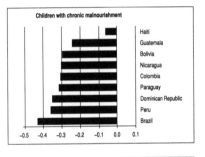

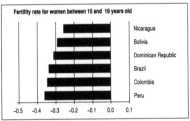

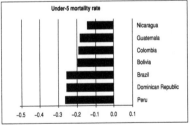

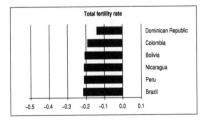

Source: Bitrán, Giedion, Valenzuela, and Monkkonen (2003) based on Demographic and Health Survey data (various years).

Note: Concentration coefficients measure inequality and are calculated in the same way as Gini coefficients. They range from −1 to 1, where 1 is perfect equality.

A study of São Paolo, Brazil, finds that the poor experience four times more infant mortality than the nonpoor (Stephens and others 1997). In Buenos Aires, Argentina, a study analyzing the city by neighborhood finds that rates of infant mortality, as well as pre- and postnatal mortality, are highly correlated with an index of unsatisfied basic needs (Arossi 1996). In another study in Buenos Aires, children living on titled parcels of land performed better on the weight-to-height measure and experienced fewer teenage pregnancies than children in the same low-income neighborhood who lived on untitled land (Galiani, Gertler, and Schargrodsky 2005). Health outcomes also vary across cities within the same country, most notably with city size. Evidence from the Dominican Republic, Guatemala, and Haiti suggests that large cities have significantly stronger health indicators than medium cities (Locher 2000). This finding is confirmed by Montgomery and Hewett (2003), who find that larger cities have significantly better height-to-age ratios than medium-size cities. This may be due to the fact that poverty incidence tends to decrease as city size increases (that is, the health advantage may largely reflect the wealth advantage of larger cities).

Causes of Health Outcomes among the Urban Poor

Health outcomes are influenced by a number of factors. On average, the urban population has better access to infrastructure and medical services and more money than the rural population (see chapters 1 and 3). But the urban poor can experience problems with their physical environment that are distinct from and have greater negative health impacts than those faced by their rural counterparts (see chapter 3).

Environmental pollution has been shown to have a significant effect on the health of urban populations. A study on São Paolo, Brazil, finds that an increase in airborne contamination (which is higher in cities) results in increased hospitalization due to respiratory illness and pneumonia (Gouveia and Fletcher 2000). Strong anecdotal evidence suggests that air pollution has a disproportionately large impact on lower income populations in urban areas, but little research has been conducted on the issue. Evidence does suggest that industrial waste disproportionately affects the health of the urban poor (Bazzani 1995).

Data from Cali, Colombia, reveal the relationship between illness on the one hand and income, unemployment, education, and access to basic services on the other (table 5.2). The data neither prove causality nor isolate the influence of each variable, but they do demonstrate a positive correlation between health and factors associated with poverty.

ACCESS TO INFRASTRUCTURE SERVICES
The clear negative health impacts of the lack of access to basic services, and the large difference in access within urban areas, make this factor one of

Table 5.2   Correlation between illness and poverty-related factors in Cali, Colombia, 1999
(percent)

Factor	Income quintile					
	1	2	3	4	5	All
Unemployment rate	35.9	22.4	18.4	11.8	5.8	17.1
Years of education of household head	6.4	6.6	7.3	8.4	10.3	8.0
Toilet in the house	93.9	98.8	98.6	99.6	100	98.2
Water connection	73.3	81.1	84.3	89.6	95.1	84.7
Sick within the past 4 months	28.9	24.3	26.6	21.3	19.3	24.1

Source: Hentschel 2000.

the better researched determinants of urban health. The World Resource Institute decries deficiencies in the physical environment in marginalized urban areas as one of the main causes of death among the urban poor (WRI 1997). UN-HABITAT (2001) finds that high child mortality is directly correlated to low environmental quality (lack of wastewater treatment, sewerage, and sanitation).

Sattherwaite (2003) emphasizes the huge variation in access to services between and within urban areas of Brazil. He examines Puerto Alegre, a city whose government encouraged citizen participation and focused on poverty alleviation. Life expectancy in Porte Alegre was 74 years in 2000, and the infant mortality rate was 20 per 1,000 live births. In contrast, in other urban areas in Brazil, such as Rio de Janeiro, the severe dearth of basic water and sanitation services is associated with a life expectancy of 54 years and an infant mortality rate of 100 per 1,000 live births.

Average access to services is better in urban areas of Brazil than in rural areas. But the extremely large variation in services by income groups in urban areas helps explain why the health indicators of the urban poor of Brazil are as bad as and sometimes worse than those of their rural counterparts (figure 5.4).

Transportation and electricity infrastructure improve health indirectly. Improved public transportation makes access to and staffing of clinics easier. It also reduces carbon dioxide emissions, which affect acute respiratory infections and lead pollution, both of which are particularly harmful to children. Access to electricity reduces indoor air pollution and makes boiling water easier. Access to electricity and transportation can increase study time and improve access to education, improving health (for a review, see Brenneman and Kerf 2002).

Access to water and sanitation is now clearly understood as a precondition to health (WHO/UNICEF 2004). In a review of studies on access to

Figure 5.4   Access to basic services rises with income in Rio de Janeiro, Brazil

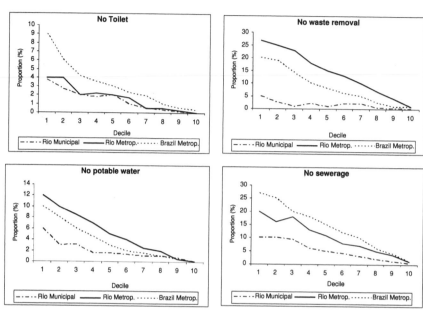

Source: Heutschel 2000.

water and health, Esrey and others (1991) find an average 22 percent reduction in diarrheal morbidity from improved drinking water and sanitation. A study conducted in Argentina used the natural experiment of improved coverage and quality of water services—mainly for the poor—generated by the privatization of several municipal utilities. This improvement led to a drop in child mortality from 9 percent to 5 percent in areas that privatized their water services (Galiani, Gertler, and Schargrodsky 2005). The reduction in child mortality was associated with significant reductions in death from infectious and parasitic diseases and uncorrelated with deaths from causes unrelated to water conditions.

An analysis of the determinants of child health by Leipziger and others (2003) includes variables for water and sanitation, electricity, quality of dwelling, female literacy, malnourishment, variables describing the child's medical attention, and controls for income quintile and country level variables, such as GDP per capita and inequality. Their results show that access to water explains about a quarter of the difference in infant mortality between the poorest and richest quintiles and about 37 percent of the difference in child mortality. They also show that the variation

---

Box 5.1   Improving Hygiene Practices as part of a Water Supply and Sanitation Project in Peru

PRONASAR, a seven-year rural water supply and sanitation project in Peru, is designed to increase the sustainable use of new and rehabilitated water and sanitation facilities in rural areas and small towns, improve hygiene practices, and strengthen training in operation and maintenance. Launched in 2003, the project is funded by the World Bank, the government of Peru, local communities, the Canadian International Development Agency, and local municipalities.

This intersectoral project works closely with the Ministry of Health as a partner in the Handwashing Initiative for Peru. It demonstrates the type of innovative approach that may maximize the health benefits of improved access to basic services. Hygiene education components like the one included in this rural project should be considered as components of all water and sanitation projects in urban areas.

Source: World Bank 2003.

---

in access to sanitation between the first and fifth quintiles accounts for 20 percent of the difference in child malnutrition; the quality of housing accounts for 10 percent of the difference.

Leipziger and others also find that the impact of infrastructure on child health is likely to be higher if combined with health and education interventions. An interaction term between variables for infrastructure and education regressed on health indicators is positive and statistically significant, showing that the impact of infrastructure on health increases with education. In fact, when the interaction term is included, the infrastructure variable ceases to be statistically significant, suggesting that infrastructure alone is not enough. This implies that policy interventions are needed that reinforce the complementary effect of access and education (box 5.1).

EFFECTIVENESS OF AND ACCESS TO HEALTH SERVICES
Health care systems in Latin America have been slow to adapt to the epidemiological transition that is occurring in urban areas (Gribble and Preston 1993). Programs that incorporate elements of a new approach have been cost-effective and successful at improving child health (box 5.2).

Although the urban poor use health services more than the rural poor, they do so much less than the rich (Bitrán, Giedion, Valenzuela, and Monkkonen 2003). In addition, although the evidence is not specific to urban areas, health care systems in Latin America provide an unequal distribution of benefits: the gap between the need for and utilization of services is much larger among the poor (Suárez-Berenguela 2000). Simply

---

Box 5.2 Providing Preventive Health Services in Low-Resource Communities in Brazil

A program in the Brazilian state of Ceará that began in the 1990s presents a model of care for other areas of Latin America that lack resources. The program is based on the new paradigm of prevention and continuity of care. As part of the program, auxiliary health workers, supervised by trained nurses and integrated with teams of physicians, made monthly home visits to families to provide essential health services. This represented a departure from previous approaches, which addressed health problems only when they became urgent. The program improved child health status and vaccinations, prenatal care, and cancer screening. It was inexpensive, as health workers were only paid the minimum wage.

Source: WHO 2002.

---

increasing access to health care services may not increase the utilization of them, since the poor do not take advantage of health services to the same extent as the rich. These results suggest that education programs must accompany increased access to services in order to maximize their benefits.

Conclusions, Research Directions, and Policy Recommendations

This chapter illustrates the importance of the local dimension of public health and shows how averages hide important differences in health within urban areas. In Bolivia, Guatemala, Nicaragua, and Peru, the urban poor perform better on health indicators than the rural poor. But in Brazil, Colombia, and the Dominican Republic, some indicators of health are weaker among the urban poor than among their rural counterparts.

Even in countries that do not exhibit evidence of an urban penalty, the urban poor perform significantly worse than the nonpoor on all health indicators. Although the reasons for this have not been completely accounted for, one of the main causes appears to be the physical environment of the poor—lack of access to basic infrastructure, poor hygienic practices and pollution. Another factor is use of health services: the urban poor access health services much less than the nonpoor (though more than the rural poor). Moreover, health care systems in Latin America and the Caribbean may be focusing on the wrong problems and lack the ability to address urban pathologies.

Research on public health in Latin America and the Caribbean is sparse and scattered, especially with respect to the urban poor (Bitrán, Giedion, Valenzuela, and Monkkonen 2003). In addition, research on specific topics tends to concentrate on one region (urban mental health in Brazil, air pollution problems in Chile, nutrition in Guatemala). While this work reinforces the notion of the heterogeneity of the health sector, it points to the need for more and better integrated research into the public health of the urban poor in Latin America and the Caribbean.

Research directions that warrant pursuing include the following:

- Multidisciplinary research into the factors (access to services, education, personal behavior) that influence health and the interaction between them.
- Analysis of the health effects of specific characteristics of urban areas, such as density, heterogeneity, and spatial segregation.
- Analysis of why some countries exhibit an urban penalty and other countries do not, as well as the policy implications of these differences.
- Deeper analysis of the relationship between city size and health, and the rural-urban continuum.
- Collection of benchmark data on health inequalities within geographic and socioeconomic strata in order to better inform policy.

Despite the need for more research into specific issues surrounding the health of the urban poor, some issues are clear enough to justify policy recommendations. In particular, reducing inequalities in urban health outcomes requires more than just increasing access to health care by the poor. The evidence reviewed in this chapter suggests that urban upgrading projects will have an important effect on public health. It may therefore make sense to include a health education component in such projects. More generally, intersectoral programs that seek to maximize the beneficial effects of nonhealth-specific interventions on health need to be promoted.

A first step for concerned authorities may be to evaluate particular cities' health needs. Some resources are already available to do so. They include the Environmental Health Project's Urban Health Assessment (http://www.eh-project.org/) and the WHO's City Health Profile (http://euro.who.int/document/e59736.pdf). While these resources are not poor specific, they are useful in evaluating the health of a city and provide evidence and credibility for serious efforts to promote health at the local level.

Endnotes

1. The term was coined in nineteenth century England, when urban mortality rates, particularly from tuberculosis, were much higher than rural ones. Public health measures, improved water and sanitation, and socioeconomic change led to declines in infant mortality rates, so that by 1905 rural and urban infant

mortality rates were similar (see http://www.unhabitat.org/programmes/guo/ for more details).

2. For a discussion of urban violence, see chapter 4.

References

Aguilar, R., D. Chacón, and S. Romero. 1998. "Cuentas nacionales en VIH/SIDA: Estimación de flujos de financiamiento y gasto en VIH/SIDA El Salvador." SIDALAC (Iniciativa Regional sobre SIDA para America y el Caribe), Mexico City.

Arrossi, S. 1996. "Inequality and Health in the Metropolitan Area of Buenos Aires." *Environment & Urbanization* 8 (2): 43–70.

Bazzani, Roberto. 1995. "Health and Habitat." International Development Research Center. Ottawa.

Bitrán, Ricardo, Ursula Giedion, Rubi Valenzuela, and Paavo Monkkonen. 2003. *La problemática de salud de las poblaciones urbanas pobres en América Latina.* Washington, DC: World Bank.

Brenneman, Adam, and Michel Kerf. 2002. "Infrastructure and Poverty Linkages, A Literature Review." World Bank, Washington DC.

Cotlear, Daniel, and Evangeline Javier. 1999. "Improving Health Care Financing for the Poor: A Peru Sector Study." World Bank, Washington, DC.

Esrey, S.A., J.B. Potash, L. Roberts, and C. Shiff. 1991. "Effects of Improved Water Supply and Sanitation on Ascariasis, Diarrhoea, Dracunculiasis, Hookworm Infection, Schistosomiasis, and Trachoma." *Bulletin of the World Health Organization* 69 (5): 609–21.

Filmer, Deon, Jeffrey Hammer, and Lant Pritchett. 1997. "Health Policy in Poor Countries: Weak Links in the Chain." Policy Research Working Paper No. 1874, World Bank, Washington, DC.

Flores, W. 2000. "Governance and Health in an Urban Setting: Key Factors and Challenges for Latin American Cities." In *Democratic Governance and Urban Sustainability*, ed. Joseph S. Tulchin, Diana H. Varat, and Blair A. Ruble, 89–96. Washington, DC: Woodrow Wilson International Center for Scholars.

Florez, C.E and T. Tono. 2002. "La equidad en el sector salud: Una mirada de diez años." Working Paper No. 6, CEDE-Universidad de Los Andes/Centro de Gestión Hospitalaria, Ford Foundation/Corona Foundation, Bogota, Colombia.

Galiani, Sebastian, Paul Gertler, and Ernesto Schargrodsky. 2005. "Water for Life: The Impact of the Privatization of Water Services on Child Mortality." *Journal of Political Economy* 113 (1): 83–120.

Galiani, Sebastián, and Ernesto Schargrodsky. 2004. "Effects of Land Titling on Child Health." Latin American Research Network Working Paper No. R-491, Inter-American Development Bank, Washington, DC.

Gouveia, N., and T. Fletcher. 2000. "Respiratory Diseases in Children and Outdoor Air Pollution in São Paulo, Brazil: A Time Series Analysis." *Occupational Environmental Medicine* 57: 477–83.

Gribble, James, and Samuel Preston. 1993. *The Epidemiological Transition: Policy and Planning Implications for Developing Countries*. Washington, DC: National Academies Press.

Hentschel, Jesko. 2000. "Using Rapid City Household Surveys for Municipal Social Policy Making: An Application in Cali, Colombia." Paper presented at World Bank Seminar, Washington, DC, May 2.

Kawachi, Ichiro, and Bruce Kennedy. 1997. "Socio-Economic Determinants of Health: Why Care about Income Inequality?" *British Medical Journal* 314 (April 5) : 917–21.

Leipziger, Danny, Marianne Fay, Quentin Wodon, and Tito Yepes. 2003. "Achieving the Millennium Goals: The Role of Infrastructure." Policy Research Working Paper No. 3163, World Bank, Washington, DC.

Locher, U. 2000. "Are the Rural Poor Better Off than the Urban Poor?" *Labor, Capital, and Society* 33 (1): 107–35.

Mendoza, T. 2000. "Cuentas nacionales en VIH/SIDA: Estimación de flujos de financiamiento y gasto en VIH/SIDA Perú 1999/2000." SIDALAC (Iniciativa Regional sobre SIDA para America y el Caribe), Mexico City.

Montgomery, Mark, and Paul Hewett. 2003. "Looking beneath the Urban Averages: The Effects of Household and Neighborhood Poverty on Health." World Bank, Urban Research Symposium, Washington, DC.

Musgrove, P. 1991. "Feeding Latin America's Children: An Analytical Survey of Food Programs." Latin America and the Caribbean, Technical Department Regional Studies Program No. 11, World Bank,Washington, DC.

O'Donnell, A., and E. Carmuega. 1998. "La transición epidemiológica a la situación nutricional de nuestros niños." *Boletín CESNI* (Centro de Estudios sobre Nutrición Infantil) Vol. 6 (March): . 1^24/.

PAHO (Pan-American Health Organization). http://www.paho.org/english/ad/dpc/nc/nc-unit-page.htm.

Phipps, S. 2003. "The Impact of Poverty on Health: A Scan of Research Literature." Canadian Institute for Health Information, Ottawa.

Pritchett, Lant, and Lawrence Summers. 1996. "Healthier Is Wealthier." *Journal of Human Resources* 31 (4): 841–68.

RCAP (Rural Center for AIDS/STD Prevention). 1997. "RCAP Fact Sheet." www.indiana.edu/~aids/fact/fact10.html.

Ruel, M. T., and P. Menon. 2000. "Towards the Development of a Child Feeding Index: Using the Demographic and Health Surveys from Latin America." International Food Policy Research Institute (IFPRI), Washington, DC, and Division of Nutrition Sciences, Cornell University, Ithaca, NY.

Sattherwaite, David. 2003. "The Links between Poverty and the Environment in Urban Areas of Africa, Asia, and Latin America." *Annals of the American Academy of Politica and Social Science* 590: 73–92.

Suárez–Berenguela, Rubén. 2000. "Health System Inequalities and Inequities in Latin America and the Caribbean: Findings and Policy Implications." Health and Human Development Division, Pan American Health Organization, Washington, DC. Available at http://www.paho.org/English/HDP/HDD/suarez.pdf

Stephens, C., and others. 1997. "Urban Equity and Urban Health: Using Existing Data to Understand Inequalities in Health and Environment in Accra, Ghana, and São Paulo, Brazil." *Environment and Urbanization* 9 (1): 181–202.

Stephen, C., and others. 1994. "Environment and Health in Developing Countries: An Analysis of Intra-Urban Differentials using Existing Data." London School of Hygiene & Tropical Medicine.

Stillwagon, E. 2000. "HIV Transmission in Latin America: Comparison with Africa and Policy Implications." *South African Journal of Economics* 68 (5): 985–1011.

UN-HABITAT Istanbul Declaration +5. 2001. www.unhabitat.org/Istanbul+5/declaration.htm.

WHO (World Health Organization). 2002. *Innovative Care for Chronic Conditions: Building Blocks for Action.* Global Report. Noncommunicable Diseases and Mental Health, Geneva.

———. 2004a. "Why Is Tobacco a Public Health Priority?" Geneva. http://www.who.int/tobacco/health_priority/en/.

———. 2004b. *The World Report on Road Traffic Injury Prevention.* Geneva: WHO.

WHO/UNICEF. 2004. "Meeting the Millennium Development Goals Drinking Water and Sanitation Targets: A Mid-Term Assessment of Progress." New York and Geneva.

World Bank. 2003. "Getting the Best from the Cities." In *World Development Report 2003: Sustainable Development in a Dynamic World: Transforming Institutions, Growth, and Quality of Life,* 107–32. Washington DC: World Bank.

World Resources Institute. 1997. "A Guide to the Global Environment: The Urban Environment." Washington, DC.

———. 1998. "Environmental Change and Human Health." Washington, DC. population.wri.org/pubs_content_text.cfm?ContentID=1366.

6
Relying on Oneself:
Assets of the Poor

Marianne Fay and Caterina Ruggeri Laderchi

To an individual, anything is wealth which, though useless in itself, enables him to claim from others a part of their stock of things useful or pleasant.

John Stuart Mill (1848)

Assets: "Rights or claims related to property, concrete or abstract. These rights or claims are enforced by custom, convention or law."

Michael Sherraden (1992)

Assets are at the core of households' strategies to survive, meet future needs, improve their lot, and reduce exposure to or minimize the consequences of shocks. Many classifications of assets are possible. One commonly used typology divides them into natural assets (such as freely available natural resources); human assets (such as education and skills); financial assets; physical assets (housing, equipment, consumer durables); and social assets (interpersonal ties with individuals and groups that can be called upon to help). The institutional, cultural, and economic context in which a household lives and the types of risks to which it is exposed affect the relative desirability and usefulness of specific types of assets.

This chapter and the following two examine the assets of the urban poor, the characteristics of these assets, and the role they play in the livelihoods of the poor. This chapter focuses on physical and financial assets. Chapter 7 examines social capital, and chapter 8 looks at the role of social safety nets (public programs to help households mitigate risk and the effect of poverty). Human capital, which conditions poor urban households' access to jobs and the quality of the jobs they can access, is

Marianne Fay is a Lead Economist and Caterina Ruggeri Laderchi an Economist at the World Bank. The authors are grateful to Sonia Hammam and Paavo Monkkonen for comments and suggestions.

discussed in chapter 3. Since natural assets are less important in the urban economy than in the rural one—common property resources are rare, and households are integrated into the monetary economy—they are not directly discussed here.[1] Physical and financial assets together constitute material wealth. In economic terms they represent purchasing power stored for future use: by putting money in a savings account, for example, households forgo current consumption, storing their wealth in a form in which they can access it later. This process of transferring purchasing power over time is subject to risks. These include the risk of being unable to sell the asset for its original value (risk of depreciation), the risk that the expected increase in the value of the asset is not realized (uncertain returns), and the risk that the claim to the resources stored in the asset cannot be realized (lack of enforceability). Liquidating an asset usually involves transaction costs, particularly when the market is thin or illiquid.

Despite these possible drawbacks, financial and physical assets represent the first source of security for households in weathering shocks and financing predicted future expenditures related to life-cycle events. The 2001 U.S. Survey of Consumer Finances finds that the two main reasons for savings are for retirement and for liquidity reasons, such as the sudden need for cash or to cope with unemployment or illness. Other types of assets require a more complex process of transformation to yield purchasing power. For example, to draw on human capital, one needs to first find an employer and then to perform the necessary labor. Human capital thus provides less flexibility than other types of capital.

Households also accumulate physical and financial assets (henceforth referred to as "assets" unless otherwise specified) for reasons other than consumption smoothing and security.[2] They save in order to improve consumption over time (through the accrual of capital gains); acquire a higher social status (either by displaying some sign of "wealth" or by contributing to networks of reciprocity); provide resources for one's children; and accumulate in order to finance future entrepreneurial activities or the future purchase of costly items. As poor households are likely to be constrained in their access to credit for either business or consumption, this last motive can play an important role in their accumulation strategies.

This chapter examines how the poor accumulate assets and the use they make of them. It then reviews the types of assets available to the urban poor and analyzes whether these are in fact good assets. The third section addresses the three key policy questions: how to increase the ability of the poor to save; how to improve the quality of the assets they hold, in terms of liquidity, riskiness, and rate of return; and how to broaden the range of assets available to them.

Good Times and Bad: How the Urban Poor Accumulate and Use Assets

The bulk of the literature on the savings and coping behavior of the poor is based on rural studies. Little research has been conducted specifically on the saving behavior of the urban poor and on the type of assets they accumulate. This is all the more unfortunate given that saving patterns and instruments of the urban poor are likely to differ from those of the rural poor, for a variety of reasons:

- The high (if not total) integration of the urban poor into the market economy is likely to result in accumulation patterns in which financial assets are a priority. The availability of cash can limit access to key resources (such as food or health care). In urban areas it plays a primary role in dealing with shocks. In contrast, in rural settings there is greater reliance on natural resources and in some cases traditional institutions (such as healers) as service providers.
- The causes of vulnerability are different in urban and rural settings, requiring different types of assets and coping strategies. The urban poor are more affected by what Glewwe and Hall (1998) call "market-induced vulnerability" rather than weather variability. This tends to result in idiosyncratic shocks (such as a household member losing her job) rather than covariant shocks (such as a large set of households suffering because of a bad crop). Poor urban households seem to engage in risk management strategies based on diversifying income sources.
- The savings instruments of the poor face different challenges in urban and rural areas. Informal arrangements (either savings or insurance based), for example, are less susceptible to covariant risk, due to the diversification of activities in urban areas, but they face greater problems in terms of enforcement, due to the higher mobility of individuals (Morduch 1999).

Acquiring Assets: The Savings of the Poor

The poor clearly save—how else would they cope with the occasional need for lump sums of money? Indeed, savings are likely to represent the most important way in which poor people today can accumulate assets (other ways of accumulating assets include inheritance, marriage, or redistribution by some third party, generally the state).

The difficulty comes in measuring their savings, since the poor are usually excluded from formal financial markets. As a result, they save by accumulating anything from consumption goods (such as food) to semidurables (such as clothing) to durable goods (such as furniture, equipment, and housing), as well as cash or contributions to informal institutions or networks of reciprocal obligations.[3] It is therefore difficult to identify how and whether poor people are saving, given that the assets they hold have both consumption and investment value (box 6.1). More generally, the measurement of savings through household survey data is complicated and plagued by concerns over measurement error (McKay 2000).[4]

There is little quantitative evidence on the savings of the poor in Latin America and the Caribbean, and what there is may not capture the complex means by which the poor save. Szekely (1998) suggests that the bottom 30 percent of Mexicans are unable to save at all. This notion is hard to reconcile with the fact that homeownership among poor Mexican households is more than 65 percent (World Bank 2005).

Both demand and supply factors affect the extent to which poor people can save. On the demand side, scarce resources and the need to satisfy immediate survival needs limit the extent of savings. Poor households, however, function in a highly volatile environment, which is likely to provide a strong incentive for saving to build up buffers against consumption shocks (Morduch 1999). This motivation is all the more powerful if access to credit and insurance markets is limited or costly. Furthermore, poor people's reported risk aversion, arising from the potentially disastrous consequences of not being able to face adverse

---

Box 6.1 How the Poor Save and Draw on Their Assets: Illustrations from *The Children of Sánchez*

The Children of Sánchez, by Oscar Lewis, is an account of the life of a poor family in Mexico City. Although the book, a classic of anthropology, was published in 1961, excerpts from it sound remarkably contemporary:

"I spent the whole night in a sea of confusion and tears, wondering how to get the money. I would sell or pawn my clothes or borrow from a loan shark no matter how high the interest was."

—Consuelo

"I hated to sell the watch, because it was only one week old. The week before I had received 400 pesos from a *tanda* [rotating savings pool] I had joined with other neighbors, and I used the money to buy myself a watch and a jacket.

To get off to a good start...Baltasar offered to pawn his new radio and pay five months rent in advance, so that we would have a place to live.

We did not have a single *centavo* in the house, and Baltasar had no money to work with, so we sold the pig my father had given us, before it was fully grown."

—Marta

shocks when living conditions are already so precarious, should provide a further incentive to save.

The evidence on this issue is conflicting. A few studies (see Lawrance 1991 and literature quoted therein) have sought to test differences between rich and poor in terms of their "time preference" (interpreted as the willingness to forgo current consumption in favor of future consumption). They find that all else equal, poor people are less "patient" than the rich and therefore less willing to forgo consumption and save. This conclusion may be due to the fact that these studies do not disentangle poor people's preferences from all the other factors that may distinguish them from the nonpoor, notably the immediacy of their needs.

On the supply side, institutional features, such as the lack of good savings instruments and the costs associated with the available ones, constrain poor people's ability to save. In the United States it has been estimated that the difference in asset accumulation by rich and poor can be ascribed largely to differences in the ability to accumulate assets rather than to different ways of responding to incentives (Ziliak 1999). The importance of supply constraints for savings is supported by the microcredit literature highlighting poor people's ability to save when appropriate tools are provided (Johnson and Rogaly 1997). Furthermore, some of the informal institutions that poor people rely on can actually prevent accumulation: reciprocity networks can prevent enhancement of one's economic position because of network members' claims to the resources generated by "successful" members (Rosenzweig 2001).[5]

Bad Times or Opportunities: Drawing on Household Assets in Times of Need

Much can be learned about the role of assets in poor people's livelihoods by considering how they are used. The (rural-based) literature on responses to famine highlights two important ways in which households behave when they need liquidity or have to cope with adversity.

- *Tradeoffs*. Households trade off short- and long-term objectives when choosing which asset to draw on, as well as when choosing asset depletion over other coping strategies (for example, taking a child out of school to work). This is particularly evident when productive assets are involved and choices have to be made between changing consumption patterns and depleting the asset stock.
- *Sequencing*. Assets differ in terms of their liquidity, "lumpiness," and risk (Devereux 1993), as well as in the perceived irreversibility of their sale and its consequences for a household's future income streams.

Households, therefore, do not draw on their assets randomly but rather sequence their responses based on their overall portfolio of assets and their characteristics (such as the type of productive activity they engage in and the other coping strategies they have adopted).

Poor households in Argentina and Uruguay adopted a variety of asset-based strategies in response to the economic crisis in 2002 (box 6.2). In Argentina changes in consumption patterns appear much more frequently than any of the asset-based strategies (90 percent of households in the first quintile decreased food consumption, with 98 percent of them buying cheaper food products). In Uruguay having lived off savings in the past increased the chances of relying on selling, mortgaging, or pawning assets.

The fact that households make rational decisions in choosing a coping strategy, however, does not mean that these strategies are necessarily optimal (Morduch 1999; Skoufias 2003). They may jeopardize earning prospects or have deleterious consequences on certain household members (by reducing learning as a result of decreasing spending on learning inputs, for example). Policy interventions may be needed to provide households with alternative assets or coping strategies (as discussed in the last section of this chapter). Such interventions may be all the more necessary as households may be accumulating assets whose value and returns are vulnerable to the effects of the crisis, so that their effective possibilities of coping are curtailed.

Bicycles, Houses, and Cash: The Assets of the Urban Poor

Households' well-being and security ultimately depend on the combination of assets in their portfolios. Unfortunately, the portfolio held by the poor may be suboptimal, because poor people need to limit income risks and smooth consumption and they lack access to appropriate savings instruments or credit and insurance markets (Rosenzweig 2001). Thus a household may forgo acquiring an asset with secure returns if such an item could be difficult to liquidate in case of need. The returns to an asset depend on the complementarity with other assets held (for example, between human capital and access to credit) as well as the complementarity between the private and public assets available (for example, tools and electricity). In Peru, Escobal, Saavedra, and Torero (1999) find that the cross-elasticities between one additional year of education and access to land are positive and progressive (that is, higher for the poor than for the rich).

The implication, then, is that the characteristics of a good asset depend on the particular needs of a household, the context facing it, and the available

Box 6.2 Drawing on Assets Following the 2002 Economic Crisis in Argentina and Uruguay

Following the economic crisis in 2002, households in Argentina and Uruguay were asked about the coping strategies they adopted. The results of the specialized surveys are summarized below.

Argentina

- The crisis resulted in a significant increase in the use of asset-based coping strategies: the percentage of households selling or pawning belongings rose by a factor of four (to 2.8 percent). Alternatives included informal borrowing from family or friends (11 percent of households); relying on store credit (7 percent); drawing on savings (5 percent of households, representing 12 percent of those who reported having savings); and borrowing from banks (2 percent).
- The use of coping strategies varied by income level. Among those in the bottom quintile, 6 percent sold assets (1 percent in the top quintile), 3 percent drew on their savings (8 percent in the fourth quintile), and 15 percent relied on store credit (1 percent in the top quintile). Interestingly the second quintile relied most heavily on borrowing from banks (3.6 percent), while just 2.0 percent of the top quintile borrowed.
- Multivariate analysis shows that households whose members lost a job had a 40 percent higher probability of liquidating their assets by selling or pawning and were 3.4 times more likely to draw on savings. In contrast, households that reported a generic loss of income but not a job loss following the crisis were 2.6 times as likely to sell or pawn assets and 16 percent more likely to draw on savings. These differences may be due to the different expectations about future income flows by people who experienced different types of income shocks.

Uruguay

- Some 68 percent of households reported to be relying on at least one strategy based on financial or physical assets (drawing on savings or selling, mortgaging, or pawning goods), and 53 percent of those who did cited living expenses as the reason for doing so. Taking informal loans and monetizing the value of assets were the two most important "new" strategies that people adopted after the crisis.
- Multivariate analysis shows that rich people were more likely to draw on savings and credit, while people in the bottom three quintiles of the wealth distribution were more likely to sell, mortgage, or pawn assets.
- Households appear to be sequencing their responses. All else being equal, those who experienced negative income shocks were more likely to draw on savings. Households experiencing an emergency, particularly a severe emergency, that was more serious than they were used to relied on monetizing the value of their physical assets. Having lived off savings in the past increased the chances of relying on selling, mortgaging, or pawning assets.

Sources: Fiszbein, Giovagnoli, and Adúriz 2002; Fiszbein, Giovagnoli, and Thurston 2003; Ruggeri Laderchi 2003.

portfolio choice. In addition, there are some "absolute" characteristics that make an asset more or less desirable.

For assets to perform their primary function as a store of value, they should provide adequate returns, or at the very least, not depreciate. Inflation presents the greatest threat of depreciation for financial savings. For physical assets, such risks depend on the depth and volatility of the secondary market in which the asset can be liquidated. In the case of a large covariant shock, if many affected households sell their belongings in a shallow market, prices fall significantly. Financial savings, therefore, represent a better asset than physical assets, provided there is macroeconomic stability and a reliable banking system.

Poor households facing a limited choice of savings instruments are often willing to hold assets even when their returns are low (as, for example, in the case of rotating savings schemes). Valuation of an asset also needs to take into account its nonmonetary returns, whether in kind (for example, the use value of housing or appliances), in status within the community, or in inclusion in some reciprocity network. Risk aversion may also play a role in poor households' holding of low-risk, low-return assets.

For poor people who have limited access to formal financial savings and credit instruments, another important role of assets is to help them manage small balances and deal with cash flow problems. Good assets for the poor allow for high-frequency operations of limited size and for flexibility. Examples of assets that offer the possibility of high-frequency operations are rotating savings pools, such as Mexico's *tandas*, to which 20 percent of urban Mexican households belong. In order to be appropriate for frequent small-scale operations, good assets should involve moderate transaction costs. This can represent a barrier to the expansion of formal financial services to the poor, as instruments devised for larger operations, such as creditworthiness assessments, may involve lengthy and expensive administrative procedures. To avoid these costs, microcredit programs rely on alternative ways to assess whether they can trust their clients, such as group responsibility.

Consumer Durables

Durables (furniture, consumer appliances, bicycles) play an important role in the asset portfolios of the urban poor, because they offer the opportunity to invest relatively small amounts and can be easily pawned or resold. Uruguayan households' responses to crises suggest that poor households are more likely than richer ones to sell home furnishings but less likely to sell more expensive durables, such as cars. Where labor is cheap, the life of durables can often be extended with small improvements and repair. The stream of consumption benefits and the option of selling the asset can therefore be extended almost indefinitely. Extending the life of semidurable goods (such as clothes or dishes) offers an opportunity for households to resort to an "internal capital market" (Browning and Crossley 1999).

Housing

Housing is likely to be the most valuable single possession that poor urban households have. In addition to providing shelter, it also plays a more standard role as an asset, one whose main modality of acquisition for the urban poor (progressive housing, discussed in chapter 3) offers the opportunity for small incremental investments. Evidence from specialized surveys on risk management in Chile and Peru finds that investment in housing and other residential property acts as a substitute for formal retirement systems (Gill, Packard, and Yermo 2004). Indeed, as discussed in chapter 3, most landlords tend to be small scale and substantially older than their tenants or other homeowners.

But is housing such a great asset to hold? Being a homeowner does have a variety of advantages. It provides a constant flow of services, and it frees low-income households, who typically improve their houses gradually based on the cash on hand and generally "own" their home outright, with no debt and mortgage, from the constraint of having to generate a fixed sum for rent every month. This can be important, especially at times of crisis. For example, in Uruguay 10 percent of renters declared that they had to move following the crisis in order to cut down on housing costs, and 4 percent of households (7 percent in the bottom quintile) declared they had to merge with other households rather than just rent a cheaper home. Furthermore, housing services can be monetized quite easily, by taking renters or additional household members in.

Being a homeowner may also have some downsides, particularly in the presence of thin or poorly developed resale or rental markets. Home ownership can tie the poor to undesirable locations—locations that are unsafe because of crime and violence or the risk of natural disasters, locations that are removed from the main labor market centers, or locations that may carry stigma, making job search more difficult.[6] It is unclear how liquid or buoyant housing markets are, particularly in poor neighborhoods. Work on the *favelas* of Rio shows the picture to be complex. In some *favelas*, rental and sales prices are higher than in parts of Copacabana or Botafogo (middle-class neighborhoods). In others, residents complain about the stigma associated with their neighborhood, which makes it difficult to get a job ("If you interview for a job, and they see your address, they say the job has been filled"), or the exploding crime and violence, which make it difficult to sell their homes (Perlman 2003).

There is a debate in Europe and the United States as to whether homeownership limits labor mobility and therefore contributes to a high equilibrium unemployment rate. One argument is that homeownership makes it expensive to move (Oswald 1996,) and is therefore correlated with higher unemployment, at least for middle-age households (Green and Hendershott 2001). Most studies, however, find either no relationship between homeownership and unemployment (Robson 2003 for the United Kingdom; Flatau, Forbes, and Hendershott 2003 for Australia) or that homeowners actually fare better than renters in the labor market (Coulson and Fisher 2002 for the United States; Van Leuvensteijn and Koning 2004 for the Netherlands; Munch, Rosholm, and Svarer 2003 for Denmark). One explanation is that even if homeownership reduces labor mobility, individuals may accept lower reservation wages in order not to have to move (see Munch, Rosholm, and Svarer 2003 for a review of the literature).

Labor mobility is much more likely to be affected by the buoyancy and dynamism of the housing market. In fact, there is evidence that regions with relatively high housing prices exhibit lower unemployment (Robson 2003). In addition, while the incidence of private rental shows no relation with unemployment, public (social) rental and rent control tend to be associated with higher unemployment (Robson 2003; Munch, Rosholm and Svarer 2003). Thus the issue is clearly not simply one of owning or renting one's home.

There is very little research on the liquidity or buoyancy of low-income housing markets in developed or developing countries. The only source of systematic analysis is from the United States, where recent work has sought to determine whether housing is a good asset for low-income families (box 6.3). Some of the limited data and research in the developing country context are reviewed here.

HOUSING EXCHANGE VALUE

Little information is available on the secondary housing market in poor neighborhoods. The presumption is that the market is not very developed, given poor households' preference for progressive housing. The limited research available suggests that low-income settlements tend to be dominated by a land market rather than a housing one, as low-income households prefer to acquire land for self-help housing rather than finished housing (Gough 1998). The research also shows that about half of households that do acquire finished housing in low-income neighborhoods previously built a home themselves, having originally entered the housing market through self-help construction.

Box 6.3 Low-Income Homeownership: Examining the Unexamined Goal

Homeownership is a valued and promoted goal of the U.S. government, which has aggressively developed policies to make it an attainable goal for all, including poor households and minorities. Access to credit is generally no longer a binding constraint; keeping up mortgage payments and finding inexpensive homes to buy are now the key issues for poor households. Until recently, no research had documented whether homeownership is in fact good for low-income buyers, for their communities, or indeed for the country. A large research project funded by a number of housing-related organizations has attempted to shed light on the issue.

Building Families' Financial Capital

Behind the push for homeownership for the poor is the notion that it is a good asset-building strategy for them. Because the poor seldom hold any kind of financial wealth and are much less likely to have pensions, the question of whether they manage to build housing wealth through homeownership is an important one. The answer in the United States is yes, in most cases. Although housing prices do fluctuate, most lower income owners benefited from housing price appreciation and actually fared better than those who bought higher priced homes. Homeownership also constitutes enforced savings. And despite the fact that the housing market has historically earned lower returns than the stock market, and an even poorer risk-adjusted return, low-income households receive a host of financial benefits from owning—most of all the promise of fixing the housing cost, so that it does not rise with inflation or population pressure. Finally, in the United States, where mortgages are available with very low down payments, low-income borrowers are able to risk relatively little money on a home today in pursuit of potentially high leveraged returns later. This option is not available to poor people investing in financial instruments.

Building Families' Social Capital

Advocates firmly believe that homeownership makes families happier and more stable and children more successful at school. Yet is that stability desirable? Is a renting family better able to move to find better jobs or schools? Research finds that children in owner-occupied homes do better in school, but this could be because of a self-selection factor: parents are more concerned and therefore seek a home in a safer neighborhood with better schools. Similarly, while there is evidence that homeownership provides people with a greater sense of control over their lives, spurs them to greater civic participation, and helps their children do better, it is also true that delinquencies and default—something the poor are at risk of—have the opposite effect. Overall, however, the answer to whether homeownership is a positive thing for families seems to be a tentative yes, if only because children of homeowners have a much higher propensity to become homeowners themselves later on.

(box continues on the following page)

Box 6.3 (*continued*)

Contributing to Community Capital

Mayors and city councilors generally exhibit blind faith that homeownership will resurrect neighborhoods in decline, although there are few studies of the issue. Recent seminal work does show a demonstrable positive impact. But homeownership alone is no panacea. Renovation and rehabilitation of housing, combined with promotion of homeownership, can be potent forces.

In sum, it appears that the popular dream of owning a home is probably a rational aspiration for low-income families and that the renewed efforts in the United States to bring low-income homeownership rates closer to that of better-off families should continue.

Source: Adapted from Retsinas and Belsky 2002.

The relative importance of the land and housing market may be linked to the age of a settlement (Gough 1998). Turnover is quite high in recently occupied settlements (especially invasions), where residents attempt to cash in on the value of the land by selling the rudimentary shelters they have built to establish their claim. Subsequently, little exchange of houses takes place for decades, because even in later stages of consolidation, most newcomers acquire land rather than finished housing (Datta and Jones 2001; Gough 1998). One of the very few studies of the low-income housing markets, conducted in Pereira, a medium-size city in Colombia, finds that only about a quarter of households in poor neighborhoods had bought their house (peaking at 59 percent in areas settled through invasion). In addition, 87 percent of homeowners had performed major renovations or extensions on the purchased property, suggesting that they had not purchased finished housing (Gough 1998).

The limited evidence available is not very conclusive, although it does suggest that the low-income housing market is not very liquid. In the Pereira study, for example, selling a home was difficult. In addition, that study and others suggest that few households actually want to sell: the hardships suffered during acquisition and consolidation result in a strong attachment to the property (Gough 1998; Datta and Jones 2001).

Nevertheless, a survey of Mexican *barrios* indicates that a good share of new arrivals and recent movers purchase used housing: more than a quarter of households that had migrated in the past five years and owned the home they live in lived in a house that predated their arrival. Even more encouraging, three-quarters of the home-owning households that had moved the previous year moved to a preexisting home (Ruggeri Laderchi 2003). However, given the small number of households that migrated or changed homes recently, these figures cover no more than about 3.5 percent of all owner-occupied homes in poor neighborhoods.

The development of secondary markets for low-income housing is likely to be affected by limitations on new constructions and illegal settlements. Such limitations work against new arrivals and in favor of older settlers. Other factors are the availability of housing finance and possibly the strengths of property rights, discussed below.

Most housing finance systems in Latin America and the Caribbean work against the development of a secondary market for low-income housing, because they generally do not serve the poor; where they do, they tend to explicitly exclude financing for "used housing." One of the key aspects of the more promising low-income housing finance schemes, such as those in Chile and Costa Rica (discussed in chapter 3), is to allow for purchases of used housing.

Security of tenure increases the exchange value of a house in several ways. First, recognized property rights contribute to creating a market. The data from Mexico's *barrios* show that the share of households that own a house built before their arrival is higher in older settlements, where supposedly more mature institutional arrangements prevail and property rights, formal and informal, are better established. Second, there is a presumption that prospective buyers would be willing to pay a premium in order to purchase property whose ownership is clearly established. Evidence from many surveys supports this claim. Following the massive titling campaign that occurred in Peru between 1996 and 2001, 64 percent of newly titled homeowners considered that the title increased the value of their home, and three-quarters believed that the title increased ownership security (Mosqueira 2003).

Security of tenure also has additional indirect effects on the value of a home, through "neighborhood quality." Titles often make it easier to access utilities—in some countries, such as Mexico, utilities, road, and transport services cannot be provided until a settlement's status is legalized—so that as communities become legalized they tend to benefit from more public services. Hoy and Jimenez (1996) provide evidence from squatter communities in Indonesia where increased titling led to increased availability of local public goods. This, combined with the fact that secure homeownership often translates into more investment in homes, results in a price differential between nonsquatting and squatting sectors of cities.

The advantages conferred by formal tenure vary, however. Recent analysis has identified a number of factors other than formal titling that contribute to tenure security, including age of the settlement, existence of public services, and presence of community leaders (Lanjouw and Levy 2002). This work, conducted in Guayaquil, Ecuador, finds that the age of the community, the presence of a community organizer, and a formal title substitute for each other as sources of transferable claims to sell or rent property. Thus the value of a title is lower in older, more established, and better organized communities. Household characteristics seem to matter too, since having a title is associated with larger gains in expected sale prices for female-headed households, who presumably may be less able to enforce their claim to a house.

OTHER RETURNS TO HOUSING
The returns to housing as an asset include the flow of housing services it provides, some of which can be monetized in case of need by taking in tenants or extended household members who share in the upkeep of the household. Indeed, as discussed in chapter 3, the bulk of landlords in Latin America and the Caribbean are homeowners who let out rooms or parts of their house (Rakodi 1995). While surveys and interviews with these small-scale landlords suggest that this is not a very profitable way of investing their resources, renting is perceived as offering a number of benefits (box 6.4).

Returns to housing also include better access to credit by providing collateral, although this is generally dependent on having formal tenure. In Peru access to formal credit increased from 7 percent to 42 percent among beneficiary households, while recourse to informal credit decreased from 31 percent to 9 percent following the titling campaign (Mosqueira 2003).

Formal tenure can also affect the returns of the overall portfolio of resources by freeing up labor otherwise engaged in protecting insecure property rights and allowing home businesses to move into more appropriate locations. In Peru formal titling increased labor force participation, due to

---

Box 6.4 How Profitable Is Small-Scale Landlordism?

Surveys and interviews with small-scale landlords in Guadalajara and Puebla, Mexico, reveal that they believe renting is not a very profitable activity but that it offers a number of advantages. Renting out a room or a floor of their house generates resources for housing improvements. It also provides temporary income in times of need and makes use of accommodations built to one day house a child's or relative's family. A number of landlords indicated that rental accommodations could provide a modest income during their old age. Many seemed to admit that beyond investing in bricks and mortar they did not know what to do with their limited savings. Small-scale landlords are thus motivated by a mixture of factors related to family, old age, and the lack of perceived alternatives.

Source: Gilbert and Varley 1991.

the reduced need for constant presence in the house (to demonstrate ownership) and the time required to pursue formalization. The result was a substantial increase in family income, as well as a significant decline in child labor, for which adult labor was substituted (Field 2002; Mosqueira 2003).

Finally, homeownership in the United States has been shown to be associated with higher social capital and better educational outcomes for children, possibly due to greater social capital and stability (see box 6.3). Whether such findings are applicable to poor neighborhoods in developing countries is unclear.

Financial Assets

Financial exclusion and the reliance on informal financial tools and physical assets are likely to result in portfolios whose return and liquidity characteristics do not compare favorably to those of the better-off. Matin, Hume, and Rutherford (1999) argue that improved access to financial services induces the following changes in the composition of a household's assets and liabilities:

- A decline in the holding of assets with lower risk-adjusted returns.
- A shift away from assets held for precautionary savings toward assets held for speculative purposes.
- A decline in the level of credit obtained at high cost (usually from informal sources).
- A decline in the frequency and amount of asset sales at low price.

When looking at financial services for the poor, savings, credit, and insurance need to be considered as a continuum. Lacking access to insurance, the poor typically rely instead on a combination of savings and credit as alternatives. As a result, the main motivation in using financial services tends to be risk management rather than the expected return of the financial service; the "protective role" dominates over the "promotional role" (Matin, Hume, and Rutherford 1999). This is likely to be equally true of the rural and urban poor.

The vast majority of households in Latin America and the Caribbean have no access to formal financial services, either savings or credit. This is certainly the case in rural areas, but even in cities access to financial services is limited: 80 percent of households in metropolitan Mexico City and 60 percent in urban Brazil are "financially excluded" (World Bank 2003a, 2003b). In contrast, only about 13 percent of families in the United States and 7 percent in the United Kingdom have no bank account.

Financial exclusion is a phenomenon that primarily, although not exclusively, affects the poor. In urban Brazil only 15 percent of the population in the lowest decile have bank accounts, while about 80 percent of the top decile do. In Mexico City the situation is even worse: only about 6 percent of the bottom half of the income distribution have access to formal financial services, while 34 percent of the upper half do. The poor account for about 16 percent of the population with bank accounts, suggesting that being poor does not preclude interest in banking services or make it necessarily unaffordable.

Lacking a bank account has costs. It makes it more expensive to engage in many transactions, such as paying or being paid.[7] Most important for the topic at hand, it makes it more difficult to save while maintaining the value of an asset. As a result, a relatively small proportion of people without bank accounts hold financial savings (28 percent in urban Mexico) (World Bank 2003a).These financial savings are held in a variety of ways: cash under the mattress, loans to relatives or friends, and informal savings institutions. Cash under the mattress loses value with inflation, and it is vulnerable to theft. In a survey of access to banking services in Brazil, two-thirds of respondents identified security as the main reason for wanting a bank account (World Bank 2003a). Little information is available about informal loans to relative or friends; it is unclear whether interest is charged or repayment is timely. As to informal savings institutions, their attractiveness in terms of products offered varies (box 6.5).

The microfinance "revolution" has increased access to loans for small businesses and, to a lesser extent, low-income households. Microfinance expansion is occurring along four different paths: servicing of "downscale" customers by commercial banks; licensing of nonbank financial intermediaries, including transformed microcredit NGOs and specially licensed microfinance institutions; start-up commercial microfinance institutions; and alliances between commercial banks and nonbank financial intermediaries, through agents or on-lending relationships.

These approaches have resulted in more efficient and broader outreach and the development of products better suited to small-scale borrowers. Lending to households by microfinance institutions is now showing more dynamic growth than microenterprise credit. Further progress can certainly be made; the reach of microfinance varies substantially across countries, and more can surely be done to further increase access to credit for the poor in a way that neither puts the poor in an unreasonable level of indebtedness nor threatens the creditworthiness of the lenders (CGAP 2001). Overall, it is clear that there is now a model that works and can be further rolled out.

Similar progress has not been made in increasing the poor's access to saving instruments. Such access is probably even more important than access to credit, particularly for the poorest.[8] For people living in urban

---

Box 6.5 Informal Savings Institutions in Mexico: *Tandas,* *Clubes,* and *Cajas de Ahorros*

Tandas are rotating savings pools that operate as both loans and savings instruments. A *tanda* might work as follows: a group of 20 people agree to contribute Mex$200 a week to a common pool for 20 weeks. Each week the proceeds are given to one member of the pool (who does not contribute that week). *Tanda* members who receive funds early effectively receive a loan that they pay off in equal monthly installments until the end of the cycle. Those who receive money at the end of the cycle effectively save with each pool contribution until the final withdrawal.

Anecdotal evidence suggests that *tandas* are usually made up of 5–20 "partners," each contributing Mex$10–Mex$20 on a weekly or biweekly basis. The prevalence of *tandas* in low-income communities shows that the poor have both the capacity and the willingness to use financial services, even with small amounts.

The *tanda* is critical to many poor Mexicans. In their own words:

"My *tanda* is sacred. I cannot fail to make a payment because it hurts the others."

"I participate only if I know I can fulfill my obligation. I'd rather not eat than fail to make a payment."

"My savings are small, but drop by drop they make a puddle. In the bank they want us to save large quantities and they ask for a lot of papers. I prefer my *tanda*."

Clubes are similar to *tandas* but are managed by stores. A group of individuals makes regular and equal payments to the store in return for an article for sale. The articles may vary from person to person, but the amounts paid are usually the same. *Clubes* select the weekly or biweekly winner in different ways, but most involve a social meeting and a game of chance, such as a door prize or bingo.

Cajas de ahorros include 15–50 members associated by a common place of work or through a church. Unlike a *tanda*, a *caja* usually requires a full year's commitment, after which members can withdraw their accumulated savings with interest, depending on the *caja*'s earnings throughout the year. *Cajas* also make loans to members and nonmembers (when recommended by a member).

Source: World Bank 2003b.

---

slums, it is very difficult to protect savings from theft, inflation, or the demands of everyday living. Because the poor tend to hold their financial savings in cash or in informal arrangements, they tend to be less protected than the rich against macroeconomic instability. Uruguay offers a case in point: 53 percent of those in the top wealth quintile but just 36 percent of those in the bottom decile declared not to have been affected by the 2002 financial crisis (Ruggeri Laderchi 2003). Most surveys show that a savings account is the product people without bank accounts are most interested in (after payment services) (World Bank 2003a, 2003b).

More, Broader, and Better: How to Improve the Poor's Asset Base

Increasing savings is hard for poor households, given scarce resources, the demands of everyday living, vulnerability to shocks, and the lack of good instruments. The pattern of accumulation is often suboptimal, because the poor are excluded from credit and insurance markets and because available savings instruments do not meet their needs. Given these mismatches and market failures, policies to strengthen and expand poor urban households' asset bases can play an important role. The key issues are how to increase household savings; how to broaden the range of assets accessible to the poor, particularly savings instruments; and how to make housing a better asset, since regardless of alternatives, housing remains the largest store of value held by all but the richest households.

More: How to Increase the Urban Poor's Asset Base

In general, it may be difficult to devise targeted policies to increase the savings of specific groups (Banks, Smith, and Wakefield 2002). In the case of the urban poor, however, policy changes could relax some constraints.

Increasing household resources is a first obvious way in which a household's ability to save could be increased. Policies of this type also help reduce the inherent tension between households' long- and short-term (survival) needs.[9] A wide variety of policies can be classified under this heading. Conditional cash transfers, such as Mexico's Oportunidades, discussed in chapter 7, in which poor households receive monthly cash allocations in exchange for continuous school and preventive health clinic attendance, increase income while promoting positive behavior. Creating employment and increasing access to education and training, providing security of tenure for housing, and providing basic services and infrastructures are other examples of policies that raise the returns to households' assets, either directly or by freeing household resources for other uses. For example, the provision of water or secure property rights allows household members to find more productive uses for their time. Indeed, recent work by Calderón and Servén (2004) shows that improved access to infrastructure, particularly water and sanitation, reduces income inequality.

Decreasing households' vulnerability to risk and protecting assets at times of crisis can also help increase savings by providing greater incentives for households to save in different assets than they would otherwise. As part of their risk management strategy, households save in relatively liquid items, which tend to be low risk and low return. Additional instruments, such as insurance mechanisms (including catastrophic insurance for the poor, discussed in chapter 3) or public schemes (including workfare and noncontributory pension schemes, reviewed in chapter 7), could provide households with incentives to create more efficient portfolios. Efforts currently under way to develop microinsurance programs could also improve the risk management options available to the poor (http://www.microinsurancecentre.org).

Better: The Housing Issue

Housing tends to be the most valuable asset held by the poor, and it is likely to remain so even if the poor are provided with good alternative savings instruments. Even in developed countries, such as Belgium and the United Kingdom, the only form in which the poor hold wealth is home ownership (Van den Bosch 1998). Thus improving the assets held by the poor will necessarily entail making the low-income housing market more liquid. Policy options for doing so include housing finance schemes for the poor that allow a secondary market to develop (such as the schemes in Chile and Costa Rica), titling, slum upgrading, and better provision of services (see chapter 3). Improving services, including transportation links in poor neighborhoods, will typically translate into both an increase in property values and easier resale. Reducing crime and violence in poor neighborhoods can help a secondary market develop.[10]

Broader: Increasing Access to Financial Services

How can policy makers broaden the range of assets that the poor can access? Savings, access to credit, and insurance mechanisms form a continuum in helping the poor cope with risk and vulnerability. Access to credit has increased significantly thanks to the "microfinance revolution," but more can be done. And much more needs to be done to increase access to good savings instruments and insurance, which lag behind credit.

A full discussion of the policy reforms that can help promote more access to banking services by the poor is beyond the scope of this chapter (for a discussion in the context of Latin America and the Caribbean, see World Bank 2003a, 2003b). Briefly, some of the approaches that have been advocated for the formal banking sector include the following:

- Reduce the cost of banking products. This can be done by encouraging banks to offer "lifeline" accounts with low or no minimum balance requirement and no option for overdrawing the account; promote competition and the use of new technology (personal digital assistants, smart cards, and handheld computers) by banks to reduce transaction costs.
- Reduce the remoteness of banks from the poor, by setting up automatic teller machines in vans and supermarkets, for example, and creating a less formal atmosphere in banks targeting poorer clients.
- Reduce the lack of familiarity between poor households and banks, by creating financial literacy programs, publishing information on the profitability of reaching down, and encouraging large employers to pay their employees through electronic transfers rather than checks.

The reach of microcredit could be increased by adopting best practice approaches (see, for example, www.cgap.org). Given their proximity and cost structure, microfinance institutions are better placed than formal banks to offer savings services to the poor. The poor save, but they do so in small, uneven increments. A savings instrument that fits their needs is one that allows frequent deposits with low transaction costs. This requires physical proximity and accounts that do not require high minimum balances. In addition, the microfinance institutions would benefit from the additional sources of funding that savings deposits would create. Unfortunately, microfinance institutions in most countries are either prohibited by law from offering savings accounts or are limited by high levels of minimum capital required to accept deposits. Countries in which the sector is sufficiently mature should contemplate letting microfinance institutions accept deposits. Doing so may require modifying the regulatory structure.

In sum, the urban poor do accumulate assets, but they are constrained in their choices—because of their lack of resources, their risk aversion, and the lack of savings and insurance instruments adapted to their needs. As a result, they probably overinvest in housing and durable goods and underinvest in financial assets. Policy measures to make housing a more liquid asset and increase access to financial services are therefore essential to help the urban poor cope with poverty and vulnerability.

Notes

1. There is nevertheless evidence of the importance of urban and peri-urban agriculture in providing access to food and incomes for the poor (Bakker 2000), pointing to the importance of access to land for more than housing purposes.

2. Matin, Hume, and Rutherford (1999) suggest three main motivations: life-cycle needs, such as burial, childbirth, education, and old age; emergencies, including personal emergencies, such as sickness or injury, death of a breadwinner, loss of employment, theft, and impersonal emergencies, such as war, floods,

and fires; and opportunities to invest in a business or acquire a plot of land on which to buy a house. See also Browning and Lusardi (1996) on the motivations for saving.

3. As Matin, Hume, and Rutherford (1999) put it, the poor have three common methods for accessing the lump sums they need: selling assets they already hold (or expect to hold), taking a loan by mortgaging or pawning those assets, and turning their many small savings into large lump sums, through savings deposits, loans, or insurance.

4. Kochar (2000) notes the difficulty of obtaining accurate measures of the income of the self-employed, of the consumption of self-produced goods, and of the market value of inputs that are not perfectly marketable.

5. Interestingly, rotating saving associations are seen by some as ways of avoiding more traditional networks and the social obligations they entail. See chapter 8 for a discussion of these issues.

6. A comment by a resident of a Rio slum is telling: "The violence is so bad here that no one will deliver anything to my house. They are afraid of being robbed" (Perlman 2003).

7. A survey of Mexico City finds that 88 percent of people without bank accounts are paid by check. While it is not clear how much banks charge to cash checks, there is a cost, if only in terms of having to go to a bank or check cashing service (World Bank 2003b).

8. There is general agreement among donor institutions and microcredit agencies that microcredit is not necessarily the most appropriate instrument to reach the very poor. See Dugger (2004) for a discussion of the debate on the issue.

9. This tension can often have a gender or intrahousehold allocation dimension. For example, assets can be accumulated while the needs of some household members go unmet.

10. For a discussion of community-based and municipal strategies to cope with crime and violence, see chapter 5 and Van Bronkhorst (2003).

References

Bakker, Nico, ed. 2000. *Growing Cities, Growing Food: Urban Agriculture and the Policy Agenda*. Feldafing: German Foundation for International Development.

Banks, James, Zoë Smith, and Matt Wakefield. 2002. "The Distribution of Financial Wealth in the UK: Evidence from 2000 BHPS Data." Working Paper W02/21, Institute of Fiscal Studies, London.

Browning, Martin, and T. Crossley. 1999. "Shocks, Stocks, and Socks: Consumption Smoothing and the Replacement of Durables During an Unemployment Spell." Canadian International Labour Network. Hamilton, Ontario.

Browning, Martin, and A. Lusardi. 1996. "Household Saving: Micro Theory and Micro Facts." *Journal of Economic Literature* 34(4):1797–1855.

Calderón, Cesar, and Luis Servén. 2004. "The Effects of Infrastructure Development on Growth and Income Distribution." World Bank, Washington, DC.

Cannari, L., F. Nucci, and P. Sesito. 2000. "Geographic Labour Mobility and the Cost of Housing: Evidence from Italy." *Applied Economics* 32(14):1899–1906.

CGAP (Consultative Group to Assess the Poorest). 2001. "Commercialisation and Mission Drift: The Transformation of Microfinance in Latin America." Occasional Paper No. 5. Washington, DC. www.cgap.org.

Coulson, N. Edward, and Lynn M. Fisher. 2002. "Tenure Choice and Labour Market Outcomes." *Housing Studies* 17(1):35–49.

Datta, Kavita, and Gareth A. Jones. 2001. "Housing and Finance in Developing Coutnries: Invisible Issues on Research and Policy Agendas." *Habitat International* 25(3):337–57.

Devereux, Stephen. 1993. "Goats before Ploughs: Dilemmas of Household Response Sequencing During Food Shortages."*IDS Bulletin* 24(4):52.

Dugger, Celia. 2004. "Debate Stirs over Tiny Loans for World's Poorest." *New York Times*. April 29.

Escobal, Javier, J. Saavedra, and M. Torero. 1999. "Los activos de los pobres en el Perú." Inter-American Development Bank, Washington, DC.

Field, Erica. 2002. "Entitled to Work: Urban Property Rights and Labor Supply in Peru." Department of Economics, Princeton University, Princeton, NJ.

Fiszbein, Ariel, P.I. Giovagnoli, and I. Adúriz. 2002. "Argentina's Crisis and Its Impact on Household Welfare." Working Paper No. 1/02, World Bank, Washington, DC.

Fiszbein, Ariel, P. Giovagnoli, and N. Thurston. 2003. "Household Behavior in the Presence of Economic Crisis: Evidence from Argentina, 2002." World Bank, Washington, DC.

Flatau, Paul, Matt Forbes, and Patrick H. Hendershott. 2003. "Homeownership and Unemployment: The Roles of Leverage and Public Housing." NBER Working Paper No. w10021, National Bureau of Economic Research, New York.

Gilbert, Alan, and Ann Varley. 1991. *Landlord and Tenant: Housing the Poor in Urban Mexico*. London: Routledge.

Gill, Indermit S., Truman Packard, and Juan Yermo. 2004. *Keeping the Promise of Old Age Income Security in Latin America: A Regional Study of Social Security Reforms*. World Bank, Washington, DC. wbln0018.worldbank.org/LAC/LAC.nsf/PrintView/146EBBA3371508E785256CBB005C29B4.

Glewwe, Paul, and Gillette Hall. 1998. "Are Some Groups More Vulnerable to Macroeconomic Shocks than Others? Hypothesis Tests Based on Panel Data from Peru." *Journal of Development Economic (Netherlands)* 56(1):181–206.

Gough, Katherine. 1998. "House for Sale? The Self-Help Housing Market in Pereira, Colombia." *Housing Studies* 13(2):149–60.

Green, R.K., and P.H Hendershott. 2001. "Home Ownership and Unemployment in the U.S." *Urban Studies* 38(9):1509–20.

Hoy, Michael, and Emmanuel Jimenez. 1996. "The Impact on the Urban Environment of Incomplete Property Rights." World Bank, Washington, DC.

Johnson, Susan, and Ben Rogaly. 1997. *Microfinance and Poverty Reduction*. Oxford: OXFAM.

Lanjouw, Jean O., and Philip I. Levy. 2002. "Untitled: A Study of Formal and Informal Property Rights in Urban Ecuador." *Economic Journal* 112 (482):986–1019.

Lawrance, Emily C. 1991. "Poverty and the Rate of Time Preference: Evidence from Panel Data." *Journal of Political Economy* 99(1):54–77. Lewis, Oscar. 1961. *The Children of Sánchez*. New York: Penguin Books.

Matin, Imran, David Hume, and Stuart Rutherford. 1999. "Financial Services for the Poor and Poorest: Deepening Understanding to Improve Provision." Finance and Development Working Paper No. 9, Institute for Development Policy and Management, University of Manchester, United Kingdom.

McKay, Andrew. 2000. "Should the Survey Aim to Measure Total Income?" In *Designing Household Survey Questionnaires for Developing Countries: Lessons from 15 Years of the Living Standards Measurement Study*, ed. Margaret Grosh and Paul Glewwe, 83–104. Washington, DC: World Bank.

Mill, J.S. 1848. *Principles of Political Economy: With Some of Their Applications to Social Philosophy.* New York: Collier & Son.

Morduch, Jonathan. 1999. "Between the State and the Market: Can Informal Insurance Patch the Safety Net?" *World Bank Research Observer* 14(2):187–207.

Mosqueira, Edgardo. 2003. Presentation made at conference in Mexico City, May.

Munch, J.R., M. Rosholm and M. Svarer. 2003. "Rent Control and Unemployment Duration." Working Paper, Department of Economics, University of Aarhus, Denmark.

Oswald, Andrew. 1996. "A Conjecture on the Explanation for High Unemployment in the Industrialized Nations: Part 1." *Warwick Economic Research Papers 475.* Department of Economics, University of Warwick, Coventry, United Kingdom.

Perlman, Janice. 2003. "Marginality: From Myth to Reality in the *Favelas* of Rio de Janeiro, 1969–2002." In *Urban Informality: Transnational Perspectives from the Middle East, Latin America, and South Asia*, ed. Ananya Roy, 105–46. Lanham, MD: Lexington Books.

Rakodi, Carole. 1995. "Rental Tenure in the Cities of Developing Countries." *Urban Studies* 32(4–5):791–812.

Retsinas, Nicolas P., and E.S. Belsky. 2002. "Examining the Unexamined Goal." In *Low Income Homeownership: Examining the Unexamined Goal*, ed. N.P. Retsinas and E.S. Belsky, 1–12. Washington, DC: Brookings Institution Press.

Robson, Martin T. 2003. "Housing Markets and Regional Unemployment Flows in Great Britain." *Manchester School* 71(2):132–55.

Rosenzweig, Mark R. 2001. "Savings Behaviour in Low-Income Countries." *Oxford Review of Economic Policy* 17(1):40–54.

Ruggeri Laderchi, Caterina. 2003. "Drawing on Financial and Physical Assets after a Crisis: The Case of Uruguay." World Bank, Washington, DC.

Szekely, Miguel. 1998. *The Economics of Poverty, Inequality, and Wealth Accumulation in Mexico.* New York: St. Martin's Press.

Skoufias, Emmanuel. 2003. "Economic Crises and Natural Disasters: Coping Strategies and Policy Implications." *World Development* 31(7):1087–1102.

Van Bronkhorst, Bernice. 2003. *A Resource Guide for Municipalities: Community-Based Crime and Violence Prevention in Latin America.* World Bank, Washington, DC.

Van den Bosch, Karel. 1998. "Poverty and Assets in Belgium." *Review of Income and Wealth* 44(2):215–27.

Van Leuvensteijn, Michiel, and Pierre Koning. 2004. "The Effect of Home Ownership in Labor Mobility on the Netherlands." *Journal of Urban Economics* 55(3): 580–96.

World Bank. 2003a. "Brazil: Access to Financial Services." Report No. 27773-BR. Washington, DC.

————. 2003b. "Broadening Access to Financial Services among the Urban Popu-
lation: Mexico City's Unbanked." Washington, DC.
World Bank. 2005. "Urban Poverty in Mexico." Washington, DC.
Ziliak, James P. 1999. "Income Transfers and Assets of the Poor." Discussion Paper
No. 1202-99, Institute for Research on Poverty, University of Oregon. www.
ssc.wisc.edu/irp/.

7

Calling on Friends and Relatives: Social Capital

Michael Woolcock

The urban poor in Latin America, like their counterparts elsewhere in the developing world, rely heavily on their friends and relatives to help them both "get by" and "get ahead."[1] Faced with institutions, policies, and services that are frequently hostile, inadequate, or indifferent to their concerns, the urban poor have little choice but to valiantly deploy a range of coping strategies, chief among them the use of their social networks, to provide everything from credit and physical security to information about housing and employment opportunities (Thomas 1995).

The norms and networks upholding these support mechanisms are often referred to as *social capital*, to distinguish them from other forms of capital, such as technology, material assets, and education (World Bank 2000). These other forms of capital are, almost by definition, in short supply in poor communities. In contrast, certain forms of social capital, such as kinship and intracommunity ties (popularly referred to as *bonding social capital*), may be in abundance. Other important forms of social capital, such as ties spanning spatial and demographic divides (*bridging social capital*) and power differentials (*linking social capital*), may be lacking.

From a social capital perspective, the challenge for those seeking to identify appropriate policy or project interventions is to maintain the integrity, strengths, and identities of poor communities while enhancing their capacity to engage a more socially, politically, and economically diverse range of actors and institutions. There are no universal prescriptions for achieving this, but three considerations are paramount. The first is to understand how different relational configurations (that is, social relations within and between different groups) both influence and are influenced by the local context in which poor communities reside. The second is to discern how best to articulate the resources of external actors with these relational configurations in poor communities in ways that are consistent with the communities' interests and aspirations. This is especially critical for delivering services that inherently require ongoing face-to-face relations between clients and providers, such as teaching and curative health care (see World Bank 2003b and Pritchett and Woolcock 2004). The third consideration is to recognize that success or failure will likely change the nature of those configurations, necessitating the cultivation from the outset of dynamic feedback and accountability mechanisms.

This chapter addresses three interrelated themes. The first section articulates a conceptual framework for thinking about social capital and urban poverty reduction in Latin America that builds on the distinguishing features of risk experienced by the urban (as opposed to the rural) poor. The second section explores how poor urban communities in Latin America and in Latin American immigrant communities in the United States have mobilized different forms of social capital in response to these risks. It reviews the policy and programmatic interventions that have been implemented. The third section considers a broader array of policy initiatives that stem from social capital theory and their application to poverty reduction initiatives in Latin American cities. These initiatives—such as slum upgrading programs—center on mobilizing community support, expanding economic opportunities, and improving relationships of accountability between citizens and the state. The last section concludes.

Social Capital and Urban Poverty in Latin America: A Conceptual Framework

Social capital has simultaneously become one of the most popular and one of the most contested concepts in contemporary social science in general and in development studies in particular (Bebbington and others 2004). Usually defined as the networks and norms facilitating collective action and access to resources (Woolcock and Narayan 2000), social capital draws on a wide range of theoretical traditions and has been applied to a wide range of analyses. In the process, it has generated a literature that critics (and even some erstwhile supporters) find confused and confusing. Before proceeding, it is therefore worth charting a clear path through this literature, in order to provide a useful and coherent framework within which to analyze how social capital (properly understood) shapes survival and mobility strategies in the cities of Latin America.

Defining and Clarifying Social Capital

Where some (for example, Fukuyama 1995) have portrayed social capital as a feature or property of entire countries or cultures (a view that is popular in Latin America), the emerging consensus in the literature is that both theory and evidence more strongly support understanding social capital as a "micro" phenomenon (that is, one that describes the nature and extent of relationships between individuals and groups). Having taken that step, a number of important issues arise that need to be addressed. First, it is crucial to recognize that the poor are often forced by necessity to use their social resources, because of hostility, indifference, or lack of accessibility on the part of formal institutions (both public and private) and because there are so few safe and stable employment opportunities available to them to sustain a viable livelihood. Prevailing social relationships do not exist in a political and economic vacuum.

Second, social relations can be a part of both the problem of and the solution to poverty. Just as a hammer can be used to build a house or vandalize it (and is no less a form of capital because it can yield both positive and negative outcomes), social relations can both constrain and liberate. Moreover, it is in and through people's immediate social networks that their identities, expectations, and self-worth are nurtured and sustained. These networks thus have a powerful influence on the type, range, and quality of information people receive and the options and opportunities to which they are exposed. In poor, violent communities, the often restricted but powerful networks characterizing or presiding over the lives of its members may reinforce destructive behavior (Fernandez-Kelly 1995), perpetuate distrust, or limit their "capacity to aspire" (Appadurai 2004). Not all social groups are working in society's best interests, and many of the world's most unsavory activities are planned, financed, and executed by members of (clandestine) networks. All that is "social" is not always "good."[2]

Third, important methodological implications stem from how one conceptualizes social capital. Even if we adopt a more micro focus, the question remains as to whether social capital is primarily an individual resource (levels of which may, like the unemployment rate, be able to be aggregated to larger units of analysis) or a group or community resource (that is, an ecological resource). The evidence from the public health literature shows clearly that it is both: individuals make explicit efforts to nurture and extend their networks, in the process generating unambiguously positive effects on their physical and mental well-being. By the same token, even the most isolated individuals are better off if they happen to live in communities with high levels of trust and participation (Klinenberg 2002).

Even if one accepts this evidence, the question remains as to how best to incorporate larger structural (or macro) dimensions. Some researchers (especially in Latin America) eschew the problem altogether by simply equating social capital with "institutional quality," "good governance," and "generalized trust." But this perpetuates the unhelpful notion that social capital is anything and everything (and hence nothing). A neater and ultimately more useful solution is to maintain a more restricted microdefinitional focus while embedding the story one tells about the form and function of networks within a larger framework of state and private sector institutions. This approach is adopted here.

Understanding how social capital "works" in poor urban communities in Latin America is thus not merely a matter of measuring rates of participation in soccer clubs or toting up civic membership lists or asking people whom they "trust," though these things have their place. It is about understanding how, within a particular historical, cultural, and political-economic context, the social networks and norms of poor communities are shaped and deployed as part of a broader portfolio of risk management strategies for facilitating survival and mobility in environments in which those risks are high, numerous, and often difficult to anticipate. Such an approach recognizes that the same networks and norms can be used to perpetuate fear, isolation, and elite domination. It also acknowledges that this approach has a rich historical foundation in a range of studies from a variety of disciplines that do not employ the social capital terminology per se but are nonetheless the richer for being able to integrate these different perspectives across time and discipline (see, for example, Roberts 1973; Perlman 1976). From a policy standpoint, the overriding task in seeking to understand these portfolios of risk management is to better identify ways and means by which external agents of various kinds can work with governments, firms, and the poor themselves to craft more informed, politically supportable, and administratively implementable solutions.

What Is Different about Risks and Networks in Poor Urban Communities?

Policy makers and practitioners are increasingly recognizing that social networks represent a key risk management strategy of the poor.[3] This recognition is based in part on a large empirical literature showing that households often devise various cooperative strategies to deal with poverty and uncertainty (Besley 1995), that they form networks and develop various other strategies to pool risk, and that access to informal sources of credit can play a crucial role in income smoothing during times of crisis (see, for example, Udry 1994 and Morduch 1999). In societies with limited assets, social collateral and reputation play a crucial role in determining access to credit (Coate and Ravallion 1993). Households devise various strategies of collaborating with other households, both within and outside the family, to pool risk (Rosenzweig and Stark 1989).

This literature is based largely on studies of rural households in developing countries (and, to a lesser extent, on urban households in developed countries). Do the survival and mobility strategies employed by the urban poor in developing countries differ from those of their counterparts in rural areas and the inner cities of developed countries? If they do, should policy makers and practitioners be concerned?

A fruitful point of departure is to consider the types of risks the urban poor face. Instead of risks associated with crop failure and often nonexistent public services, the urban poor are much more likely to suffer from the following types of risk:

- Poorly defined property rights, resulting in housing demolition and re-settlement.[4]
- Higher susceptibility to contagious and waterborne diseases, which are a product of unsanitary, high-density living conditions.
- Exposure to organized crime, drugs, and gang violence.[5]
- Unemployment, underemployment, and unsafe working conditions.
- Overwhelmed (as opposed to absent) public services.
- The adverse effects of regional and national macroeconomic shocks.

The use of networks to respond to these risks tends to be very different in poor urban communities in developing countries. To look at these issues, it is useful to take a step back and think about what we mean by a "network" and what roles we might expect it to fulfill.

One way to think about a network is as a series of communication links within a group of people (see, for instance, Chwe 2000). In this sense, a network is a method of disseminating information among a group of individuals. Once such a network has been formed, it may perform one or more functions. A network can be purely informational; it can be used to provide goods, such as credit or housing; or it can be used to provide services, such as security and child care. The outcomes that a network produces depend both on the nature of the communication links and the functions that the network was designed to serve. Considerable work by sociologists during the past decade has shown that outcomes that emerge as a result of network communication depend both on the number and the nature of linkages among the members of the network (Chwe 2000; McAdam 1986; McAdam and Paulson 1993).

A priori one would expect networks in urban areas to differ from those in rural villages in terms of their size, diversity, and primary functional role, for several reasons. First, urban regions (especially those in which the poor reside) tend to have much higher population densities than their rural counterparts. One consequence of this high density is that even if services are provided equally to urban and rural regions—so that, for instance, the number of doctors per capita is the same in an urban slum and a village—the number of choices that a person in an urban area faces is much higher than their rural equivalent. As a result, the informational requirements of making an appropriate choice (conditional on options) are much higher in urban areas. This magnifies the importance of a network as a means of disseminating information.

The outcomes that networks produce can be very different for urban areas. In rural areas, characterized by smaller bonding social capital networks, people tend to interact with those who have largely similar knowledge pools to draw on. Considerable effort thus has to be made to find and engage people with nonredundant information. In cities the costs of doing so are much lower, but the corresponding challenge is that competing for (often very) finite resources means that there are strong pressures to secure access to a diverse, information-rich network. Recent arrivals to the city from rural areas, for example, draw on previous cohorts of emigrants from their village to help find initial housing and employment, but they need to gain access to different and more diverse networks to secure better housing, better employment, and formal markers of citizenship (such as ration cards and property titles) (see Jha, Rao, and Woolcock, forthcoming).

Networks in urban regions tend to be less stable than those in rural communities (largely due to the fluidity of urban populations), which may change the ways in which they operate. Ethnographic research in a Jakarta slum notes that the structure of social networks may move away from kinship ties to those based on friendship and individual relations (Jellenik 1991).[6] Urban slum living is very dense, with multiple families often living in the same house. This density tends to move social relationships away from the traditional forms that characterize village networks. Marriages are much less stable, and both women and men are more likely to engage in serial monogamy. As a result, they have several circles of relatives. Relationships are forged more on the basis of the quality of reciprocal links between individuals and friends than on familial obligations. This is precisely the finding that Roberts (1973) reports for Guatemala City, where 58 percent of couples reported not marrying (even though their Catholic beliefs strongly encouraged it), because in a highly uncertain world, the costs of permanent attachment to someone who may turn out to be unreliable or irresponsible were simply too high. Eames and Goode (1973) draw a similar conclusion in their review of studies of urban poverty in Central America and the Caribbean.[7]

How Can Recognizing the Social Capital of the Urban Poor Help Craft More Effective Policy?

Much of the empirical foundation for the framework outlined above is informed by an extensive literature on how social capital in different Latin American communities shapes the direction and size of migration flows to the United States. This section considers these studies before exploring in more detail how the framework can be usefully applied to understanding contemporary responses to urban poverty in Latin America. It then shows how the lessons from both can be integrated to make recommendations for future policy initiatives.

Social Networks within Latin American Emigrant Communities

Migration is a prime risk management strategy, undertaken to diversify and increase household income streams. The success of migrant entrepreneurs from different ethnic groups in the United States constitutes the largest body of research on the urban poor in developed countries. This work focuses on the important policy question of international migration, investigating not just its demographic features (number of migrants, their skill levels, age distribution, and country of origin) but the explicit role that social networks play in shaping where migrants go, how they initially procure resources to establish housing and employment (often small businesses or farm labor), and whether and how they seek to become assimilated into their new country.[8]

Consider, for example, the case of Mexicans in San Diego and Haitians in Miami. Both groups display low levels of internal cohesiveness, despite sizable ethnic communities that could potentially offer them considerable economic resources and social opportunities. As Portes (1995, p. 264) puts it,

> neither community possesses a well-developed ethnic economy that can generate autonomous opportunities for its members. Both communities have large numbers of transient and recent arrivals and individuals without legal status...[T]he institutional development of [these] ethnic communities has been hampered by its recency, the tenuous legal status of much of its population, and widespread discrimination from outsiders.

Without a strong community group to provide initial financial resources, small businesses fail to get started or quickly go bankrupt. With "too much" freedom and "not enough" community, immigrants begin to display a short-term commitment to their host country, establishing a cycle that undermines their sense of ethnic identity and commitment to its institutions (Roberts 1995). Classic signs of alienation and indifference emerge, and the end result is, not surprisingly, modest economic performance.

It is not necessarily the case that short-term commitments to the host country result in weaker network ties. Recent work by Munshi (2003) suggests that despite the widespread prevalence of recurrent migration, Mexican immigrants maintain a dense network based on *paisanaje* (belonging to a community of common origin) that benefits incoming migrants in a number of ways. Munshi examines the impact of network status on migration and employment opportunities of Mexican immigrants in the United States using data from the Mexican Migration Project. He finds that migrants with a "better" (that is, larger and older) network are more likely to find jobs as well as financial support and housing assistance. Munshi's results suggest that the impact of these networks is large: shutting down the networks would increase unemployment from 4 percent to 11 percent and decrease nonagricultural employment by almost 25 percent (from 51 to 28 percent).

Other immigrant groups, such as the Koreans in Los Angeles (Light, Kwoun, and Zhong 1990) and the Chinese in San Francisco (Light and Karageorgis 1994), have been able to call upon and develop both cohesive internal ties and more extensive networks into the mainstream economy. Excluded from mainstream financial and civic institutions, recent arrivals move into co-ethnic enclaves (such as Chinatown), in which a range of indigenous social institutions exist for meeting basic credit and security requirements. But these resources often come at a price: longer term members of such communities have on occasion had to resort to such drastic measures as anglicizing their names in order to avoid having their modest but diligently acquired assets siphoned off by subsequent cohorts of co-ethnic immigrants (Portes and Sensenbrenner 1993).[9] Thus not only do "the same social relations that...enhance the ease and efficiency of economic exchange among community members implicitly restrict outsiders," as Waldinger points out (cited in Portes and Landolt 1996, p. 19),[10] they also explicitly restrict insiders.[11] Those who are able to forge new social ties into the wider business community, however, even in less dramatic circumstances, enjoy greater economic success. This also suggests that the need for and obligations toward group members in poor communities changes as one's economic status increases.[12] Paradoxically, then, the more successful the indigenous social institutions are in providing their members with financial and other resources, the less necessary those institutions become.[13] The regularity with which large new cohorts of low-skilled immigrants arrive, however, and their immediate need for security, housing, employment, and financial support ensures that these social institutions endure.

Granovetter (1995, p. 137) captures the essence of these dilemmas of development in his review of the ethnic entrepreneurship literature in anthropology and economic history, observing that

> individuals and groups attempting to assemble firms may face on the one hand the problem of insufficient solidarity among themselves, which produces a failure of trust, and on the other hand the problem of uncontrolled solidarity, which produces excessive noneconomic claims

on an enterprise. Under what conditions can these mirror-image problems be overcome?

Citing the example of rotating savings and credit associations (RoSCAs), Granovetter proposes a social mechanism he calls "coupling and decoupling." In this mechanism, members of economic groups draw initially on the resources of family and peers but then attempt to forge broader and more autonomous ties beyond the group as their need for larger markets and more sophisticated inputs expands.

A parallel strand of research has looked at the social structures of persistently poor urban communities and the survival strategies of the homeless. Extending the classic work of Wilson (1987, 1996), Sampson and his colleagues emphasize the role of an urban community's "collective efficacy"—its capacity to work together to address joint problems—in responding to crime, juvenile delinquency, and other social ills (Raudenbush, Sampson, and Earls 1997; Sampson, Morenoff, and Earls 1999).[14] Here again the story centers on the importance of integrated social networks and kinship systems. On the one hand, these networks and kinship systems help young people engage in pro-social behaviors, such as staying in school and resisting the temptations of drugs and gang membership. On the other hand, however, because the poor are spatially, economically, and politically isolated, these networks and systems deprive them of access to key decision makers and information about job and other opportunities. Even the most destitute of the urban poor, the homeless, have "something left to lose," namely, the close social relations they have with other homeless people, which are a crucial source of moral and material support (Dordick 1997).[15]

In short, for development to proceed in poor urban communities, the initial benefits of intensive intracommunity ties (bonding social capital) must be complemented over time by more extensive extracommunity linkages to markets and (crucially) polities (bridging and linking social capital).[16] This gradual shift in the strength, form, and direction of social ties as economic exchange becomes more complex is a highly problematic and conflict-ridden transition (Woolcock and Narayan 2000). It has tremendous importance for understanding the prospects for medium-term economic growth and governance in poor communities, especially those in which poverty alleviation strategies centering on the formation of small groups, such as microfinance, agricultural, and environmental management programs (Radoki and Jones 2002), are becoming increasingly popular.

The insights derived from the classical social theorists and contemporary studies of urban poverty and ethnic entrepreneurship suggest that a key survival and mobility strategy in poor communities entails managing the tension between the claims of kinship and locality with economic imperatives to build a more diverse "portfolio" of social and political assets. In the face of broad technological, corporate, and political forces conspiring to marginalize and isolate them, the poor need to forge and maintain linkages that transcend their communities. Doing so will enable them to resist the economic and noneconomic claims of community members when those claims undermine (or threaten to undermine) the group's economic viability and expansion. It will facilitate entry into more diverse markets and allow the poor to initiate and sustain formal political processes, especially by individuals with superior ability and ambition. Once they organize as a political force for recognition and change, their aspirations and interests are more likely to be taken seriously by those in positions of power.

A corresponding policy implication is that in successful community-level development programs, linkages to outside institutions need to be forged incrementally. A community's stock of social networks in the form of internal ties can be the basis for launching development initiatives, but it must be complemented over time by the construction of new networks, that is, connections to "outsiders" in possession of nonredundant information and resources, especially as they pertain to labor markets, factor and product markets, and public services. The construction of these networks is the task of both broad public policies that expand economic opportunities and access to services for poor people (that is, making "top-down" institutions more pro-poor) and specific programs that support front-line field workers as they seek to engage poor communities, building relationships with them that can become the basis for enhancing their confidence and organizational competence (that is, making "bottom-up" initiatives more empowering). Coordination and integration between both domains is crucial: on their own "bottom-up" initiatives are likely to be implemented piecemeal (and hence inefficiently) rather than as part of a coherent long-term regional or national strategy, while "top-down" approaches alone are unlikely to reflect the priorities of the poor or to secure the necessary mix of incentives, legitimacy, and sense of ownership required to implement and maintain service delivery mechanisms in a sustainable manner.

"Participatory" policy and project responses to urban poverty in Latin America (and elsewhere) should be seen as part of, not a substitute for, a coherent development strategy. Top-down coordination and resources need to be complemented by bottom-up information flows and accountability mechanisms. Policy makers should be wary of expecting successful participatory (and other) development projects in one setting to automatically achieve comparable results elsewhere; project success in any given environment is heavily dependent on the quality of context-specific social relationships forged between clients and providers. An innovative urban development project in Bolivia bears out these lessons (box 7.1).

Box 7.1 Participatory Budgeting in Bolivia: Getting Top-Down and Bottom-Up Right

The passage of the People's Participation Law in Bolivia in 1994—a national initiative that established 250 new municipalities in rural and urban areas across the country—had a dramatic effect on the form and management of service delivery budgets. Previously, the entire budget had been controlled at the national level. Under the new law, 20 percent was now devolved to the new municipalities (according to their population share) and within them to legally recognized area-based community organizations. These organizations assumed responsibility for priority setting and local oversight, and they contributed some of their own resources as part of the preparation of annual and five-year investment plans.

Unlike its counterpart in Brazil, the Bolivian model of participatory budgeting is a national program that determines the amount to be allocated to each municipality. By ensuring continuity, coherence, predictability, and cross-regional equity, the program is less prone to the idiosyncrasies of local political whims. It establishes incentives that encourage communities to take a strategic and long-run approach to managing their affairs rather than one that has to continually optimize in the short run. While program performance has been uneven across Bolivia—with local factors shaping the degree and form of uptake—in general the impact has been positive. Integrating top-down institutional mechanisms and bottom-up organizational structures has been key to both making the Bolivian municipal participatory planning process work and to understanding subregional variations in performance.

In the quest to scale-up and expand, the development community should not focus exclusively on the highest profile cases of participatory budgeting (such as the Brazilian city of Porto Alegre; see Santos 1998). It should also be wary of taking the Bolivian example at face value. The strengths and weaknesses of both—indeed, virtually all—projects are specific combinations of components that are technocratic (professional skills), bureaucratic (standardized procedures), and idiosyncratic (context-specific knowledge).

While every effort should be made to learn from successful and unsuccessful projects elsewhere, in the end the viability of new initiatives will turn on their capacity to craft their own appropriate mix of these elements and, perhaps most important, to set up effective feedback mechanisms that enable them to learn from themselves as their efforts unfold.

Sources: Imparato and Ruster 2003; Pritchett and Woolcock 2004.

Urban Poverty, Social Capital, and Policy Responses in Latin American Cities

A distinctive feature of urban poverty in developing countries is the nature and extent of risks experienced by the poor and the different types of social networks that can be called upon to address those risks. In rich and

poor countries alike, it is largely the capacity to manage transitions between the claims of "survival" networks and entry into different and
more diffuse types of "mobility" networks that determines their long-
term welfare. Especially important are networks providing access to improved housing, employment, and public services, by securing various
forms of "citizenship" and becoming active participants in formal political structures. The goal of policy and project interventions should be to
work directly with the poor to help them more smoothly and rapidly
manage these transitions, all the while remaining conscious of the broader
political and economic factors (such as the availability of basic employment
opportunities) that make particular risk management and transition
strategies more or less necessary (Sojo 2003).

Improved public service provision can play a central role in facilitating
this process (World Bank 2003b). Implicitly or explicitly, it is this general
understanding of the dynamics of social capital that has informed several
recent policy initiatives in response to urban poverty in Latin America.
Successful slum-upgrading projects from around Latin America provide
ample evidence of the importance of combining public service delivery
reform with initiatives to enhance the collective capacity of the poor by
expanding their networks and political participation. In a well-integrated
environment, reforms to the legal code and to service delivery mechanisms
provide the framework within which community organizations operate.
At best, these organizations serve to put pressure for reform on policy
makers and service providers and to hold them accountable for their
actions (see Imparato and Ruster 2003; World Bank 2003b) (box 7.2).

Implications for Future Policy Considerations

The central message of this chapter is the importance to policy makers
and practitioners of recognizing both how dynamic the prevailing risk
management strategies of the poor are and how limiting their networks
can be. Different types of social networks are at the core of their strategies.
Policy and project responses need to be designed so that they complement
their strengths and provide a point of articulation for more formal services
providers. The networks of the poor cannot be understood in isolation,
and they cannot be the sole focus of attention: their capacity to function
effectively is greatly enhanced by policies and institutions that expand
employment opportunities and provide good-quality services.

There is another sense in which social capital matters for poverty reduction in urban communities. Beyond understanding the social foundations of the survival and mobility strategies of the poor, social capital theory
also points to the importance of social relationships more generally. In

---

Box 7.2 The Astonishing Success of Villa El Salvador in Lima, Peru

Villa El Salvador (VES) in Lima, Peru, was constructed in 1971 in response to that city's massive population growth.[a] Founded to accommodate 4,000 families occupying land on the southern outskirts of Lima, VES was the initiative of a grassroots campaign to respond to a housing crisis. The project came to fruition through the joint efforts of grassroots organizers and representatives of the government's social development agency. From modest beginnings, in which initial residents were simply given plots of land, VES grew within the first year to a population of 70,000. Through active dialogue with the government, roads, electricity, and schools were soon provided, enabling economic opportunities in the form of small businesses and the construction of an industrial district to be started and sustained.

Though similar to other *barriadas* (informal settlements) in Lima, VES is distinctive in a number of important respects. First, from the outset it forged strong ties with the state that not only ensured political support but, crucially, gave residents the knowledge and confidence to engage the state. Second, the area was designed to function as an urban public space, not a "slum," and was able to do so because of direct community input into the design process. Third, as the need to expand VES and address ongoing development concerns emerged, strong ties between residents, NGOs, firms, and the state enabled the area development plan to be adhered to. Today, VES is a bustling city, with a population of 350,000; though it remains a low-income community, most of its members have secure property title and access to basic services.

a. This and other case study material on slum upgrading in Latin America and the Caribbean is drawn from Imparato and Ruster (2003).

---

matters pertaining to the provision of public services, certain services—or at least certain key aspects of a given service, most notably education and health care—can be delivered only through ongoing social relationships (Pritchett and Woolcock 2004).

As a host of World Bank (2003b) and other studies have shown, the well-being of the poor turns crucially on their access to public services. As such, the nature of the social relationship—between teachers and students, between health care providers and clients, between community and slum leaders and municipality representatives, between police and citizens—is central to determining whether and how services are delivered. Where and when this relationship breaks down—when mothers have to bribe doctors for medicines, when teachers fail to show up for work, when the police are part of criminal networks—the solution lies not in simply procuring more resources or upgrading training programs, though these may be useful, but in repairing, building, and sustaining a mutually respectful social relationship. Teaching, curative care, and social work simply cannot be provided except through such relationships.

Efforts to respond to youth unemployment and urban crime in Jamaica, Guatemala, and Colombia have adopted such an approach. In Kingston a range of civic groups (many headed by women whose sons, brothers, and fathers have been lost to violence) have emerged to try to stem the violence. These programs provide mentoring programs, sports facilities, music instruction, and small business training in order to strengthen prosocial ties among community members (Duncan and Woolcock 2002). The Jamaica Social Investment Fund (launched in part in response to the work of Moser and Holland 1997) explicitly seeks to harness such ties to better identify and implement community development projects.[17] In Guatemala City (Grant 2001) and Bogota (McIlwaine and Moser 2001), similar community-based initiatives have been launched in response to endemic urban violence. In both cities the initiatives have sought to work through key front-line staff members able to build durable relationships of trust between themselves and communities. These relationships have helped strengthen service delivery, improve information flows regarding employment and training opportunities, and more constructively address issues that otherwise would have given rise to conflict. Such approaches are especially important in settings such as Guatemala, where social fragility borne of civil war, high ethnic diversity, and wide economic inequality has created a low level of generalized trust (World Bank 2003a).

Conclusion

The way in which scholars and policy makers understand the role that different types of social relationships (or social capital) play in the lives of the urban poor in Latin America has evolved over the past 40 years. The persistence of primordial kinship systems and "inefficient" informal institutions was initially held to be symptomatic of the failure of the once-rural poor to adapt to the pace and conditions of urban life (the "marginality" view). This perspective gradually gave way to one in which more attention was paid to the many and varied ways the social capital of the poor was harnessed to cope with adversity ("the resources of poverty" view). Most recently, as heightened economic integration across the region and the globe has generated greater uncertainty (even if it has also created new opportunities), the limits of these network-based strategies in poor urban communities have, according to some, been reached.

This chapter argues for (and provides examples of) a twofold policy response. The goal of this response is to expand economic opportunities and make key services more accessible and accountable to the urban poor and to enhance the capacity of the urban poor to diversify their social networks and participate (directly or indirectly) in the design, implementation, and maintenance of projects affecting them. Both responses are needed, in their own right and to enhance each other's effectiveness. Increasing the quantity and quality of top-down initiatives and delivery mechanisms (by providing more resources and making them more accessible, accountable, and effective) while simultaneously striving to make bottom-up processes more inclusive and capacity-enhancing is needed to forge and sustain the spaces in and through which a broad alignment of interests and incentives to serve the poor (and the nonpoor) can occur. To deliver on these goals, it will be necessary to sustain the political will, to mobilize the administrative infrastructure, to conduct the necessary background research, and to disseminate the lessons from demonstrated successes (and failures). These tasks are vital—and ones the international community can usefully support.

As the examples provided in this chapter and elsewhere demonstrate, some of the most innovative and effective responses to the challenge of urban poverty have emerged from harnessing the respective comparative advantages of formal institutions (their resources and reach) and informal social mechanisms (their proximity to the specific concerns, capacities, and aspirations of the poor), achieving together what neither could achieve alone. The heterogeneity of the urban poor, combined with the inherently discretionary and transaction-intensive nature of the services they most need (education, health care, conflict mediation), mean that standardized policy responses can be only one part of the optimal development strategy. In addition to broader policies for encouraging economic growth and attendant employment opportunities, crafting effective context-specific solutions (whose precise form is hard to predict ex ante) to the challenge of urban poverty in Latin America and the Caribbean requires the political willingness and ability to procure adequate resources and establish adequate accountability mechanisms while devolving as much decision making responsibility as possible.

Notes

1. This terminology comes from Briggs (1998). Where possible, reference is also made to urban areas in the Caribbean.

2. See, for example, Rubio (1997) on the "perversity" of social capital in Colombia.

3. Portions of this section draw on Das, Rao, and Woolcock (2003).

4. On the broader role of weak property rights in development, see de Soto (2000).

5. See the more detailed discussion of these issues in chapter 4. See Rodgers (2003) on the rise of violence in slums in Nicaragua, in particular on the ways that in the aftermath of the civil war poor urban communities became territory to be

controlled by an entire class of young, male, ex-military personnel left without status, income, and direction. On the unusual mixture of democratic politics and urban violence in Jamaica, see Duncan and Woolcock (2002).

6. For a depiction of similar dynamics in Cairo, see Singerman (1995).

7. In a controversial book on life in the *favelas* of Brazil, Scheper-Hughes (1992) argues that extreme poverty can erode even the most primal of social attachments, that between a mother and child.

8. On this point, see, among others, Waldinger (1996), Light and Gold (1999), Portes and Rumbaut (2001), and Massey and Durand (2002).

9. For a model of "passing" and "identity switching" in this context, see Bloch and Rao (2001). For earlier ethnographic work on the benefits and burdens of social ties among the urban poor, see Hannerz (1969).

10. Waldinger (1996); Waldinger, Aldrich, and Ward (1990); Portes and Zhou (1992); and Light and Karageorgis (1994) make similar arguments. For a detailed empirical assessment, see Massey and Espinosa (1997).

11. Munshi (2003) argues that a "bad" network externality is imposed by the need to provide for newcomers, since newcomers will typically be employed in lower paying jobs.

12. Munshi (2003) suggests that this is one of the reasons for the low levels of education among Mexican migrants, despite a long tradition of migration to the United States.

13. This applies to small businesses in poor communities; ethnic enterprises already well established in the commercial sector (such as Jewish diamond merchants in New York) may benefit considerably, as may consumers, by being able to control entry and exit into their industry through informal social mechanisms (Coleman 1990).

14. This work continues a long and distinguished tradition of urban research at the University of Chicago. See also Jargowsky (1998) and Venkatesh (2000).

15. Other studies (for example, Scheper-Hughes 1992) depict a harsh world in which urban poverty is both a product of and exacerbates fragmented social networks. In this view, a vicious circle is established in which low social capital, violence, unemployment, and poverty negatively reinforce each other.

16. See Briggs (1998), Woolcock (1998), Gittell and Vidal (1998), World Bank (2000), and Saegert, Thompson, and Warren (2001).

17. On the efficacy of the Jamaica Social Investment Fund, see Rao and Ibáñez (forthcoming).

References

Appadurai, Arjun. 2004. "The Capacity to Aspire: Culture and the Terms of Recognition." In *Culture and Public Action*, ed. Vijayendra Rao and Michael Walton, 59–84. Stanford, CA: Stanford University Press.

Bebbington, Anthony, Scott Guggenheim, Elizabeth Olson, and Michael Woolcock. 2004. "Understanding Social Capital Debates at the World Bank." *Journal of Development Studies* 40(5):33–64.

Besley, Timothy. 1995. "Savings, Credit and Insurance." In *Handbook of Develop-ment Economics*, Vol. 3A, ed. Jere Behrman and T.N. Srinivasan, 2125–207. Amsterdam: Elsevier.

Bloch, Francis, and Vijayendra Rao. 2001. "Statistical Discrimination and Social Assimilation." *Economics Bulletin* 10(2):1–5.

Briggs, Xavier de Sousa. 1998. "Brown Kids in White Suburbs: Housing Mobility and the Multiple Faces of Social Capital." *Housing Policy Debate* 9(1): 177–221.

Chant, Sylvia. 1991. *Women and Survival in Mexican Cities: Perspectives on Gender, Labour Markets and Low-Income Households*. Manchester: University of Man-chester Press.

Chwe, Michael Suk-Young. 2000. "Communication and Coordination in Social Networks." *Review of Economic Studies* 67(1):1–16.

Coate, Stephen, and Martin Ravallion. 1993. "Reciprocity Without Commitment: Characterization and Performance of Informal Insurance Arrangements." *Journal of Development Economics* 40(1):1–24.

Coleman, James. 1990. *Foundations of Social Theory*. Cambridge, MA: Harvard Uni-versity Press.

Das, Jishnu, Vijayendra Rao, and Michael Woolcock. 2003. "Social Networks and Urban Poverty: What Do We Know?" World Bank, Development Research Group, Washington, DC.

de Soto, Hernando. 2000. *The Mystery of Capital: Why Capitalism Triumphs in the West and Fails Elsewhere*. New York: Basic Books.

Dordick, Gwendolyn. 1997. *Something Left to Lose: Personal Relations and Survival among New York's Homeless*. Philadelphia: Temple University Press.

Duncan, Imani, and Michael Woolcock. 2002. "The Socioeconomic Foundations of Political Violence in Kingston, Jamaica." World Bank, Development Re-search Group, Washington, DC.

Eames, Edwin, and Judith G. Goode. 1973. *Urban Poverty in a Cross-Cultural Con-text*. New York: Free Press.

Fernandez-Kelly, Patricia. 1995. "Social and Cultural Capital in the Urban Ghetto: Implications for the Economic Sociology of Immigration." In *The Economic Sociology of Immigration*, ed. Alejandro Portes, 213–47. New York: Russell Sage Foundation.

Fukuyama, Francis. 1995. *Trust: The Social Virtues and the Creation of Prosperity*. New York: Free Press.

Gittell, Ross, and Avis Vidal. 1998. *Community Organizing: Building Social Capital as a Development Strategy*. Newbury Park, CA: Sage Publications.

Granovetter, Mark. 1995. "The Economic Sociology of Firms and Entrepreneurs." In *The Economic Sociology of Immigration: Essays on Networks, Ethnicity, and Entrepreneurship*, ed. Alejandro Portes, 128–65. New York: Russell Sage Foundation.

Grant, Emma. 2001. "Social Capital and Community Strategies: Neighborhood Development in Guatemala City." *Development and Change* 32(5):975–77.

Hannerz, Ulf. 1969. *Soulside: Inquiries into Ghetto Culture and Community*. New York: Columbia University Press.

Imparato, Ivo, and Jeff Ruster. 2003. *Slum Upgrading and Participation: Lessons from Latin America.* Washington, DC: World Bank.

Jargowsky, Paul. 1998. *Poverty and Place: Ghettos, Barrios, and the American.* New York: Russell Sage Foundation.

Jellenik, Lea. 1991. *The Wheel of Fortune: The History of a Poor Community in Jakarta.* Honolulu: University of Hawaii Press.

Jha, Saumitra, Vijayendra Rao, and Michael Woolcock. Forthcoming. "Governance in the Gullies: Democratic Governance and Community Leadership in Delhi's Slums." *World Development.*

Klinenberg, Eric. 2002. *Heat Wave: A Social Autopsy of Disaster in Chicago.* Chicago: University of Chicago Press.

Light, Ivan, and Steven J. Gold. 1999. *Ethnic Economies.* New York: Academic Press.

Light, Ivan, Im Jung Kwoun, and Deng Zhong. 1990. "Korean Rotating Credit Associations in Los Angeles." *Amerasia* 16(1):35–54.

Light, Ivan, and Stavros Karageorgis. 1994. "The Ethnic Economy." In *The Handbook of Economic Sociology,* ed. Neil Smelser and Richard Swedberg, 647–71. Princeton, NJ: Princeton University Press.

Lomnitz, Larissa. 1977. *Networks and Marginality: Life in a Mexican Shantytown.* New York: Academic Press.

Massey, Douglas, and Jorge Durand. 2002. *Beyond Smoke and Mirrors: Mexican Immigration in an Era of Free Trade.* New York: Russell Sage Foundation.

Massey, Douglas, and Karin Espinosa. 1997. "What's Driving Mexico–U.S. Migration? A Theoretical, Empirical, and Policy Analysis." *American Journal of Sociology* 102(4):939–99.

McAdam, Doug. 1986. "The Recruitment to High-Risk Activism: The Case of Freedom Summer." *American Journal of Sociology* 92(1):64–90.

McAdam, Doug, and Ronnelle Paulson. 1993. "Specifying the Relation between Social Ties and Activism." *American Journal of Sociology* 99(3):640–67.

McIlwaine, Cathy, and Caroline Moser. 2001. "Violence and Social Capital in Poor Communities: Perspectives from Colombia and Guatemala." *Journal of International Development* 13(7):965–84.

Morduch, Jonathan. 1999. "Between the State and the Market: Can Informal Insurance Patch the Safety Net?" *World Bank Research Observer* 14(2):187–207.

Moser, Caroline, and Jeremy Holland. 1997. *Urban Poverty and Violence in Jamaica.* Washington, DC: World Bank.

Munshi, Kaivan. 2003. "Networks in the Modern Economy: Mexican Migrants in the U.S. Labor Market." *Quarterly Journal of Economics* 118(2):549–99.

National Research Council. 2003. *Cities Transformed: Demographic Change and its Implications in the Developing World.* Washington, DC: National Academies Press.

Neuhouser, Kevin. 1989. "Sources of Women's Power and Status among the Urban Poor in Contemporary Brazil." *Journal of Women in Culture and Society* 14(31): 685–702.

Perlman, Janice. 1976. *The Myth of Marginality: Urban Poverty and Politics in Rio de Janeiro.* Berkeley: University of California Press.

———. 2003. "Marginality: From Myth to Reality in the *Favelas* of Rio de Janeiro, 1969–2002." In *Urban Informality: Transnational Perspectives from the Middle*

East, Latin America, and South Asia, ed. Ananya Roy. 105–46. Lanham, MD: Lexington Books.

Portes, Alejandro. 1995. "Economic Sociology and the Sociology of Immigration: A Conceptual Overview." In *The Economic Sociology of Immigration: Essays on Networks, Ethnicity, and Entrepreneurship*, ed. Alejandro Portes, pp. 1–41. New York: Russell Sage Foundation.

Portes, Alejandro, and Patricia Landolt. 1996. "The Downside of Social Capital." *American Prospect* 26(May–June):18–21, 94.

Portes, Alejandro, and Min Zhou. 1992. "Gaining the Upper Hand: Economic Mobility Among Immigrant and Domestic Minorities." *Ethnic and Racial Studies* 15 (4): 491–522.

Portes, Alejandro, and Ruben Rumbaut, eds. 2001. *Ethnicities: Children of Immigrants in America*. Berkeley: University of California Press.

Portes, Alejandro, and Julia Sensenbrenner. 1993. "Embeddedness and Immigration: Notes on the Social Determinants of Economic Action." *American Journal of Sociology* 98(6):1320–50.

Pritchett, Lant, and Michael Woolcock. 2004. "Solutions When the Solution Is the Problem: Arraying the Disarray in Development." *World Development* 32(2): 191–212.

Radoki, Carole, and Tony L. Jones. 2002. *Urban Livelihoods: A People-Centred Approach to Reducing Poverty*. London: Earthscan.

Rao, Vijayendra, and Ana Maria Ibáñez. Forthcoming. "The Social Impact of Social Funds in Jamaica: A Participatory Econometric Analysis of Participation, Targeting, and Collective Action in Community-Driven Development." *Journal of Development Studies*.

Raudenbush, Stephen, Robert Sampson, and Felton Earls. 1997. "Neighborhoods and Violent Crime: A Multilevel Study of Collective Efficacy." *Science* 277 (August 15):918–24.

Roberts, Bryan R. 1973. *Organizing Strangers*. Austin: University of Texas Press.

———. 1995. *The Making of Citizens: Cities of Peasants Revisited*. London: Arnold.

Rodgers, Dennis. 2003. "Dying for It: Gangs, Violence and Social Change in Urban Nicaragua." Working Paper No. 35, Development Studies Institute, London School of Economics.

Rosenzweig, Mark, and Oded Stark. 1989. "Consumption Smoothing, Migration, and Marriage: Evidence from Rural India." *Journal of Political Economy* 97(4): 905–27.

Rubio, Mauricio. 1997. "Perverse Social Capital: Some Evidence from Colombia." *Journal of Economic Issues* 38(3):805–16.

Saegert, Susan, J. Phillip Thompson, and Mark Warren. 2001. *Social Capital and Poor Communities*. New York: Russell Sage Foundation.

Sampson, Robert, Jeffrey Morenoff, and Felton Earls. 1999. "Beyond Social Capital: Spatial Dynamics of Collective Efficacy for Children." *American Sociological Review* 64(5):633–60.

Santos, Boaventura de Sousa. 1998. "Participatory Budgeting in Porto Allegre: Toward a Redistributive Democracy." *Politics and Society* 26(4):461–510.

Scheper-Hughes, Nancy. 1992. *Death without Weeping: The Violence of Everyday Life in Brazil*. Berkeley: University of California Press.

Singerman, Dianne. 1995. *Avenues of Participation: Family, Politics, and Networks in Urban Quarters of Cairo*. Princeton, NJ: Princeton University Press.

Sojo, Carlos, ed.. 2003. *Social Development in Latin America: Issues for Public Policy* Washington, DC: World Bank.

Thomas, J. 1995. *Surviving in the City: The Urban Informal Sector in Latin America* London: Pluto Press.

Udry, Chris. 1994. "Risk and Insurance in a Rural Credit Market: An Empirical Investigation in North Nigeria." *Review of Economic Studies* 61(3):495–526.

Venkatesh, Sudir A. 2000. *American Project: The Rise and Fall of a Modern Ghetto*. Cambridge, MA: Harvard University Press.

Waldinger, Roger. 1996. *Still the Promised City? African-Americans and New Immigrants in Postindustrial New York*. Cambridge, MA: Harvard University Press.

Waldinger, Roger, Howard Aldrich, and Robin Ward. 1990. *Ethnic Entrepreneurs: Immigrant and Ethnic Business in Western Industrial Societies*. Beverly Hills: Sage.

Wilson, William Julius. 1987. *The Truly Disadvantaged*. Chicago: University of Chicago Press.

———. 1996. *When Work Disappears: The World of the New Urban Poor*. New York: Knopf.

Woolcock, Michael. 1998. "Social Capital and Economic Development: Toward a Theoretical Synthesis and Policy Framework." *Theory and Society* 27(2):151–208.

Woolcock, Michael, and Deepa Narayan. 2000. "Social Capital: Implications for Development Theory, Research, and Policy." *World Bank Research Observer* 15 (2): 225–49.

World Bank. 2000. *World Development Report 2000/01: Attacking Poverty*. New York: Oxford University Press.

———. 2003a. *Poverty in Guatemala*. Report No. 24221-GU, World Bank, Latin America and Caribbean Region, Washington, DC.

———. 2003b. *World Development Report 2004: Making Services Work for Poor People* New York: Oxford University Press.

Public Social Safety Nets
and the Urban Poor

Marianne Fay, Lorena Cohan, and Karla McEvoy

The previous chapters discussed how poor people can try to protect themselves against poverty and vulnerability by building up their asset base or calling on friends and relatives. Other strategies include relying on public mechanisms, such as social assistance or social insurance (unemployment, health, and disability insurance; pensions). Social insurance is usually available only through formal labor markets. As a result, it is out of reach for most poor families—only about 30 percent of the employed urban poor work in the formal sector in Latin America—making social assistance the key public instrument for helping the poor.

Social assistance aims to help the poor cope with poverty and vulnerability when private mechanisms and social insurance cannot—this is why it is commonly referred to as a social safety net.[1] Its design therefore needs to be informed by the availability of social insurance and private schemes. It also needs to respond to what is known about the nature of the deprivation and vulnerability affecting the target population.

This chapter reviews what is "urban" about poor people living in cities, focusing on differences that are relevant to social safety nets. It then discusses whether these differences imply a need for different types of programs or just different design of specific interventions.

Myths and Facts about the Safety Net
Needs of the Urban Poor

Before discussing the safety net needs of the urban poor, it is worth tackling two myths about the topic. Both are based on the common misconception

Marianne Fay is a Lead Economist, Lorena Cohan a Consultant, and Karla McEvoy an Operations Analyst at the World Bank. This chapter benefited from substantial inputs from Gillette Hall, Caterina Ruggeri Laderchi, and Bernice Van Bronkhorst and from comments by Christopher Chamberlain, Ariel Fiszbein, Margaret Grosch, Theresa Jones, and Helena Ribe. We are grateful to Lic. Concepción Steta Gándara for documentation and insights on the expansion of Oportunidades in urban areas.

that urban averages are representative of the conditions of the urban poor. It is also important to review some of the characteristics of urban poverty that are relevant to the design of safety nets.

Myth 1: The Greater Availability of Social Insurance in Urban Areas Makes Social Assistance Less Necessary

Publicly managed social insurance systems providing old age pensions, income support for the disabled, and health insurance are widespread in Latin America, and coverage is generally higher in urban than in rural areas.[2] These programs are therefore, at least potentially, a critical component of the urban safety net, with the capacity to vastly reduce income vulnerability and poverty in the face of catastrophic illness, disability, and old age.

However, empirical analysis of the determinants of access to social security does not find much evidence of an urban bias (Packard, Shinkai, and Fuentes 2002). Once individual characteristics, such as income, years of education, and type of employment are taken into account, regression analysis finds that the probability of having access to pension systems is greater for the urban population in five countries (Chile, El Salvador, Mexico, Paraguay, and Peru); lower in two countries (Costa Rica and Ecuador); and similar in three countries (Brazil, the Dominican Republic, and Nicaragua). In addition, these results must be interpreted with caution, given the special rules that often apply to rural workers. In Brazil, for example, rural workers are less likely to contribute to social security programs, but since they can benefit after contributing only nine years, they may enjoy some benefits nevertheless.

More important, coverage of these systems is highly regressive, leaving the vast majority of the poor—urban and rural—without coverage. This is mostly due to the fact that social insurance is usually accessed through formal labor markets and formality increases with income (from about 30 percent of employment in the first quintile to 68 percent in the top quintile). Indeed, across Latin America workers earning higher incomes and with more education are more likely to contribute to social security (Packard, Shinkai, and Fuentes 2002). Even in Chile, which has one of the most developed social insurance systems in Latin America, more than half of urban workers below the mean income level are without coverage (World Bank 2002). In countries with less-developed systems, regressivity is even more pronounced, leaving the poor virtually without coverage (Gill, Packard, and Yermo 2004).

A recent study of Peru addresses old-age poverty and the urban social insurance system (World Bank 2003b). It finds that in urban Peru, the share of the employed labor force with access to an old-age insurance system is significantly lower among workers in the poorest income quintile (3 percent) than among the top quintile (27 percent). Moreover, access has become more regressive in recent years, decreasing for the poorest and remaining constant or increasing for other social groups (table 8.1). The incidence of pension receipts among Peru's population over 65 is regressively distributed, with only about 15 percent of the elderly in the

Table 8.1   The pension system in urban Peru is highly regressive—and has become more so over time
(percent)

Year/Area	Share of employed labor force 14–65 contributing to a pension system			Share of elderly (65+) receiving pension benefit		
	Quintile 1 (poorest)	Quintile 5 (richest)	All	Quintile 1 (poorest)	Quintile 5 (richest)	All
1999						
All urban	4	26	16	22	41	32
Metropolitan Lima	8	29	18	40	47	40
Rest of urban Peru	2	24	15	9	35	25
2000						
All urban	3	29	18	14	45	33
Metropolitan Lima	6	31	20	23	52	40
Rest of urban Peru	2	27	16	6	37	27
2001						
All urban	3	27	16	15	44	32
Metropolitan Lima	5	30	19	27	53	40
Rest of urban Peru	1	23	14	6	32	22
Change between 1999 and 2001						
All urban	−25.6	1.1	−0.6	−32.1	7.0	−0.9
Metropolitan Lima	−33.8	3.4	4.4	−33.1	11.5	1.5
Rest of urban Peru	−18.8	−0.8	−6.2	−38.0	−10.0	−10.4

Source: World Bank 2003b.

bottom quintile but 44 percent of the elderly in the top quintile receiving a pension. The distribution is also heavily skewed toward metropolitan Lima, with far lower coverage rates in other urban areas. Regressivity has worsened over time, probably as a result of the regionwide increase in informality (chapter 2).

In sum, although Latin America is characterized by relatively well-developed social insurance systems that favor the urban working population, the vast majority of the urban working poor have little to no access to these programs. In addition, informality is increasing throughout Latin America, so that increased coverage of social insurance is unlikely in the near future, at least in the absence of major reforms.

A Second Myth? Social Assistance Is More Easily Accessible in Cities

There is often a presumption that the urban poor are better served by safety nets than the rural poor. This perception is partly associated with the fact that access to social insurance as well as to health and education services is indeed much greater. However, one of the first in-depth analyses of safety nets broken down by urban and rural populations, carried out for Mexico, finds that social assistance actually favors rural populations.[3] Mexico has only recently begun developing an urban poverty program, and expanding its flagship antipoverty program, Oportunidades, into urban areas.

Lacking a more general analysis of safety nets across Latin America, it is not possible to say whether Mexico is representative of Latin American safety nets. The evidence from Mexico does show, however, that an urban bias in safety nets is not automatic. More generally, many of the programs available in urban areas are poorly targeted and therefore fail to address the needs of the urban poor, so that even if there is an urban bias, it may not favor the poor (box 8.1).

Fact 1: Greater Integration into the Market Economy affects the Risks and Vulnerability of the Urban Poor

The urban poor are much more integrated into the market economy than their rural counterparts. This has several implications that are relevant to the design of safety nets.

First, greater market integration implies that lower income urban households are more susceptible to macroeconomic shocks and fluctuations in the growth rate.[4] (Seen positively, it implies that the urban poor have more opportunities to escape poverty when the economy does well.)

Box 8.1   Does Social Protection Address the Needs of the Urban Poor in Latin America and Caribbean?

Social protection in Latin America and the Caribbean consists of a wide range of programs operated by different ministries and levels of government. Almost all countries have some type of school feeding program, and many are developing school-based cash transfers. Workfare programs are also common, and most countries have some type of old-age pension and disability program. Despite significant expenditures on social protection, however, almost none of the countries in the region has explicitly matched key risks and poverty groups with appropriate programs. The table illustrates the mismatch between typical interventions for addressing risks and the circumstances of the region's urban poor.

Source: Adapted from World Bank 2001a.

Mismatch between objectives of national assistance programs and circumstances of the poor in Latin America and the Caribbean

Objective of national assistance program	Assistance type	Program characteristics	Circumstances of the poor
Raise employment	Job creation	Job targets often in the formal sector	Usually in the informal sector
Improve job skills	Training	Literacy required	Often illiterate or have very poor reading skills
Increase primary education	Elementary school assistance	Serve designated age groups before entering labor market	Eligible age groups often already in labor market
Provide credit	Loans for businesses	Serves small holders with collateral	Possess little or no material collateral
Provide social security	Medical and unemployment insurance	Serves formal sector businesses and firms	Typically work in the informal sector

Source: Campbell 2003.

It implies that faced with macroeconomic shocks, households that had been getting by may be plunged into poverty (box 8.2). Such poverty, even if only transient, can have long-lasting consequences. The cognitive potential of young children may be permanently reduced, for example, by inadequate nutrition in their first years of life.

**Box 8.2   How Do the New Poor and the Chronic Poor
Cope with Macroeconomic Crisis?**

The 2002 crisis in Argentina affected both the structurally poor and many in
the middle class, who became known as the "new poor." A study of urban
areas finds that the two groups coped with the situation differently. The new
poor engaged in new forms of generating income, such as trading products
and services, organizing informal markets to sell objects, starting homemade
production and microenterprises, putting new members of the household into
the labor force, and replacing costly products with cheaper ones. The structurally poor resorted to increased participation of women and children in subsistence activities, such as cardboard collection, increased home-made production for self-consumption, and community purchases at wholesale stores. The
structurally poor reduced their consumption of basic products, such as milk
and meat; made illegal use of electricity; and substituted natural gas with bot-
tled gas or firewood.

Source: World Bank 2003d.

This has important implications for the design of safety nets in urban
areas: first because programs that deal with transitory poverty face specific
targeting challenges (see below) and second because a major goal is to reduce households' vulnerability by helping them partake of the opportunities offered by thicker urban labor markets. This can involve job search
and job placement assistance programs, as well as measures to free up additional household members to join the labor market (a two-income
household is inherently less vulnerable). These measures include child
care and security of tenure, so that there is no need for someone to be at
home to ensure that the claim on the property is constantly established
(see chapters 2 and 3).

Second, for the urban poor the transmission of a macroeconomic shock
is usually through the labor market. The loss of work is typically one of
the most devastating shocks that can affect an urban household. But depending on the conditions of the local labor markets, a recession need not
always translate into higher unemployment. Instead it may result in
falling real wages—as happened during Mexico's 1994–95 Tequila crisis
and Argentina's 2002 crisis.[5] In Argentina three-quarters of the overall decline in household labor income was due to a fall in real wages for workers staying in the same job; only 10 percent was due to job losses. The importance of these labor market adjustments suggests that workfare
programs can play an important role in helping households cope with
the effects of the shocks. Indeed, Argentina's Plan *Jefes y Jefas de Hogar Desocupados* (unemployed heads of households) had a significant impact on
both aggregate unemployment and extreme poverty (box 8.3).

Box 8.3   How Effective Was Argentina's Jefes Program During the 2002 Crisis?

Following the crisis that hit Argentina in late 2001, the proportion of the population living in poverty rose from 37 percent in October 2001 to 58 percent a year later.[a] In response to the crisis, the government launched a major work program, *Jefas y Jefes de Hogar Desocupados* (unemployed heads of households). The program provides 150 pesos (about $50) a month to unemployed household heads or their spouses in exchange for 20 hours a week of community service work, job training, or work as a temporary employee of a private company. Eligible households are those with at least one child under the age of 18, a pregnant woman, or a member with a disability. Either the husband or the wife can participate in the program, provided that the spouse is not working.

Program eligibility criteria were not tightly enforced: about one-third of those receiving the program did not satisfy eligibility criteria. In particular, the aim of targeting only unemployed heads of households was clearly not realized, given that about half of participants were women who were previously inactive. The program is estimated to have reduced Argentina's unemployment rate by about 2.5 percentage points, a smaller impact than originally believed. Nevertheless, the effect on poverty, particularly extreme poverty, was significant: close to 10 percent of the participants would have fallen below the food poverty line without the program.

The extent of participation by people who were not formally eligible may not have been a bad thing, given the evidence that a fall in real wages, rather than unemployment, was the significant factor behind the decline in living standards. The fact that beneficiary unemployment status is hard to verify in economies with high rates of informality makes this eligibility requirement unenforceable anyway. More effective in ensuring pro-poor targeting were eligibility criteria correlated with structural poverty, such as having dependents or living in households with no members working in formal labor markets.

Overall, the program was not badly targeted, particularly compared with Argentina's overall social spending. About one half of all Jefes participants came from the poorest fifth of Argentine families, and all but 10 percent fell below the official poverty line. Among the lowest quintile, income to men from work programs increased from 2 percent of total household income to 16 percent; for women the share rose from 3 percent to 22 percent.

Sources: McKenzie 2003; Galasso and Ravallion 2004.

a. While the Jefes program is not specifically urban, the analysis discussed here is based on household surveys that cover only urban areas. Argentina, which is 90 percent urbanized, does not have a national survey.

Third, the greater integration in the market economy implies a higher monetization of food consumption, hence a greater sensitivity of food consumption to income and price fluctuations.[6] In Latin America programs based on food transfers have been quite popular. Many such programs, started following crises as part of social fund initiatives, have become institutionalized. While these programs do not always represent the most effective use of resources, their design can include features that enhance their effectiveness, such as building on local self-help groups (as in the case of Peru) that offer women the opportunity to work outside the home. The choice of the items to be distributed can make the programs self-targeting or help them cater to the nutritional needs of especially vulnerable groups, such as children. Finally, although food rations may cause household expenditures to be reallocated between items or adjusted to compensate for the fact that particular household members are targeted by food programs, food transfers can still represent a practical way of distributing resources to poor households (Ruggeri Laderchi 2001).

Fact 2: Cities Are Much More Diversified Socioeconomically

The urban poor are part of a much more diversified economy than the rural poor. As a result, as discussed in chapter 1, different urban groups can be affected very differently by a given macro shock. In contrast, a rural economy affected by a weather-related disaster or a collapse in the price of a particular crop is likely to be affected in a much more homogeneous manner. The heterogeneity of the potential beneficiaries of safety nets and the difficulty of predicting which groups will be affected most has important consequences for the design of safety nets. In particular, safety nets need to be mostly self-targeted, so that whoever is in need can access them.

Socioeconomic diversity also implies that untargeted interventions result in much higher leakages, given the much lower urban poverty incidence. To the extent that the land and rental markets result in sorting by neighborhood, geographic targeting at a sufficiently disaggregated level can help. Within neighborhoods, however, substantial variation in living standards is likely to exist (see chapter 1). In Mexico, for example, where the issue has been studied in the context of Oportunidades, the government's flagship antipoverty program, just 26 percent of residents of "marginal" urban neighborhoods are below the poverty line, and only about 77 percent of eligible households live in such neighborhoods (Gutiérrez, Bertozzi, and Gertler 2003).

Proxy means-testing through indicators of unsatisfied basic needs, which are often used in Latin America, may not be very precise, since, as

discussed in chapter 3, access to services in urban areas is more closely related to the age of the settlement than to income.[7] In sum, targeting in urban
areas requires a good dose of self-targeting, given the greater socioeconomic heterogeneity of the population and the sheer number of people involved, which make both errors of inclusion and means testing very costly.

Fact 3: Weaker Family Ties Leave a Greater Proportion of the Elderly without Family Support

One reason for the emergence of pensions in the developed world was
urbanization and the attendant decline in the role families played in social insurance. As discussed in chapter 7, social networks tend to be
much less stable in cities than in rural areas because of greater population mobility. Density tends to move social relationships away from traditional familial ties to ones based on the quality of reciprocal links. One
result is that the proportion of elderly living alone and unsupported by
familial networks tends to be much higher in urban areas. In Mexico, for
example, about two-thirds of households formed of only people over 65
live in cities.

Expectations are also different in urban and rural areas. The results of
a specialized survey in Chile show that while 47 percent of rural respondents expect to live with their children in their old age, only 19 percent of
urban respondents do. And while 67 percent of rural respondents expect
some sort of care by their children, only 34 percent of urban respondents
do (Gill, Packard, and Yermo 2004). Combined with the fact that everyone
ages (whereas only some people are ever unemployed or disabled), this
makes the elderly poor a particularly important target group for public
policy. The aging of the Latin American population and the longer life-
span of urban residents compared with their rural counterparts suggests
that the elderly will become one of the fastest growing vulnerable groups
in the region. And, as discussed earlier, the relatively high coverage of
pensions in cities still leaves the vast majority of the urban population
(poor or nonpoor) without any coverage.

Fact 4: Diversity and Density Imply Greater Social Risks of Child-Rearing

Three-quarters of Latin America's children and youth live in cities. They
are a group of particular concern in poor urban areas, for a number of
reasons (box 8.4). First, relative to the urban population as a whole, they
are disproportionately affected by poverty. In 1999, 50 percent of 13- to 19-
year-olds lived in poverty, almost twice the overall urban poverty rate.

Box 8.4   Who Are "At-Risk Youth"?

At-risk youth are teenagers and young adults who face "environmental, social, and family conditions that hinder their personal development and their successful integration into society as productive citizens" (p. 5). They tend to exhibit an increased propensity to engage in or be subject to harmful situations, including violence, substance abuse, unemployment, early school-leaving, and risky sexual behavior. The age "youth" may differ from country to country. The United Nations defines youth as people between 15 and 24.

Source: World Bank 2005.

Poor urban youth exhibit particularly poor health status and educational achievements.

Second, data on violence rates consistently find that youth who are poor, marginalized, and live in cities are at greater risk for both violence perpetration and victimization than any other demographic group (Guerra 2004).[8] Urban youth are more exposed to gangs, organized crime, drugs, firearms, and risky reproductive health behavior than other groups, especially in Latin America, the most violent region in the world by most indicators (chapter 4).

The commonly used indicator of at-risk youth—the inactivity rate—is disturbingly high in most of urban Latin America. In Brazil it is about 20 percent for poor 13- to 17-year-olds; in Central America it ranges from 19 to 25 percent. The regional youth unemployment rate (which is usually about twice the national unemployment rate) grew from 14 percent to 20 percent between 1994 and 1999, reaching almost 25 percent in some countries (Marques 2003).

Social policy has a key role to play in targeting at-risk youth. The issues tend to be quite different in urban and rural areas. In terms of health and education, the rural challenge tends to be the lack of access to services (schools, clinics, social workers) and intrafamily violence. In urban areas the issues are overwhelmed services, environmental health problems, gangs, guns, drugs, and pervasive interpersonal violence.[9]

Fact 5: The More Complex Economy and the Greater Sophistication of Local Governments Affects the Design of Interventions

The urban economy is more complex than the rural one—more sophisticated designs are required to provide water and sanitation, build a bridge, and provide other services. Decisions on public works involve more actors and more sources of financing, and they require more planning. These considerations make the design of workfare programs more complex, particularly when they are directed toward infrastructure or services managed by local governments (box 8.5).

On the other hand, one possible advantage of urban areas might be the greater resources—financial and human—and sophistication of their local governments. These advantages may make cities better able to administer some programs or even develop some of their own to respond to local needs.

The evidence is mixed as to the appropriate role of local governments in social safety nets. The presumption is that they should be involved in identifying recipients and their needs rather than in financing programs.[10] In Latin America the more successful safety nets tend to be centralized ones (which need not imply that they could not be made more efficient through decentralization). Given the huge variety in performance across otherwise similar urban local governments, their ability to successfully contribute to the social safety net is probably determined by the quality of the particular administration in place. In sum, while local governments could potentially play a much greater role in urban areas, there is no clear evidence on what the optimal role should be.

Addressing the Needs of Urban Dwellers

The discussion of rural-urban differences suggests that the main challenges in developing a safety net system that addresses the needs of the urban poor are design ones. This includes targeting issues as well as the need to adapt the internal mechanics of programs such as workfare or conditional cash transfers to the urban reality. There are, however, some specifically urban issues and groups that need addressing. One issue is food vulnerability associated with income shocks. One urban group is at-risk youth (since the risks confronting the urban poor are different enough to require altogether different types of programs). In addition, while the problem of the elderly poor is not urban per se, it is particularly acute in urban areas, where the family structure is weaker and the share of the population covered by pension schemes is declining.

Design Issues for Urban Safety Nets

TARGETING URBAN SAFETY NET PROGRAMS
A broad array of targeting instruments is available, all of which can be useful in designing various types of safety net programs (box 8.6). The

Box 8.5   Argentina's Experience with Workfare: The Trajabar Program

In 1996 the government of Argentina established a workfare program known as Trabajar. Through the execution of small infrastructure facilities, Trabajar sought to improve the living standards of the communities in which subprojects were located and create opportunities for temporary employment for poor workers in both urban and rural areas. The program was managed and implemented by the Ministry of Labor and Social Security through staff at the national, regional, and provincial levels. Subprojects were proposed by municipalities, communities, national agencies, and civil society organizations. The subprojects were designed to be labor intensive and relatively small, with the average project costing less than $100,000 and employing an average of 20 workers. The types of subprojects eligible for financing included rehabilitation, expansion, and new construction of community or public infrastructure, such as sewerage, latrines, potable water, housing, roads, urban works, irrigation, schools, and health centers. The wage rate was set at the same low level for urban and rural areas (the idea being that if the rate was not attractive to urban dwellers, perhaps they were not so poor).

Trabajar encountered a number of difficulties in larger municipalities (cities with more than 100,000 residents). First, larger municipalities found it difficult to insert Trabajar projects, the review and evaluation of which occurred on a monthly basis, into municipal and master plans that had already been formulated and that included mostly fairly complex works. Second, Trabajar projects were small, and larger municipalities found they did not fit well into the large-scale projects that made up their capital investment plan. Third, in larger municipalities, infrastructure projects fell under the purview of the public works agencies, not the social assistance agencies, as was the case for smaller municipalities, and the public works agencies often concluded that the benefits from a Trabajar project did not outweigh the cost of proposing and implementing one. Finally, larger municipalities found it easier to contract out the work rather than employ low-skilled workers in need of more supervision. Despite these difficulties, Trabajar was still popular in large urban areas.

The Trabajar program staff developed a proposal to address these issues. That proposal involved changing the project cycle for larger municipalities so that they would have an opportunity to work with a projected financial envelope of Trabajar funds and integrating them into master plans. It also allowed financing of a series of small stand-alone projects that could be part of a larger infrastructure project. These changes were never implemented, however, because the new government replaced Trabajar with the Jefes de Hogares program.

Source: Interviews with World Bank staff, July 2003.

choice of a particular instrument depends on the program to be targeted, the information available, the administrative capacity of the country or agencies charged with targeting, and the cost of the targeting instrument. In some cases, political considerations affect the choice of instrument, as when policymakers and legislators require program administrators to select beneficiaries individually (on the basis of poverty indicators, for example) and require the use of the same system for all regions or municipalities seeking to achieve uniform treatment nationally.

Verified means testing, the gold standard of targeting, has the advantage of being able to detect the new poor who lack money to buy basic

---

Box 8.6   Types of Targeting Methods

Verified means testing collects (nearly) complete information on a household's income, wealth, or both and verifies the information collected against independent sources, such as pay stubs or income and property tax records. This method requires verifiable records in the target population, as well as the administrative capacity to process and continually update this information in a timely fashion.

Proxy means testing denotes a system that generates a score for applicant households based on fairly easy to observe characteristics of the household, such as the location and quality of the dwelling, ownership of durable goods, the demographic structure of the household, and the education and possibly occupations of adult members. The indicators used in calculating this score and their weights are derived from statistical analysis of data from detailed household surveys. The drawbacks of this method include the high administrative capacity required to build initial registries and keep them updated; the higher costs compared with other targeting methods, such as geographic targeting; and errors of inclusion and exclusion, since welfare scores are predictions with high standard errors.

Community based-targeting uses a group of community members or a community leader whose principal functions in the community are not related to the transfer program to decide who in the community should benefit and who should not. The idea is that local knowledge of families' living conditions may be more accurate than what a means test conducted by a government social worker or proxy means test could achieve. The drawbacks of community-based targeting are a possible lack of transparency and elite capture or political interference due to the lack of systematic criteria for selection. In addition, community-based targeting may be more complex in urban areas, where the notion of a "community" may not correspond to a clear geographic area (as in a village).

(box continues on the following page)

Box 8.6   (continued)

Categorical targeting refers to a method in which all individuals in a specified category—say, a particular age group or region—are eligible to receive benefits. It involves defining eligibility in terms of individual or household characteristics that are fairly easy to observe, hard to manipulate, and correlated with poverty.

Geographic targeting combines census data with household survey information. The variables and parameters can be derived from household surveys to estimate poverty. With these parameters, the probabilities of being poor can be estimated for people in selected geographical areas, and these areas can then be ranked on the mean probability of being poor in that area. Poorer areas can then be selected for program eligibility. Although a registry of beneficiary households is still needed (to verify residence and detail identification and addresses of beneficiaries), this is an inexpensive method that can be used in urban areas, as poverty maps can be made for small areas if recent census information is available.

Under *self-targeting*, a program is open to all, but the design discourages people who are not poor from participating in the program. This is accomplished by recognizing differences in the private participation costs between poor and nonpoor households. For example, wages on public works schemes can be set low enough so that only those with a low opportunity cost of time due to low wages or limited hours of employment will apply. Services can be delivered in areas where the poor are highly concentrated, so that the nonpoor have higher (private and social) costs of travel. Inferior or less popular goods can be distributed, such as food that is consumed predominantly by the poor.

Note: Adapted from Coady, Grosh, and Hoddinott 2004.

foods or to pay for basic public services, such as water and electricity, which are critical in a highly monetized environment. However, the vast majority of urban poor are in the informal sector, which makes it difficult to verify income or wealth. In addition, verified means testing is very expensive, requiring qualified personnel to conduct interviews, make home visits, and verify information with independent sources. This option is valid for small programs that involve a large transfer.

Proxy means testing can be a good instrument in urban areas, particularly when done through a two-step process. In the first step the variables that determine poverty scores and weights are identified using a random sample of households. In the second step a poverty map is drawn based on census information and the parameters calculated in the first step. Households residing in areas identified as poor are then actively recruited into the social programs. In some cases, households outside the area are free to apply. This is the methodology used in urban Mexico for its conditional cash transfer program Oportunidades (box 8.7).

There are three main drawbacks to applying proxy means tests in urban areas. First, the main scoring variables, determined from national household surveys, are generally linked to the availability of public services.

Box 8.7   Expanding a Model Cash Transfer Program from Rural to Urban Areas: Mexico's Oportunidades

The Programa de Desarrollo Humano Oportunidades was the first large-scale conditional cash transfer program in Latin America and one of the most successful, according to several external evaluations. Initiated in 1997 under the name Progresa, its main objectives are to promote the development capacity of extremely poor households in education, health, and nutrition. Monetary benefits are conditioned on human capital investment by beneficiary families (school enrollment of children and youth and regular attendance at health clinics).

Progresa/Oportunidades targeted only the rural poor until a gradual roll-out to urban areas in 2002. The main challenges to expanding into urban areas involved targeting and adapting the program to the needs of the urban poor.

Oportunidades retains the basic principle of geographic and household targeting used in rural areas, but it adjusted the mechanisms in recognition of the greater difficulty and cost of targeting in urban areas. Census information is first used to identify poor neighborhoods, where Oportunidades temporary offices or "modules" are set up and advertising is carried out to let households know they can apply for benefits. Applicants can also come from outside the neighborhood. Individuals arriving at the module are administered a questionnaire about their socioeconomic conditions, the answers to which are immediately entered into a computer to determine the household's eligibility. Households deemed eligible then receive a verification visit, generally within two weeks. A recent evaluation estimates that this approach captures about 65 percent of eligible households, compared with 77 percent when all households in eligible areas were administered questionnaires. The module approach costs about one-third less than administering the questionnaire to all households in poor neighborhoods (Gutiérrez, Bertozzi, and Gertler 2003).

At the end of 2003, the package of benefits offered was the same in urban and rural areas, but results were different. In particular, the impact on school enrollments, graduation, and drop-out rates was much smaller than in rural areas (Parker 2004). This probably is due more to the fact that opportunity costs are higher in urban areas than to differences in enrollment between rural and urban poor, which is remarkably similar in Mexico, even at higher grade levels.[a] In addition, street violence and distance from schools makes it necessary for children and youth to take a bus to school, the cost of which is reported to absorb as much as 80 percent of the school grant (Escobar Latápi and González de la Rocha 2004).

(box continues on the following page)

Box 8.7   (continued)

Unexpectedly, one of the strongest impacts of Oportunidades on urban households has been home improvements, which occurred to a much greater degree among beneficiary than nonbeneficiary households. Improvements include regularizing property, acquiring infrastructure services, and upgrading construction materials. The evaluation study argues that this specifically urban impact on housing reflects the fact that the irregular status of a home or its poor quality is perceived as an obstacle to overcome or a source of vulnerability to a much greater extent in urban than in rural settings (Escobar Latápi and González de la Rocha 2004).

A difficulty encountered during the urban expansion of the program has been the need to adapt the requirements imposed on participants to the urban work reality. In particular, some working mothers did not join or dropped out of the program because they could not attend medical appointments or educational talks held during working hours. An additional problem is that of saturation of clinics in poor urban areas, which poses a significant problem, since regular medical check-ups are a requirement of the program (Escobar Latápi and González de la Rocha 2004). In addition, program administrators cite the need to adjust the content of the educational talks on public health issues to the urban reality (emphasizing coping with drug use and street violence rather than boiling water, for example).

a. See in particular section 1.1 in http://www.oportunidades.gob.mx/pdfs/prog_oportunidades.pdf (in Spanish).

However, the main problem facing the urban poor is usually not lack of connections to public services, but the poor quality of services or their inability to pay for them. Second, the static nature of poverty score measures makes them ill suited for programs designed to help cope with transitory poverty. While this problem could be addressed by including income, unemployment, and occupation variables or updating registries regularly (say, every year or so), few countries have been able to do so. Third, mobility is high within and between cities, and many poor people lose their benefits when they move. This occurs because poverty scores need to be recalculated for the new residence of the family, and most benefits are not portable.

Geographic targeting (small area poverty map) is a preferred targeting method for urban social infrastructure but one that results in high errors of both inclusion and exclusion in urban areas. Apart from the usual public service infrastructure, geographic targeting is often used to target community-based child care centers (such as those in Colombia and Guatemala) and school lunch or snack programs in poor areas, among other programs.

Self-selection is used for many safety net programs that are open to anyone who thinks they meet the eligibility requirements and wants to participate. Programs include workfare, such as Argentina's Trabajar, youth training, and many others. The main drawbacks of this method are that it may be difficult to inform the poorest people about the program and they may not apply for lack of money for travel, lack of time, or other reasons.

In practice, these targeting instruments are often used in combination. Table 8A.1 describes their use in several urban safety net programs.

ADAPTING PROGRAMS TO THE URBAN CONTEXT: WORKFARE AND CONDITIONAL CASH TRANSFERS

Trabajar and social investment funds suggest that public works require more careful planning in an urban setting. In addition, to the extent that a macro shock affects not only employment levels but also real wages, a narrow requirement that workfare be open only to the unemployed (and not the inactive) may not be appropriate. As to conditional cash transfers, they may need to adapt to different needs and opportunity costs in urban areas, as illustrated by Mexico's Oportunidades program.

PROVIDING CHILDCARE

Interventions to help poor people take greater advantage of the jobs available in cities are particularly important in urban areas. In addition to education and training and programs that directly target labor market insertion (such as job placement schemes, discussed in chapter 2), child care is essential to allow women to access better quality jobs. An impact evaluation of a child care program in Guatemala shows that the program raised the income of working mothers by 30 percent (Ruel and others 2002). Such programs have the additional advantage of helping improve future educational achievements and reducing the incidence of crime and violence among youth.

HELPING THE POOR COPE WITH FOOD VULNERABILITY

Programs to help households cope with food vulnerability can take a variety of forms, including general food price subsidies, rations and food stamps, vouchers, and community kitchens. Although they tend to be popular with policy makers, most of these programs suffer from high operational costs and leakages to the nonpoor, and they are generally considered inefficient. In addition, concerns have been raised about the labor market disincentives of some programs (Sahn and Alderman 1995) (such concerns are not exclusive to food transfers).

Empirical analysis shows that the disincentive effect depends on program design, targeting, and the relative size of the transfer. For some food programs, no disincentive effect is found (Ruggeri Laderchi 2001). In addition, program benefits may be underestimated, due to the frequent failure to include the impact of improved nutrition on productivity and health (Cornia and Stewart 1995). Important design elements that can maximize effectiveness include using commodities consumed primarily by the poor; locating ration shops in poor areas; providing incentives for shop owners to accept ration cards; minimizing transactions costs (through queues, for example); and periodically revising eligibility criteria to identify vulnerable groups. Supplementary feeding programs targeting infants and children are recognized as a low-cost, high-impact food program, particularly if coupled with health services and other complementary inputs, such as nutritional education (Lorge Rogers and Coates 2002).

Targeting At-Risk Youth

Most Latin American and Caribbean countries offer some sort of social safety net program targeting at-risk youth. These programs run the gamut from provision of school meals to assistance with school fees, grants to tertiary education students, welfare programs (including food stamps), and economic and social assistance. Unfortunately, many of these programs suffer from lax application of eligibility criteria, duplication of benefits, targeting problems, a mismatch between the risk faced and the intervention offered, and very limited coverage (Marques 2002; World Bank 2000, 2001a; Blank 2001; Murrugara 2000). Furthermore, many government programs targeting at-risk youth focus on repression (for example, "zero tolerance" anti-gang laws recently put into place in many Central American countries) rather than prevention, even though prevention strategies are known to cost less and produce better outcomes.

In order to design effective interventions to prevent risky behavior among youth (violence, early school leaving, substance abuse, unsafe sex), it is important to understand the underlying causes of these behaviors. One of the most popular approaches to understanding risky youth behavior is based on a public health model that identifies a set of risk and protective factors: individual characteristics, family and peer setups, and community and societal factors that increase or decrease the probability of engaging in risky behaviors. Best-practice interventions have been identified for each of these sets of factors (Guerra 2004).

Effective interventions focused on the individual provide a curriculum (through formal or nonformal education) that includes information on human relations, legal issues, job markets, life skills, civic education, and problem solving, all of which have been shown to improve grades, foster greater school involvement, and decrease delinquent behavior (Guerra 2004). Another type of intervention tries to prevent risky youth behavior by influencing the relationships youths have with their families, peers, and mentors. Interventions include parent-school partnerships that encourage parental involvement in children's education and learning, mentoring programs that provide role models for at-risk youth, parent training programs, and gang prevention programs. Interventions focused on the community and societal factors seek to improve schools and communities through neighborhood revitalization programs, community policing, economic development projects, housing programs, and opportunities for recreation and positive engagement for young people (recreation, learning, and employment).

A recent World Bank review of international programs targeting at-risk youth shows that successful programs emphasize the completion of secondary education as a fundamental development need. These programs pay young people to participate in vocational or training activities (at-risk youth often need immediate income support for their personal survival or to assist their families) and include, along with training, long-term support on life skills, education, and job orientation (World Bank 2003a). The review concludes that orienting youth toward self-employment is not usually effective, given the difficulties they face obtaining credit and developing managerial skills to run their own businesses.

No single program is likely to solve all the problems at-risk youth face. But certain key elements need to be in place, such as connectedness to a responsible or nurturing adult and the involvement of the family, the community, or both. In addition, some instruments seem effective across different areas of intervention. For example, mentoring has been shown to be equally successful in preventing substance abuse and early school-leaving (Guerra 2004). Given that youth have more in common with adults than with children, many types of social safety net programs traditionally designed for adults can be adapted to include youth as beneficiaries.

Conditional cash transfer programs offer a good example of the type of social safety net program that is traditionally geared toward adults but can also target at-risk youth. These programs can provide incentives for youth to attend secondary school. Increased secondary school attendance benefits not only the individuals themselves but society as a whole.

A good example of such a program is Brazil's Agente Jovem Program, created in 1999. The program seeks the active participation of vulnerable youth between 15 and 18 to help ease the transition from school to work or back to school. Beneficiaries serve as "agents of change" by providing community service in exchange for cash transfers. The eligibility criteria include age and means-tested income (family per capita incomes must be less than half the minimum wage). Priority is given to youth who are out of school but not yet in the labor force, those who have graduated from other social programs (especially PETI [Program for the Eradication of Child Labor]), those who have committed criminal acts or are under state protection, and those who have participated in sexual education and awareness programs. The program components include a monthly cash transfer of R$65 (about $20) per beneficiary, training, and social services (World Bank 2003c).

Another type of intervention involves tackling youth unemployment directly by generating employment opportunities through existing safety net programs, notably social investment funds. France, for example, subsidizes the creation of job opportunities for people between 18 and 25 (www.travail.gouv.fr/civis.pdf).

MEETING THE NEEDS OF THE ELDERLY

Given the large percentage of the workforce in urban areas that does not participate in the formal pension system, as well as the high fiscal dependence of contributory pension systems (box 8.8), it makes sense for governments to consider noncontributory benefits to prevent poverty in old age. Some Latin American countries have implemented such noncontributory pension programs (table 8.2). In some cases (as in Brazil), however, these programs explicitly target rural populations.

Although noncontributory pension schemes can still be improved in many ways (mainly by increasing coverage and reducing costs), in 2000 and 2001 noncontributory pensions lowered the poverty rates among the elderly by 95 percent in Brazil, 69 percent in Chile, 67 percent in Argentina, and 21 percent in Costa Rica. These statistics clearly signal that this type of pension scheme should be considered more often by Latin American governments as a way to prevent their elderly populations from falling into poverty (Gill, Packard, and Yermo 2004).

Box 8.8   Latin America's Costly—and Regressive—Social Insurance Systems

Social insurance programs absorb a significant share of total social protection spending in most Latin American and Caribbean countries. Mexico, for example, spends three times more on social insurance than on social assistance. This is due to the generous benefit structure and insufficient contribution rates, which require additional transfers from public revenues to operate, even though these social insurance systems were designed to be funded from participant and employer contributions. This is particularly true for pension systems. In Peru the government spends 1.4 times the amount set aside for all poverty alleviation programs each year on deficit financing for the country's public pension regimes. In Brazil pensions absorb 56 percent of public social spending, and social security is very poorly targeted: less than 1 percent reaches the poorest 10 percent, while 50 percent goes to the richest 1 percent. The regressive nature of the program has recently prompted controversial attempts to reform the system by realigning contribution and benefit levels.

Sources: The Economist 2003; World Bank 2004a.

Table 8.2 Noncontributory assistance pensions in Latin America cover a significant proportion of pension recipients

Country	Beneficiaries as share of all pension recipients (percent)	Elderly beneficiaries as share of elderly poor
Argentina	10.1	47.0
Brazil		
Rural	33.0	86.3
Other	11.1	
Chile	22.6	36.5 urban; 78.7 rural
Costa Rica	31.2	44.5
Uruguay	9.0	17.3 Montevideo; 11.9 interior

Source: Adapted from Gill, Packard, and Yermo 2004.

Policy makers are often reluctant to implement noncontributory pension systems for fear that providing a noncontributory benefit for the elderly could eliminate household incentives to contribute to the pension system or to save outside the system. More generally, such programs are considered "charity" toward groups with weak political constituencies and are therefore vulnerable to budget cuts. Policy makers also fear that such programs may be unaffordable.

Recent work shows that there are ways to design programs to minimize both their fiscal cost and the potential disincentives to save or work in old age. Gill, Packard, and Yermo (2004) suggest offering a universal flat minimum pension to all. The advantage of such a system over a system targeted to the very poor is that it minimizes transaction costs, reduces opportunities for corruption, and eliminates the disincentives to save and accumulate wealth or work in old age that means-testing creates. This approach can be made more affordable by offering a benefit that is much lower than the average contributory pension, by making benefits available at a later age than the usual retirement age for the contributory pension, and by taxing pensions like any other source of income.

Where Do We Go From Here?

What can we learn from the preceding discussion? First, urban bias is a myth as far as the urban poor are concerned. Social insurance is indeed more broadly available in cities but not to the urban poor, who are largely outside the formal labor markets through which social insurance is accessed. The data are not available to determine whether there is an urban bias in social assistance, although in one country (Mexico) the bias, if there is one, may be a rural one.

Second, the urban poor face a different set of risks and opportunities than the rural poor. Policy makers must understand these risks and opportunities if they are to create effective social safety nets. The urban poor are more integrated into the market economy, which makes them more sensitive to macroeconomic shocks, positive and negative. These shocks are transmitted mostly through the labor market, suggesting that a safety net strategy should focus on increasing labor market participation. Cities are also more complex economically and physically than rural areas, complicating the design of classic safety net programs, such as workfare or conditional cash transfers. The environment facing the urban poor is much more diversified socioeconomically, making targeting more difficult. Finally, density and diversity create weaker family ties, leaving more elderly people without family support. Combined with classic urban perils (drugs, crime and violence, gangs), these weaker family ties increase the social risk associated with child-rearing and create the problem of at-risk urban youth.

Does this mean the urban poor need different types of safety net programs? Or can existing safety net programs simply be adjusted to respond to urban needs? The answer is: a bit of both. In terms of design adjustment, targeting is more complex and more necessary. Conditional cash transfers may need to adapt their requirements and offerings to the urban reality. Workfare must to take into account both the greater complexity of public works in urban areas and the fact that a fall in real wages rather than just unemployment may be the labor market shock it needs to help cope with. As for the elderly poor, they are not unique to urban areas, but they are less likely to receive family support in cities, making them more dependent on public support.

At-risk youth stand out as requiring tailored solutions in urban areas, not because children and adolescents are necessarily better off in rural areas, but because the needs of urban at-risk youth and the dangers they face and pose to others are different.

Finally, the greater integration of the urban poor into the market economy argues for urban safety net packages that focus on facilitating their participation in the labor market. Integrating the urban poor requires labor market policies, such as those discussed in chapter 2 (training, job search assistance). It also requires associated measures, such as transportation, child care, security of tenure, and other measures that encourage investments in human capital.

Annex

Table 8A.1   Targeting Instruments for Safety Net Program in Urban Areas

Program	Targeting instrument	Special considerations
Early child development programs (0–5 years)	Geographic for program-based centers, proxy means or means for vouchers	Could be a small area poverty map of the city or a nutrition-based map. Vouchers are ideal for incorporating private providers.
Nutrition programs (fortified foods for pregnant mothers and small children)	Growth monitoring indicator taken at health center or urban health post.	For undernourished children or children at high risk of under-nutrition
Primary and secondary school scholarships	Proxy means or means test for poverty-related targeting, others for merit-based targeting and reducing drop-out rate.	Not all scholarships are for the poor. Some are for high-performing students or to deter drop-outs and improve continuation in school.
School lunches and snacks	Geographic. In some mixed areas, proxy means or means test used to provide discount coupons for school meals to poor families.	Individual selection for school lunches is difficult because of stigma and administrative problems.
Youth training in urban areas	Self-selection and or proxy means or means test	Other criteria, such as unemployment, are generally used.
Public works in urban areas	Self-selection when wage paid is lower than that usually paid for similar work done by poor workers.[11] Proxy means or means test when minimum	In some countries it is not possible to use self-selection, because the program has to pay the minimum wage. In this case, there is a need to apply additional

(table continues on the following page)

Table 8A.1   (continued)

Program	Targeting instrument	Special considerations
	wage needs to be paid.	targeting instruments, such as work requirements, which are generally used.[12]
Cash transfers (conditional and unconditional)	Proxy means or means test	Most cash transfers require some kind of individual or household identification and selection. In DC, it is hard to apply means test because of the lack of reliable information due to the high share of self-employed. Proxy means are sometimes the best alternative.
Assistance pensions for the elderly	Proxy means or means test for direct subsidy or center-based subsidy in nursing homes	Special efforts need to be made to find and reach elderly poor in need of assistance. Local communities, churches, and others can identify potential recipients. Subsidies can be higher for elderly with dependents.
Health-related subsidies (fee hospital waivers, health insurance)	Proxy means or means test plus other health-related indicators (disabilities, pregnancy)	Proxy means or means tests are generally hard to apply for emergency services, since hospitals are not well prepared to apply tests. In some countries, such as Colombia, proxy means tests are coupled with home visits.

Table 8A.1   (continued)

Program	Targeting instrument	Special considerations
Subsidies for public services (water, electricity, gas)	Proxy means or means test. When good geographic targeting system exists, it can be used.	Generally hard to apply, but most useful for new poor, who may not have the money to pay full cost of services and other necessities.
Low-income housing subsidies	Proxy means or means test plus other tests (savings)	Generally require effort by families, such as savings.

Endnotes

1. See the World Bank Social Protection Web site (http://www1.worldbank. org/sp/safetynets/). Social insurance programs such as contributory pension schemes or unemployment insurance are related largely to earnings and need not include any transfers from the general budget (although many contain some cross-subsidization). Others define safety nets to include both social assistance and social insurance (see, for example, World Bank 2001b).

2. This urban bias is due to the fact that access is tied to participation in the formal labor market, which is higher in urban areas. Formal sector employment represents about 55 percent of overall employment in Latin America's cities but only 36 percent in the countryside (chapter 2).

3. Overall, social expenditures exhibit a slight bias in favor of the rural poor (relative to the urban poor, not to the population as a whole), although the allocation may be fair given relative shares of the poverty gap. Social expenditures include health and education expenditures, pensions, and monetary transfers, while social assistance includes only monetary transfers (Procampo and Opportunidades) (see World Bank, 2004b).

4. This is captured by the much higher elasticity of poverty to growth in urban areas, discussed in chapter 1.

5. See the World Bank Social Protection Web site (http://www1.worldbank. org/sp/safetynets/) for Mexico and McKenzie (2003) for Argentina. Fallon and Lucas (2002), quoted in McKenzie (2003) find that the main impact of financial crises is a cut in real wages.

6. In contrast food consumption by the rural poor is more sensitive to changes in household size. See Musgrove (1991) for a discussion.

7. A household that acquires a shack in a new, unserviced neighborhood that it will improve over time may have higher income than another household that rents rooms in a more established neighborhood in which services are available. Critics of Oportunidades have argued that the selection of beneficiaries, which is done on

the basis of assets, the type of urban services available, crowding indicators, and dependency indicators, favors households in irregular settlements and settlements in the process of regularization, acquisition of services, and home improvements. Increasing the weight of income would increase the share of urban households eligible, particularly those living in *vecindades* (tenement-like buildings, often in poor conditions but with services) (Escobar Latápi and González de la Rocha 2004).

8. Poor health and education outcomes are very much linked to violence, with causality running in both directions.

9. In countries with guerilla problems or civil war, rural violence can be a serious problem as well.

10. Local financing would imply that areas most in need would not be able to afford much in terms of social programs. For this reason there is widespread agreement that funding should be national. There is much less agreement as to the role of local entities in implementation. The success of any given assignation of responsibility probably depends largely on the clarity of roles and the match between purposes, skills, and resources. For a discussion, see "political economy and institutions" in www.worldbank.org/safetynets.

11. Whether this requires being able to pay less than the minimum wage depends on the country (in Argentina, for example, the minimum wage is set very low so most workers earn more).

12. It is hard to enforce an unemployment criteria since it is hard to check (except for formal sector workers). As such, the only way to ensure the beneficiary is unemployed (if indeed this is the requirement chosen) is by enforcing a full work load requirement that makes it unlikely that the person has another job.

References

Blank, Lorraine. 2001. "Jamaica Social Safety Net Assessment." World Bank, Washington, DC.

Campbell, Tim. 2003. *The Quiet Revolution, Decentralization, and the Rise of Political Participation in Latin American Cities.* Pittsburgh: University of Pittsburgh Press.

Coady, David, Margaret Grosh, and John Hoddinott. 2004. *Targeting Transfers in Developing Countries: Review of Lessons and Experience.* Washington, DC: World Bank.

Cornia, G. Andrea, and Frances Stewart. 1995. "Two Errors of Targeting." In *Public Spending and the Poor: Theory and Evidence,* ed. Dominique Van de Walle and Kimberly Nead, 350–82. Washington, DC: World Bank.

Escobar Latápi, Agustin, and Mercedes González de la Rocha. 2004. "Evaluación cualitativa de programa oportunidades en zonas urbanas, 2003." In *Resultados de la evaluación externa del programa de desarrollo humano oportunidades, 2003, Documentos Finales,* 265–99. Instituto Nacional de Salud Publica, Oportunidades, Centro de Investigación y Estudios Superiores en Antropología Social. Mexico D.F., Mexico.

Fallon, Peter, and Robert E.B. Lucas. 2002. "The Impact of Financial Crises on Labour Markets, Household Income and Poverty: A Review of Evidence." IED Discussion Paper 103, Boston University.

Galasso, Emanuel, and Martin Ravallion. 2004. "Social Protection in a Crisis: Argentina's Plan Jefes y Jefas." World Bank, Development Research Group, Washington, DC.

Gill, Indermit S., Truman Packard, and Juan Yermo. 2004. *Keeping the Promise of Old Age Income Security in Latin America: A Regional Study of Social Security Reforms*. Washington, DC: World Bank.

Guerra, Nancy. 2004. "Module on Youth Violence in LAC." World Bank, Capacity-Building Program in Municipal Crime and Violence Prevention in Latin America and the Caribbean, Washington, DC.

Gutiérrez, Juan Pablo, Stefano Bertozzi, and Paul Gertler. 2003. "Evaluación de la identificación de familias beneficiarias en el medio urbano: evaluación de resultados de impacto del programa de desarrollo humano Oportunidades." Instituto Nacional de Salud Publica, Government of Mexico, Mexico City.

Hall, Gillette, and Ana-Maria Arriagada. 2001. "Social Protection." In *Mexico: A Comprehensive Development Agenda*, ed. Marcelo Giugale, Olivier Lafourcade, and Vin Nguyen, 479–504. Washington, DC: World Bank.

ILO (International Labour Office). 2002. *Pensiones no contributivas y asistenciales: Argentina, Brazil, Chile, Costa Rica y Uruguay*. Geneva: ILO.

Lorge Rogers, Beatrice, and Jennifer Coates. 2002. "Food-Based Safety Nets and Related Programs." Social Protection Discussion Paper Series No. 0225, World Bank, Washington, DC. http://siteresources.worldbank.org/SOCIALPROTECTION/Resources/SP-Discussion-papers/Safety-Nets-DP/0225.pdf

Marques, José Silveiro. 2002. "Honduras, vulnerabilidad, riesgos, y pobreza: evaluación de la red de protección social." World Bank, Washington, DC.

———. 2003. "Social Safety Net Assessments: Cross-Country Review of Empirical Findings." World Bank, Washington, D.C.

McKenzie, David. 2003. "Aggregate Shocks and Labor Market Responses: Evidence from Argentina's Financial Crisis." Department of Economics, Stanford University, Stanford, CA.

Murrugara, Edmundo. 2000. "Social Protection in Uruguay." World Bank, Washington, DC.

Musgrove, Philip. 1991. "Feeding Latin America's Children: An Analytical Survey of Food Programs." World Bank, Latin America and the Caribbean Region, Technical Department Regional Studies Program No. 11, Washington, DC.

Packard, Truman, Naoko Shinkai, and Ricardo Fuentes. 2002. "The Reach of Social Security in Latin America and the Caribbean." Background paper to the Regional Study on Social Security Reform, World Bank, Washington, DC. wbln0018.worldbank.org/LAC/LAC.nsf/ECADocByUnid/004EE0215E94B07D85256C750071B747?Opendocument.

Parker, Susan, 2004. "Evaluación del impacto de oportunidades sobre la inscripción escolar." Instituto Nacional de Salud Públic (INSP) y Centro de Investigación y Docencia Económicas (CIDE), Mexico.

———. 2003. "Case Study: The Progreso Program in Mexico." Paper presented at the conference Scaling Up Poverty Reduction, Shanghai, May 25–27.

Ruel, Marie T., Benedicte de la Briere, Kelly Hallman, Agnes Quisumbing, and Nora Coj. 2002. "Does Subsidized Childcare Help Poor Working Women in Urban Areas? Evaluation of a Government-Sponsored Program in Guatemala City." IFPRI Discussion Paper No. 131, Food Consumption and Nutrition Division, International Food Policy Research Institute, Washington, DC.

Ruggeri Laderchi, Caterina. 2001. "Killing Two Birds with the Same Stone? The Effectiveness of Food Transfers on Nutrition and Monetary Poverty." QEH Working Paper No. 74, Queen Elizabeth House, Oxford University, Oxford.

Sahn, David E., and Harold Alderman. 1995. "Incentive Effects on Labor Supply of Sri Lanka's Rice Subsidy." In *Public Spending and the Poor: Theory and Evidence*, ed. Dominique Van de Walle and Kimberly Nead, 387–408. Washington, DC: World Bank.

The Economist. 2003. "Lula Comes Under Friendly Fire." July 17.

World Bank. 2000. "Managing Social Risks in Argentina." Washington, DC.

———. 2001a. "A Review of Selected Poverty Programs in Nicaragua's PRSP Portfolio." Washington, DC.

———. 2001b. "Social Safety Net Assessment: A Toolkit for Latin America and the Caribbean." Latin America and the Caribbean Regional Office, Social Protection Group, Human Development Department, Washington, DC.

———. 2001c. "Social Safety Nets in Latin America and the Caribbean: Preparing for Crises." Washington, DC.

———. 2002. "Chile, Household Risk Management, and Social Protection." Report No. 25286, Washington, DC.

———. 2003a. "Caribbean Youth Development: Issues and Policy Directions." Washington, DC.

———. 2003b. "Peru: Restoring the Multiple Pillars of Old Age Income Security." Report No. 27618-PE, Washington, DC.

———. 2003c. "Program Document for a Proposed First Programmatic Human Development Sector Reform Loan to the Federative Republic of Brazil." Report No. 25351-BR, Washington, DC.

———. 2003d. "Argentina: Crisis and Poverty 2003. A Poverty Assessment." Report No. 26127-AR, Washington, DC.

———. 2004a. "Brazil: Equitable, Competitive, Sustainable: Contribution for Debate." Washington, DC.

———. 2004b. "Urban Poverty in Mexico." Washington, DC.

———. 2005. "Youth at Risk in Brazil." Washington, DC.